STEADFAST DEMOCRATS

PRINCETON STUDIES IN
Political Behavior

Princeton Studies in Political Behavior

Tali Mendelberg, Series Editor

Steadfast Democrats

How Social Forces Shape Black Political Behavior

Ismail K. White

Chryl N. Laird

PRINCETON UNIVERSITY PRESS

PRINCETON AND OXFORD

Published by Princeton University Press
41 William Street, Princeton, New Jersey 08540
6 Oxford Street, Woodstock, Oxfordshire OX20 1TR

press.princeton.edu

Library of Congress Cataloging-in-Publication Data

Names: White, Ismail K., author. | Laird, Chryl Nicole, author.
Title: Steadfast Democrats : how social forces shape Black political
    behavior / Ismail K. White and Chryl N. Laird.
Description: Princeton, New Jersey : Princeton University Press, 2020. |
    Series: Princeton studies in political behavior | Includes
    bibliographical references and index.
Identifiers: LCCN 2019033702 (print) | LCCN 2019033703 (ebook) |
    ISBN 9780691199511 (hardback) | ISBN 9780691201962 (ebook)
Subjects: LCSH: African Americans—Politics and government. | Party
    affiliation—United States. | Group identity—Political aspects—United
    States. | Democratic Party (U.S.)
Classification: LCC E185.615 .W456 2020 (print) | LCC E185.615 (ebook) |
    DDC 323.1196/073—dc23
LC record available at https://lccn.loc.gov/2019033702
LC ebook record available at https://lccn.loc.gov/2019033703

British Library Cataloging-in-Publication Data is available

Editorial: Bridget Flannery-McCoy and Alena Chekhanov
Jacket Design: Layla Mac Rory
Production: Erin Suydam
Publicity: Nathalie Levine and Kate Farquhar-Thomson

This book has been composed in Adobe Text and Gotham

Printed on acid-free paper. ∞

Printed in the United States of America

10 9 8 7 6 5 4 3 2 1

For our mothers, Doris and Adassah
Your unconditional love knows no bounds.

In memoriam
Marion Overton White and Troy D. Allen
May you rest with the ancestors.

CONTENTS

ACKNOWLEDGMENTS

This book has been many years in the making, and it certainly would have taken many more were it not for the assistance, guidance, helpful feedback, and support of many others. First, we would like to thank the numerous scholars, colleagues, and reviewers who generously offered their time to review early drafts of the manuscript. Tali Mendelberg has been a major supporter of our work from the beginning of the writing process. We are so thankful for your commitment to our work and your guidance through the publishing process.

We are grateful to the numerous scholars who read and commented on various iterations of our article in the *American Political Science Review* that began this work and on drafts of our book manuscript. We would like to thank Antoine Banks, Vince Hutchings, and Julian Wamble for taking the time to engage our work and offer insightful advice, commentary, and critique. Additionally, we appreciate the suggestions from Fred Harris and Ahmed White regarding historical cases that exemplified our framework.

The Mamdouha S. Bobst Center for Peace and Justice at Princeton University was outstanding, providing us with the financial support and venue for a book conference to receive extensive feedback. The attendees were dynamic, insightful, and encouraging. We are incredibly grateful to the dynamic attendees, Chaya Crowder, Martin Gilens, Daniel Gillion, Patrick Egan, Sally Nummah, LaFleur Stephens, Ali Venezuela, and Omar Wasow, who offered invaluable advice and recommendations on an early draft.

We owe a debt of gratitude to the scholars who attended presentations of this project at annual professional meetings over the last several years, including the Annual Meeting of the American Political Science Association, the Annual Meeting of the Midwest Political Science Association, and the National Conference of Black Political Scientists.

We have had the privilege of presenting our work at workshops, invited talks, and conferences at universities across the country, including the research workshop organized by Michael Dawson and Cathy Cohen at the

University of Chicago; the 2012 Symposium on the Politics of Immigration, Race, and Ethnicity; and the 2015 Princeton Conference on Identity and Inequality. Your observations, comments, and questions challenged us to grapple with our line of inquiry.

We also want to thank the two anonymous reviewers who dedicated the time to assessing our manuscript for Princeton University Press. Your thoughtful feedback helped guide us in making improvements to our project and providing further clarity in our framework.

Data procurement for our experiments was quintessential for the completion of our project, and we would like to thank Conrad Jones, Southern University, the Frank W. Hale Jr. Black Cultural Center, Larry Williamson Jr., and the Mershon Center for International Security Studies for their assistance and support. We would also like to thank those who provided us onsite support for our fieldwork. Vincent Shaw, thank you for providing us with room and board. Our experiments would not have been possible without the research assistance from Nyron Crawford, Kris Kay, Yalidy Matos, and Julian Wamble. We are grateful for your service in our study and to our undergraduate students who assisted as confederates.

Access to survey data and information was an essential component of our research, and we would like to thank Spencer Overton and the Joint Center for Political and Economic Studies for their support. We would also like to thank the American National Election Studies and the Pew Research Center for their continued provision of public access to their survey databases.

We would like to thank our departments, the Department of Political Science at Duke University and the Government and Legal Studies Department at Bowdoin College, for their continued support of our research project.

Media interest in our project has been great, and we would like to thank Gene Demby, Seth Masket, NPR *CodeSwitch*, and Vox.com for providing us with opportunities to discuss our work.

We would also like to acknowledge the work of our copyeditor, Leanne C. Powner. You went over our book with a fine-tooth comb and helped to elevate our delivery and execution.

Special thanks go to Corrine M. McConnaughy. Her brilliant insights can be found in every chapter of this book. Without her encouragement, we would have not begun this project, and without her guidance, invaluable feedback, and support, we surely would not have completed it. Thank you!

We would like to acknowledge and honor the late Troy D. Allen. Troy was coauthor on our first paper in the *American Political Science Review*, which inspired this book project. He was an extraordinary scholar, mentor, father, brother-in-law, and friend. Troy, you remain at the heart of this scholarship. We miss you dearly.

Lastly, this book project would have not been possible without the support of our families over the years. To our partners and children, Corrine, Khalil, Meara, Amelie, Cornelious, and Carter, thank you for your continued support, encouragement, and motivation to finish the book.

STEADFAST DEMOCRATS

Introduction

On December 12, 2017, the state of Alabama held a special general election for the U.S. Senate seat vacated by Attorney General Jeff Sessions. The race, which had Republican Roy Moore running against Democrat Doug Jones, had already captured national attention. It was supposed to be an easy seat for the GOP to retain—a long-held seat in a deeply conservative state. Then, in November, the *Washington Post* published the story of a woman who claimed Moore had initiated a sexual encounter with her when she was a young teen and he was thirty-two (McCrummen, Reinhard, and Crites 2017). As more allegations of pedophilia and sexual assault against Moore surfaced, some Republican leaders endeavored to convince the candidate to remove himself from the ballot. He would not. With a Senate seat on the line, President Donald Trump came through with a public endorsement of Moore. And despite the controversy, the likelihood of Moore winning the race in the Republican stronghold remained common knowledge. Trump, after all, had taken the state by a 28-point advantage in 2016. Republican Mitt Romney had carried it by 22 points in his 2012 bid (*New York Times* 2017).

But Moore lost.

The crucial politics that delivered Jones's historic upset of Moore, it turns out, were the politics of Alabama's black citizens. NPR reported on the exceptional nature of black support for Jones: "Black voters made up 29 percent of the electorate in Alabama's special Senate election, according to exit polling. That percentage is slightly more than the percentage of Black voters in the state who turned out for Barack Obama in 2012. And a full

1

96 percent of Black voters in Alabama Tuesday supported Jones, including 98 percent of African-American women" (Naylor 2017). The essential role of black voters in the Jones win was undeniable in retrospect, if not anticipated in advance. Democratic National Committee chairman Tom Perez (2017) pronounced via Twitter, "We won in Alabama and Virginia because #BlackWomen led us to victory. Black women are the backbone of the Democratic Party, and we can't take that for granted. Period."

How black voters came to determine the outcome of the Alabama Senate race became both an engaging and an important story to tell. The near-unanimous black support for Jones came with turnout among black voters that far surpassed predictions. Indeed, the *New York Times* reported in the weeks before the election that six out of ten black voters were unaware that the election was even scheduled to take place. Analysis after the election, however, revealed that black turnout had been subsequently fueled by relentless on-the-ground mobilization efforts of black organizations and black social networks. In its postelection coverage, the *Times* gave this vivid description of the role black social networks played in getting out the black vote:

> The word traveled, urgently and insistently, along the informal networks of black friends, black family and black co-workers: Vote. Joanice Thompson, 68, a retired worker at the University of Alabama at Birmingham, scrolled Tuesday through the text messages on her phone from relatives reminding each other what needed to be done. Byron Perkins, 56, a trial lawyer, said his Facebook feed was clogged with photos of friends sporting the little "I Voted" stickers given out at polling places. Casie Baker, 29, a bank worker, said her family prodded and cajoled and hectored each other until the voting was done. (Faussett and Robertson 2017)

Black churches had also provided space for Jones to appeal to black voters on Sundays leading up to the election, and reports indicated that there were significant mobilization efforts by local NAACP chapters and other black political organizations (Faussett and Robertson 2017).

Steadfast support for the Democratic Party by black Americans that defies standard political expectations—such as that on display in the 2017 Alabama Senate race—is the subject of this book. The unique social doing of politics among black Americans, whereby blacks' high degree of social interconnection and interdependence creates unique racialized social incentives for black political behavior, will be our focus. Through the lens on modern black politics we offer, Jones's victory over Moore may not end up looking completely predictable, but we contend that it will not look politically unusual.

In short, what we offer is a theoretical framework for understanding how black Americans as a group have succeeded in solving a basic sociopolitical dilemma: how to maintain group unity in political choices seen by most as helping the group in the face of individual incentives to behave otherwise. We do this by elucidating the process by which black Americans have produced and maintained their overwhelmingly unified group support for the Democratic Party in the post–civil rights era. Ours is a social explanation of constructed black unity in party politics that centers on the establishment and enforcement of well-defined group expectations—norms—of black political behavior. We contend that among black Americans, support for the Democratic Party is a well-understood behavioral norm with roots in black liberation politics. Nonetheless, individual black Americans face a range of incentives—some of them increasing over recent decades—for abandoning the common group position of Democratic Party support. Yet the steady reality that black Americans' kinship and social networks tend to be populated by other blacks means they persistently anticipate social costs for failing to choose Democratic politics and social benefits for compliance with these group expectations. Within this framework, then, in-group connectedness provides not just a salient racial self-concept or informational cues but also social accountability as a constraint on black political behavior. We refer to this process by which compliance with norms of black political behavior gets enforced via social sanctioning within the black community as *racialized social constraint* in politics. It is this process within black politics that we empirically illuminate and assess—the same one that featured in the *Times* coverage of how on-the-ground mobilizing of black support delivered the first Democratic senator from Alabama in decades.

Why Black Democratic Unity Is a Question

That black Americans are remarkably unified in their support for the Democratic Party, and have been since the mid-twentieth century, seems a rather straightforward fact of American politics. It is a rather simple one to illustrate, as we do in Figure 0.1 with data from the American National Election Studies (ANES) surveys from 1952 through 2016. By the late 1960s the ANES data placed identification of black Americans with the Democratic Party in the neighborhood of 80 percent. It has remained in that neighborhood ever since. The coincidental timing of such stark black alignment with the

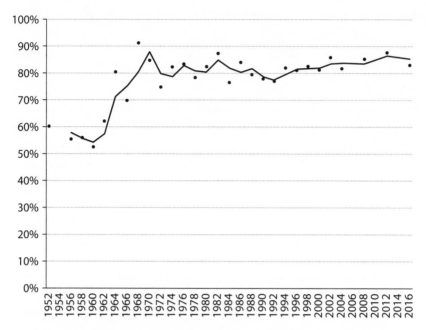

FIGURE 0.1. Percentage of self-identified black Democrats (including leaners), 1952–2016

Democratic Party and the deliverance of civil rights policy by Democratic administrations in the 1960s tempts a simple explanation that those policies made Democrats of blacks. Two important empirical observations complicate the matter.

First, the increasing tendency of black voters to support the Democratic Party predates the civil rights gains of the 1960s. Franklin Roosevelt's New Deal electoral coalition included significantly more black voters than previous Democratic presidential candidates'. That political reality seems to have been made possible in part by Republican Herbert Hoover's favoritism of the "lily white" faction of the Southern wing of the party—to the particular detriment of the Southern black politicians who had clung to influence in the national party via the "black and tan" faction (Walton 1975). Political scientist Ralph Bunche argued in his report *The Political Status of the Negro*, prepared in the late 1930s for the study of black Americans sponsored by the Carnegie Foundation and headed by Gunnar Myrdal, that Hoover "spelled the doom of the Black influence in Southern Republican organization." Among his included evidence were testimonies of blacks who had held positions in the Southern organization, including the first black woman to serve as a Republican committeewoman, hailing from Georgia, who reported, "I have always voted the Republican ticket. In 1932 Walter Brown and Herbert

Hoover lily-whited the party in Georgia. . . . I have stomped this entire state for the Republicans—but I wouldn't do it now" (quoted in Walton 1975, p. 163). And Eric Schickler (2016) has shown that reliable black partisan preferences for Democrats—not just votes swung in their direction—had begun to consolidate by the late 1940s. In other words, the civil rights politics of the 1960s may have crystallized black Democratic partisanship, but they can't stand alone as *the* political driver.

Second, in the years since the civil rights gains that supposedly defined black partisanship as Democratic, black Americans have grown more politically and economically diverse. This has surely provided new incentives to abandon the centrality of civil-rights-defined group interest in party identification in favor of some other self-interest, ideological, or alternate group position as the basis for partisan defection. That such defection has not occurred, we argue, should be seen as a bit of a puzzle.

Consider, for example, the remarkable growth of business interests within the black community. In the years before the 2008 Great Recession, the number of black-owned businesses in the United States had been growing at an especially rapid rate. According to the U.S. Census Bureau (2011), "From 2002 to 2007, the number of black-owned businesses increased by 60.5 percent to 1.9 million, more than triple the national rate of 18.0 percent." This prompted Thomas Mesenbourg, the deputy director of the U.S. Census Bureau at the time, to issue a statement saying, "Black-owned businesses continued to be one of the fastest growing segments of our economy, showing rapid growth in both the number of businesses and total sales during this time period" (U.S. Census Bureau 2011). These black business owners likely experience a tension between their desire for the expanded tax relief policies promoted by the Republican Party and its candidates and the Democratically endorsed social justice and welfare programs that disproportionally benefit the black community but rely heavily on tax revenue.

The last forty or so years have also witnessed the emergence and rapid growth of income inequality within the black community. Figure 0.2 illustrates this reality with income data from the U.S. Census. When the Civil Rights Movement made its greatest national policy gains, income inequality across black households was decidedly modest. In the 1970s, the difference between the average household income of those in the top fifth of black households and those in the bottom fifth was about $71,000 in 2016 dollars. In the late 1980s, however, incomes of blacks in the upper percentiles began to grow rapidly. By 2016, the difference in the average household income of those in the top fifth of black households and those in the bottom fifth had

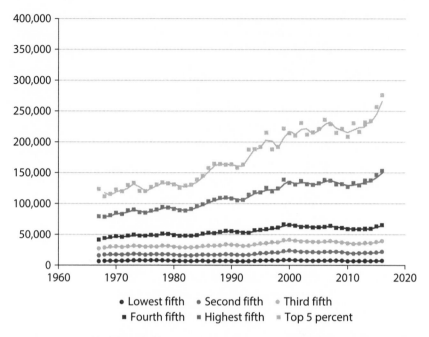

FIGURE 0.2. Mean black household income in 2016 dollars. *Source:* U.S. Census Bureau (2018).

grown to about $145,000. The pull of economic inequality is even starker when looking at the top 5 percent of black households. From the late 1980s to today, incomes in that stratum more than doubled, moving from about $125,000 in 1981 to about $275,000 in 2016. Meanwhile, blacks in the lower percentiles experienced little or no meaningful change in yearly household income over this time period. The point: when black America consolidated a voting bloc behind the Democratic Party in the 1970s, its economic interests, at least as measured by income, were decidedly more uniform than they are today. With this growing heterogeneity in black economic interests, we might reasonably expect growing partisan heterogeneity. Those blacks in the upper stratum, who stand to benefit most from growing income inequality, it seems, should eventually see some personal benefit in supporting Republican efforts to promote policies that would expand government support for business opportunities or reduce taxes on the wealthy. And yet they generally have not left the Democratic fold.

Growing diversity within the black community is not limited to economics. The post–civil rights era has also seen a noticeable increase in ideological conservativism among black Americans (see Philpot 2007, 2017; Tate 2010). Figure 0.3 illustrates this rise via the percentage of blacks identifying as

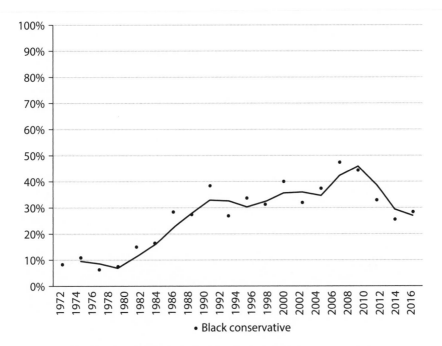

FIGURE 0.3. Percentage of blacks who identify as conservative on seven-point liberal-conservative scale, cumulative ANES. *Note:* Analysis only includes responses to face-to-face interviews. The number of valid African American responses ranges from 142 in 1974 to 560 in 2008. In 1984, as a measurement improvement, the ANES began asking a follow-up question to the initial seven-point liberal-conservative self-identification scale of moderates and those who said they did not know or haven't thought about it. The question asked, "If you had to choose, would you consider yourself a liberal or a conservative?" This resulted in more self-identified black liberals and conservatives and fewer moderates and "don't know or haven't thought about it" responses. Although this measurement change may contribute some to the increase we see here, conservative identification was increasing among blacks before the introduction of this new question.

conservative on the standard seven-point liberal-to-conservative ideological self-identification scale from the ANES. According to ANES surveys, in the early 1970s less than 10 percent of blacks identified as politically conservative. By the 2000s nearly 50 percent of black Americans described themselves as such. Although a noticeable decline in black conservativism using this measure of ideology has emerged in recent years, the ANES still estimates that nearly a third of blacks identify as conservatives. And yet partisan identification changes to align ideology with party among blacks have not followed (Philpot 2017).

When it comes to policy, the rightward shift in black political attitudes appears even more enduring. We illustrate this point in Figures 0.4a–d with

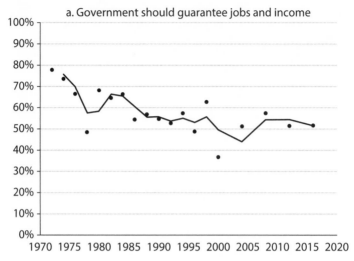

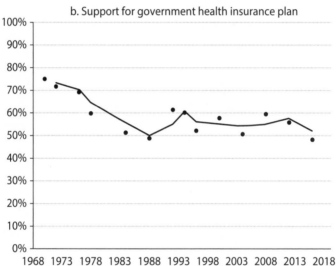

FIGURE 0.4. Percentage of black support for government redistributive initiatives

data from both the ANES and the General Social Survey. A significant majority of blacks in the 1970s backed some form of government-sponsored redistributive policy, such as government health insurance, aid to the poor, or a
government-sponsored guaranteed jobs and income program. The survey
data show that between 70 and 80 percent of blacks supported each of these
programs in the early 1970s, as Democratic partisanship solidified. By the
2000s black support for each of these initiatives had fallen off sharply.[1] In

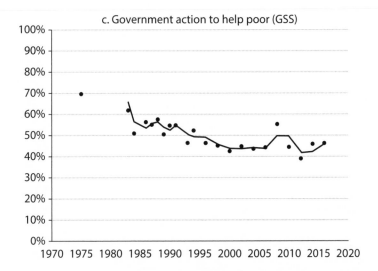

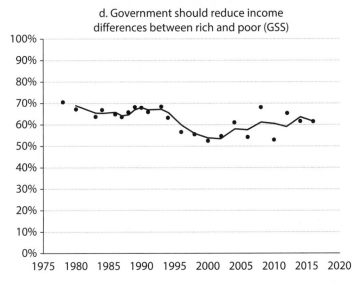

FIGURE 0.4. (*continued*)

2004, for example, only 51 percent of blacks stated that they would support a government-sponsored guaranteed jobs and income program. Similarly, only 51 percent of blacks supported a government-sponsored health insurance program, and only 43 percent of blacks supported government efforts to help the poor.

Importantly, this conservative shift in black policy positions also extends to racial issues. Again with data from the ANES and the General Social Survey, Figures 0.5a–c document a clear shift away from the government

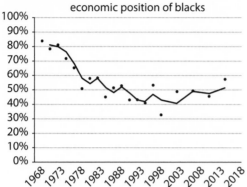

a. Government should improve the social and economic position of blacks

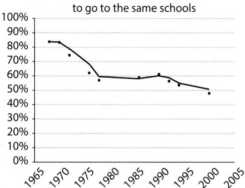

b. Government should see to it that white and black children are allowed to go to the same schools

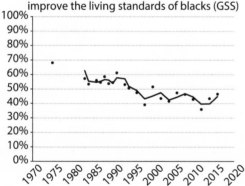

c. Government has special obligation to help improve the living standards of blacks (GSS)

FIGURE 0.5. Percentage of black support for government efforts to solve racial problems

intervention priorities that characterized the civil rights policies of the 1960s and 1970s. In the 1970s, black Americans overwhelmingly felt that government intervention was necessary to solve racial inequalities. In the early 1970s, over 80 percent of blacks supported government programs meant specifically to improve the social and economic position of blacks. Well over 80 percent of blacks in the early 1970s also felt that the government should be more active in integrating schools. By the 1990s, however, support for these initiatives had dropped off dramatically. In 2000, only about 50 percent of blacks supported government efforts to integrate schools, and today only about 50 percent of black Americans support government assistance programs targeted specifically at racial minorities. The contemporary divisions among blacks on racial issues also extend to less governmentcentric issues, such as affirmative action, where surveys regularly show that over 30 percent of blacks oppose racial preferences in hiring and college admissions.

This rather dramatic rightward shift in black political attitudes over the last half century might be explained, as some have argued, by the incorporation of black political leaders into mainstream politics, which has helped to push blacks away from the extreme liberal positions of the civil rights era by shifting their attention to mainstream political disagreements (Tate 2010). Or perhaps this conservative shift is the product of the economic prosperity experienced by those blacks who have benefited from the rising income inequality over the last several decades. Whatever is responsible for moderating black political beliefs in the 1980s and 1990s, our contention is that the politically remarkable observation is that *this conservative shift does not seem to correspond to changes in black party identification.*

That the increasing political diversity among black Americans has resulted in a unique distance between political attitudes and partisanship is a point we underscore by comparing blacks with other ethno-racial groups using data from the 2012 ANES survey. Figure 0.6 shows group differences in the percentage of self-identified liberals and conservatives who also identify as Democrats. The differences in rates of Democratic Party identification between black conservatives and conservatives of other ethno-racial groups are striking. While only 19 percent of self-identified white conservatives, 22 percent of Asian conservatives, and 48 percent of Latino conservatives identify as Democrats, an overwhelming majority—82 percent—of self-identified black conservatives identify as Democrats. In fact, the level of Democratic Party identification among *black conservatives* equals that of *white liberals*. Table 0.1 shows a similar pattern of relative difference in Democratic partisan identification by conservative issue positions. Just as

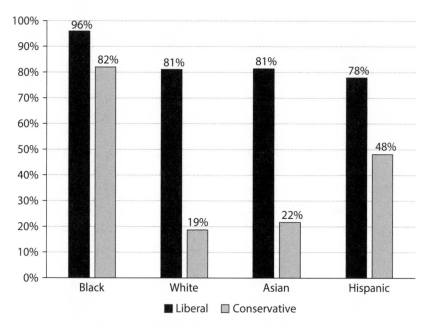

FIGURE 0.6. Percentage of Democrats by liberal-conservative self-identification (from seven-point scale) and race, 2012 ANES

TABLE 0.1. Percentage of Democratic Identification by Conservative Issue Position and Race, 2012 ANES

	Black	White	Asian	Hispanic
Govt. should let each person get ahead on own	77.4	21.6	35.7	45.5
No regulation of businesses to protect environment	74.1	15.9	10.0	37.9
Oppose increasing taxes on millionaires	82.2	10.0	8.3	43.6
Govt. should provide many fewer services	68.9	17.6	36.4	35.9
Govt. should make it easier for people to buy a gun	75.0	17.8	0.0	35.2
By law, abortion should never be permitted	72.8	21.8	18.2	51.3
Favor death penalty	85.2	37.1	46.8	57.2
Oppose laws to protect gays and lesbians	91.3	19.5	18.7	40.0
Oppose university affirmative action	87.9	32.3	41.5	52.1
Oppose workplace affirmative action	87.7	33.1	45.4	51.0
Blacks should help themselves (and not receive govt. assistance)	78.8	29.1	40.8	49.1

with the self-identified conservative ideology measure, the vast majority of black issue-conservatives identify as Democrats, while those in other racial groups do not. Across eleven different measures of issue conservativism, the percentage of blacks identifying with the Democratic Party never dips below 70 percent. Compare this with white issue-conservatives, whose rate of Democratic Party identification never exceeds 37 percent. Even blacks' conservative beliefs on racial issues fail to correspond to eroded identification with the Democratic Party. Nearly 90 percent of blacks who stated that they oppose affirmative action programs nonetheless identified as Democrats.

Why hasn't growing conservativism—even on racial issues—pushed blacks into the ranks of the Republican Party? Surely, blacks must sense the tension between their conservative political beliefs and their Democratic Party support. The question thus becomes how, exactly, have blacks maintained Democratic Party unity since the civil rights era? Answering that question is our aim.

Racialized Social Constraint and Black Democratic Party Identification

To make sense of the enduring partisan unity of black Americans, we argue, necessitates a framework that better incorporates their social groupness into our understanding of their political groupness. The idea that blacks form a political group because of collective interests defined by the American racial order is not a novel one. Nor is the idea that to make demands on government effectively, groups—such as black Americans—that have historically lacked economic and political power often come to rely particularly on forms of mass political action meant to convey unity in political preferences (Omi and Winant 1996). African Americans have often employed mass protest, boycotts, public demonstrations, and bloc voting as a means of conveying a sense that group members are unified both in their political positions and in their demands for government responsiveness to specific group concerns (Browning, Marshall, and Tabb 1984; Gillion 2013; McAdam 1982). And for black Americans this "solidarity politics" has proved to be an effective means of challenging white supremacy (Shelby 2005). From the enormous crowds that showed up in 1963 for the March on Washington to blacks' nearly unanimous electoral support for the candidacy of the first black person nominated by a major political party for president, solidarity politics have conveyed to government and the larger American population the message that black Americans not only speak with one voice but are prepared to act collectively if their concerns are not addressed.

Essential to the effectiveness of this solidarity politics strategy is the ability of the group to credibly convey that common concerns are widely *valued* by group members because it is that value that signals political commitment (McConnaughy 2013). The effectiveness of solidarity politics, in other words, rests on the credibility of the threat that the group will mete out its collective power. This logic for black politics was rather clearly articulated by Stokely Carmichael and Charles Hamilton in their 1967 guide to black political empowerment, *Black Power*. As quoted in Shelby (2005, p 101), Carmichael and Hamilton explain, "The concept of Black Power rests on a fundamental premise: *Before a group can enter open society, it must first close ranks*. By this we mean that group solidarity is necessary before a group can operate effectively from a bargaining position of strength in a pluralist society."

Defection by group members, however, is a constant threat to solidarity politics that must be managed. The challenge to black politics from defection or shirking by group members can be seen rather clearly in Martin Luther King Jr.'s final speech, where he implored the black community in Memphis to show up for a scheduled march in support of striking sanitation workers. King exhorts, "When we have our march, you need to be there. If it means leaving work, if it means leaving school—be there. Be concerned about your brother. You may not be on strike. But either we go up together, or we go down together" (Stewart 2018). King's entreaty evinces the central tension: in the grander scope of politics, only unity will deliver gains for subordinated groups, but defection for the sake of immediate individual interests is a constant threat to the group position and impairs the doing of politics in the interest of the group.

We argue that black Americans' capacity to resolve the defection conundrum is born of the same phenomenon that has created their need for political unity: the American experience of racial apartheid. The efforts of white Americans to segregate black Americans from larger American society have made black Americans uniquely socially integrated with and reliant on each other. Closed off from white social institutions such as schools, colleges, fraternal organizations, and churches, black Americans built their own indigenous institutions. Cordoned off from white neighborhoods by policies and social intimidation practices, black Americans built their own communities. Antimiscegenation laws and social denigration from white society further ensured that black Americans' kinship and social networks have remained characterized by a high degree of racial homophily. In short, black Americans remain remarkably socially interconnected with each other and segregated from white Americans. And in this social reality, we argue,

are the tools for a black politics maintained by racialized social pressure—
what we term *racialized social constraint.*

Racialized social constraint is a process of enforcing the norms of black
political behavior. It includes well-defined, racially specific social rewards
and penalties, which are used to compel compliance with group-based
expectations of political behavior. Even in the presence of individual incentives to do otherwise, the unambiguous nature of black political expectations
and the particular value assigned to the social consequences of defection
from versus compliance with this normalized group behavior place significant constraints on the political behaviors of black Americans. Social pressure *from other blacks* is the key element of this process. For an individual
whose social existence rests within the black community, the cost of defecting from the understood norms and practices of that group is greater when
it is understood that other members of that group, in particular, might be
aware of this defection. In other words, racialized social constraint rests not
on blacks concerned with whites questioning their blackness but rather on
the social costs to be paid when other blacks question their commitment
to or standing within the racial group. Well-established norms can also be
internalized into beliefs in black solidarity. Thus, racialized social constraint
functions beyond external social pressure, through an attitudinal acceptance of the importance of group solidarity. Both these mechanisms work
to increase individual-level commitment to group-based norms of political
behavior, preventing self-interested behavior that would undermine the
group's capacity to leverage unity as political power in the collective interest.

Specific norms of black political behavior exist, we argue, because black
Americans have over time been able to connect certain group-benefiting
political behaviors with racial in-group identity. Through the association of
certain behaviors with prototypical or idealized representations of blackness
(Laird 2019), those behaviors come to be defined as "good" black political
behaviors. And central among these norms in the post–civil rights era has
been that of Democratic Party identification. Maintenance of Democratic
identification as an in-group norm is surely aided by its informational basis—
that blacks "are Democrats" is repeated as fact through common descriptive
information, such as election returns that describe over 90 percent of black
voters casting ballots for the Democratic presidential candidate. But there is
more than a descriptive norm at work. Appeals that suggest that other black
Americans "died for your right to vote" and depictions of black Democratic
politicians, such as Barack Obama, that describe them as "role models" for
black youths are common elements of black political communication. Given

this normalization of black support for the Democratic Party, we contend that identifying with and voting for the Democratic Party and its candidates have come to be understood by most black Americans as in-group expected behaviors that individual blacks perform in anticipation of social rewards for compliance and sanctions for defection. Enforcement comes through social ties and black institutions, which help to define the boundaries of black social and political behavior and add institutional weight to black social connections (Cohen 1999; Dawson 1994; F. C. Harris 1994; Harris-Lacewell 2004; Mckenzie 2004).

What the Racialized Social Constraint Framework Is—and What It Is Not

Racialized social constraint as an explanation for black partisan unity is a move away from explanations of black politics that are focused almost exclusively on individual dispositions and toward one that truly incorporates social dynamics. To this point, most explanations of black partisan political behavior have focused on the roles that individual dispositions play in shaping or constraining black political beliefs and actions (see Dawson 1994; Gurin, Hatchett, and Jackson 1981; Philpot 2017; Shingles 1981; Tate 1991; Verba and Nie 1972). Among these have been individual dispositions, such as ideology, and individual-level group identity considerations ranging from simple affective closeness to beliefs in common fate, group consciousness, and solidarity. While not arguing that these attitudes are unimportant to black political decision making, we seek to resolve important empirical and theoretical difficulties.

The currently dominant attitudinal explanation of black support for the Democratic Party suggests that even blacks whose ideological, class, or individual interests do not align very well with the party's platform will nonetheless identify as Democrats as a result of an understanding that the Democratic Party is more likely than the Republican Party to represent the interests of blacks as a group (Dawson 1994; Philpot 2017; Tate 1993). One central difficulty in this model is that what "group interest" is and how it gains and *maintains* a common definition across a diverse group remain vaguely specified. What, exactly, is "black" group interest in the post–civil rights era (see Frymer 1999)? Even considering the role that Democrats played in securing black civil rights protections in the 1960s, it is not as if Republicans have not tried to position themselves as a party that represents black interests—or at least some interpretation thereof. Many of the limited government, self-help, personal responsibility, and moral arguments offered to blacks by Republicans are explicitly couched in terms of black identity politics, including black empowerment and racial group uplift. Blacks who do identify as Republicans have made concerted efforts to convince other black Americans that it is in both the individual and the group interests of blacks to support the Republican Party (see Fields 2016). And still, even most blacks who share many of the Republican Party's conservative political positions remain solidly in support of the Democratic Party. Existing dispositional models of black politics do not tell us why and *how* that is so. Our framework seeks to do just that.

Broadly, the basis of group-identity models of politics is the observation that humans are by nature social and that group membership and identification help to fulfill a basic need to belong (Tajfel and Turner 1979). But groups provide more for individuals than simply psychological belonging—they structure both daily experiences and access to resources and power. Thus, understanding the implications of group memberships for politics necessitates a set of analytical tools that clarify how the social workings of specific group memberships translate into individual political behaviors. Our racialized social constraint framework takes the specificity of the black American experience—with its history of slavery and racial segregation—and spells out its implications for the doing of group-based politics by individuals. It integrates not only the common set of beliefs but also the common practices and social relations that define what it means to be a black person in America (Franklin and Moss 1994). It makes the *structure* of the lived experience of blackness central to the politics of black Americans. Fundamentally, our framework seeks to better explain how the social experience of blackness translates into the homogeneity we observe in black partisan identification and behaviors.

As much as it is important to say what racialized social constraint is, it is equally important to clearly articulate what it is not. We are not suggesting that black Americans are mindlessly following the dictates of the group. Quite the contrary. Unlike many dispositional explanations of black political behavior, which suggest that group unity stems from some sort of affective tie to the racial group or from black Americans not making individually optimal decisions (Dawson 1994), ours is a rational explanation of black political decision making. Adherence to group norms of political behavior is produced through black Americans making realized trade-offs between their ideological or individual self-interests and the potential for racialized social consequences that might accrue to them personally as the result of their decision. Importantly, social sanctions are dealt out to group members for defection from political choices understood to be in the interest of the group, and social rewards are given for compliance with these expectations. Indeed, we will show in later chapters how racialized social constraint produces compliance not with just *any* political behaviors but rather with those that have specific group-interest meaning.

Our account also does not suggest that black Americans lack any real agency in deciding their own partisanship. While deviating from in-group expectations can have real social costs for black Americans, the racialized social constraint model still implies that black Americans make *choices* about the trade-offs they are willing to accept between social costs and rewards, on the one hand, and self-interests, on the other. We demonstrate empirically that although black Americans are highly responsive to racialized social pressure, many nonetheless freely defect from group-based expectations. For some black Americans, defection is enabled by having more racially diverse social connections. Others appear to defect simply because they more greatly value their individual ideological or material self-interests over any social cost of defection. The modern black experience of racialized social constraint certainly implies trade-offs to navigate. It does not, however, engender a coercive system meant to suppress individual choice and agency entirely.

Lastly, despite our invocation of unique features of black groupness, we offer this framework as an adaptable tool for the general explanation of group-based behavior. Its utility in explaining the politics of other social groupings depends on the extent to which there are well-defined norms of political behavior and socially homogeneous institutions and networks that enable the maintenance and enforcement of those norms. As we discuss the conditions necessary for our racialized social constraint model to hold, we highlight how groups such as Southern whites, white evangelical Christians, trade union members, and certain localized racial and ethnic groups exhibit elements of social constraint similar to those exhibited by black Americans. In the concluding chapter of the book, we discuss in some detail how our framework applies to some of these groups.

Making Racialized Social Constraint Visible

Our central task in this book is demonstrating how a distinct set of social processes, embodied in our racialized social constraint explanation, constrains black behavior and prevents defection from the Democratic Party.

Demonstrating this is not simple. Given that nearly all black Americans identify as Democrats—and have for some time—isolating the conditions under which this identification is created and maintained is empirically difficult. There simply is not much variation in the outcome that can be used to observe under what conditions black Americans identify with the Democratic Party and under which they do not. Our approach resolves this difficulty by adopting a fundamentally counterfactual perspective. To understand and assess how blacks' high level of Democratic partisanship is maintained, we first identify the social and political conditions that might result in lower levels of black Democratic Party support. Then we create those conditions and observe what happens. In short, by offering black Americans, under controlled conditions, realistic incentives to defect from the Democratic Party and social situations in which they can feel free to defect, we find some black Americans significantly less likely to identify with and behaviorally support the Democratic Party. That is, by providing conditions that are less likely to occur "in the real world," we can observe how the "real-world" conditions are effectively maintaining the distribution of black Democratic identification and support.

The experiments we conducted give us causal evidence of how racialized social constraint produces partisan unity among black Americans. By operationalizing racialized social constraint through a set of constructed racialized social interactions, to which we randomly assigned black American study participants, we were able to directly test its ability to constrain partisan defection. Our experiments cover a broad range of manifestations of the racialized social constraint concept. We assess how even everyday existence in a racially homophilic environment imposes constraint by observing the effect of the simple presence of another black person bearing witness to a political behavior that implies a choice between supporting the group interest and supporting a self-interest. We gain insight into the constraining effects of black institutions by observing the effect of study participants being made aware that their choices in a group-interest versus self-interest situation will be made known through the student newspaper of a historically black university. Each experiment offers a unique piece of empirical leverage. Together they tell a coherent story of racialized social constraint as a fundamental force in the production of black partisan unity.

While the experiments are the core of our empirical assessment of racialized social constraint's causal effects on black political behavior, we embed them in the context of relevant descriptive realities of the black American political experience. The plausibility and explanatory value of our framework depend on a range of descriptive facts—from the extent of ongoing racial homophily in the social environments of black Americans to black Americans' basic awareness of what other blacks do and expect of them in the realm of partisan politics. Thus data drawn from the "real world" of the black American experience are just as much a part of the empirical case we offer as are the results of experiments wherein we construct the details of our study participants' experiences.

Outline of Book

In the next chapter, we offer a detailed explanation of our racialized social constraint model of black political behavior. As an answer to our central question of the role of black unity in partisan politics, we argue that black support for the Democratic Party has over time become a normalized form of black political behavior for which blacks actively hold one another accountable. In developing this argument, we first review the relevant literature on African American political behavior and discuss how many of the insights gained from this research point to the importance of group-based expectations in ensuring compliance with group norms of black political behavior. We then engage the microfoundations of black political behavior, building on insights from mainstream political behavior and social psychology to identify the precise mechanism by which black partisan homogeneity is likely maintained. Our focus is on *how* various incentives for compliance with group norms and sanctions for defection from these norms result in the maintenance of black political unity. We also discuss the unique way that these norms relate to black identity, building on insights from the psychological theory of role identities. All of this leads to a set of general expectations for what we should observe if our framework for understanding black political behavior holds.

In Chapter 2 we begin with a discussion of the social and political circumstances that have necessitated black political unity, norms of black political behavior, and the emergence of racialized social constraint. Placing its historical origins in slavery, we discuss how racialized social constraint has developed from a tool for navigating the complicated social and political world of forced labor communities into an instrument for facilitating racial group-based collective action politics among black Americans. We connect norms of racial group constraint formed under slavery to mechanisms for mobilizing blacks into the protest activities of the 1960s Civil Rights Movement and tools for facilitating specific forms of engagement in modern electoral politics. From the combined insights provided by our historical review of black Americans' efforts at collective action and our racialized social constraint model, we derive specific predictions of how racialized norms of political behavior constrain black partisan support in modern electoral politics. Finally, we highlight two basic facts that speak to the explanatory potential of our framework. First, we show that black Americans indeed share a common awareness that most other blacks regularly support Democratic candidates. Second—and, we think, more telling—we show that black Americans report not only that they are regularly solicited by friends and family to support the Democratic Party but also that they are concerned about the social consequences of friends and family finding out if they were to choose not to support the Democratic Party and its candidates.

Building on research that focuses on the social and cultural underpinnings of political preferences, we take racial segregation and the isolation of African Americans in racially homogeneous communities to be crucial in ensuring the continued effectiveness of racialized social pressure at constraining black political behavior. Thus, Chapter 3 offers our empirical assessment of the connection between racial homophily in black social networks and homogeneity in black party support. We show a strong link between racially homogeneous social networks and black Democratic Party support. Among our findings is that the more racial in-group members within a black person's close social network, the more likely that individual is to identify as a Democrat. Further, the composition of networks seems most predictive among those blacks who have ideological incentives to defect from the norm of Democratic support. Among black conservatives, we find, those with more racially diverse social networks are more likely to defect from the norm of supporting the Democratic Party.

In Chapter 4 we begin to dig into the process by which racialized social constraint works to inhibit the defection of black Americans from the norm of Democratic Party support. Empirically, we take advantage of the social interactions within survey interviews—between black respondents and either black or non-black interviewers—as a window into exactly how racialized social constraint works to inhibit blacks' defection from the Democratic Party. Pooling more than thirty years of face-to-face survey data and twenty years of phone survey data, we show that the simple presence of a black interviewer exerts considerable pressure on black respondents to conform to the norm of supporting the Democratic Party. Not only do we find that black respondents express significantly greater identification with the Democratic Party when in the presence of a black interviewer, we further demonstrate that the effect is most pronounced among those blacks who have the greatest incentive to defect from the norm of Democratic Party support: black conservatives.

In Chapter 5 we move from racialized social constraint's influence on the simple expression of black party identification to its ability to increase political action in support of the Democratic Party and its candidates. To demonstrate the existence of an in-group norm of active support, we turn once again to data about the race of the interviewer. These data show that the mere presence of another black person—even a complete stranger—leads black Americans not only to express an increased desire to act in support of Democratic candidates before an election but also to overstate their actual involvement in campaign activities following the election. We then push deeper into the causal process of racialized social constraint using a lab-in-the-field experiment that enables us to directly test the effect of racialized social pressure on blacks' willingness to engage in political action. Using the behavior of contributions to the Obama campaign as a black group-norm-consistent behavior, and using personal monetary incentives to defect from this norm to induce a self-interest conflict, we vary whether black study participants must make their choice in front of another person who has made his or her own political choice clear, as well as whether that person is a racial in-group member. We find that, indeed, social pressure from other blacks uniquely reduces self-interested behavior and results in greater group-norm-consistent political behavior. Importantly, we also show that social pressure from other blacks only works to increase group-norm-*consistent* behavior. It does not encourage defection.

Chapter 6 takes up black social institutions as central locations where in-group political norms are defined and propagated. We outline a basic history of black social institutions, including how their creation was a direct response to the denial of access to white spaces. We note the importance of these institutions as sites for in-group political discourse and the enforcement of norms. These institutions are places where blacks are reminded of group expectations. Using survey data, we demonstrate the frequency with which blacks Americans interact within black institutions. Our analysis shows that black institutions continue to be centers for daily engagement, reinforcing black social ties. This also, of course, makes them sites wherein black Americans are likely to anticipate social sanctions for their political behaviors. Indeed, we show that participation or membership in black institutions is related to greater adherence to norms of black political behavior, including Democratic partisan identification. We then turn to another lab-in-the-field experiment to directly test the power of black institutions to facilitate racialized social constraint. Using a prominent black institution, a historically black university, to implement racialized social constraint, we find that black institutions can indeed be especially effective as conduits for the enforcement of compliance with norms of black political behavior.

In the final chapter, we examine the broader implications of this research, both empirical and normative. We discuss the potential for our theoretical framework to further understanding of the political behavior of other social groupings in America. In particular, we consider how our theory of racialized social constraint could explain the behavior of Southern whites in their modern allegiance to the Republican Party. We also consider the framework's applicability to understanding the political homogeneity of localized racial groupings—where ethno-racial political unity might not be possible on a national scale but should be expected under local circumstances. If the foundational mechanism of political power through unity is that identified by our framework—coracial social ties—then desegregation and the loss of black institutions are a fundamental challenge to the doing of black liberation politics. We discuss what this might mean for the future of black politics. In so doing, we also engage arguments about the harms of coracial policing and weigh how to think about balancing those concerns against the reality that the political unity that has consistently enabled black political power relies on a process of social sanctioning. Finally, we consider the questions future research might answer by engaging and applying our theoretical framework and chart a course for future progress.

1

Black Political Decision Making

> There must be a climate of social pressure in the Negro community
> that scorns the Negro who will not pick up his citizenship rights and
> add his strength enthusiastically and voluntarily to the accumulation of
> power for himself and his people.
> —MARTIN LUTHER KING JR., *WHERE DO WE GO FROM HERE: CHAOS
> OR COMMUNITY?*

Black Americans' loyalty to the Democratic Party in the post–civil rights
era has become a well-documented and well-known fact of American politics (Tate 1993). Black Americans nearly unanimously support Democratic
presidential candidates. Unified black support for the Democratic Party
extends to midterm elections and down-ticket contests at the state and
local levels. Indeed, black Americans' partisan commitment to Democrats overrides race in the sense that they will most often support white
Democrats over black Republicans. For example, in the 2016 American
National Election Studies (ANES) Pilot Study, black respondents were
asked whom they would support in a head-to-head contest between potential Republican presidential nominee Ben Carson, an African American
neurosurgeon who was well respected within the African American community before his run for the Republican nomination, and presumptive
Democratic nominee Hillary Clinton. Only 10 percent of black Americans
favored Carson over Clinton. Notably, Carson's support among potential
black voters was only 2 percentage points greater than that of Donald

Trump, who received only 8 percent of black support in the same preelection matchup with Clinton.

The long-standing nature of blacks' electoral loyalty to the Democrats can present itself as somewhat of a puzzle. Pundits, political commentators, and even some scholars have argued that blacks' loyalty to the Democratic Party has produced little in the way of substantive policy changes with regard to race over the last several decades (see Frymer 1999). By some measures the material condition of blacks has indeed improved very little if at all over this same time period.[1] Speculation about when black support for the Democratic Party will falter finds a regular home in media coverage of American elections. Some have even surmised that if blacks were a little more strategic with their vote, perhaps by giving the impression that they might be willing to support Republican candidates, they could force the parties to compete for their support and leverage more substantive policy outcomes. Yet year after year the outcome is the same: nearly unanimous support for Democratic candidates.

To explain the perhaps perplexing loyalty of black Americans to the Democratic Party, scholars have generally turned to the dominant political parties' positions on issues of race. Although these explanations have come in different flavors—some behavioral or psychological, some institutional, and some sociological—they commonly frame black support for the Democratic Party as rooted in both the race-and-labor politics taking place within Northern cities the mid-twentieth century (Schickler 2016; Walton 1975) and the partisan commitments made in reaction to the demands of the 1960s black rights movement (Rigueur 2015). In such accounts, the racially charged nature of the 1964 presidential campaign and Democratic support for both the 1964 Civil Rights Act and the 1965 Voting Rights Act were defining moments that helped to crystallize black political support for the Democratic Party. Indeed, despite some disagreement over when and how black Americans' alignment with the Democrats began, the importance of these events in the foundational consolidation of African American support for the Democrats is difficult to question. What remains unclear in the scholarly literature is how, nearly fifty years after the end of the Civil Rights Movement—generations later—and in the face of growing political conservatism within the black community (Philpot 2007, 2017; Tate 2010), black Americans have been able to *maintain* their nearly unanimous support for the Democratic Party.

Our purpose in this book is to answer this question of how black unity in partisan politics has been maintained over decades. In this chapter, we outline the theoretical framework we use to do so. We argue that because black Democratic Party identification consolidated under the heightened group consciousness of the Civil Rights Movement, supporting the Democratic Party became defined as a well-understood norm within the African American community—an expectation of black political behavior, compliance with which blacks actively hold one another accountable for. This in-group accountability, we argue, helps to constrain black political behavior by making salient the possible social benefits of conformity and the likely social consequences for defection. Those who may have ideological or self-interested reasons to defect from the in-group norm of supporting the Democratic Party (e.g., black conservatives or black business owners who might want lower taxes) nonetheless maintain their support for the Democratic Party in pursuit of social acceptance or approval from other group members or in an effort to avoid negative social sanctions for defection from this group norm. This process, which we call *racialized social constraint*, is a social explanation of black political behavior in which individual blacks conform to norms of black political behavior out of an expectation that conformity has the potential for increased social standing within social relationships with other African Americans and that non-conformity or defection has the potential for loss of social standing.

What makes this process effective as a tool for maintaining black party unity, we contend, is the American system of race that has produced and reproduced the segregation of blacks from the dominant white society. The black American experience remains one marked by racial homophily in social networks, kinship ties, and social institutional belonging. This fact imparts a uniquely high social value to in-group connections for blacks. Upholding the in-group norm of supporting the Democratic Party is a choice on the part of blacks to preserve that social value. Public displays of normalized group behavior—such as publicly supporting the Democratic Party—signal to other blacks a commitment to the social group and ultimately work to authenticate one's place in this social grouping. Normalization of black Democratic Party identification within the black community thus renders black social and political identities nearly inseparable. Conforming to norms of black political behavior such as supporting Democratic candidates has come to be understood as a salient way that black Americans can affirm their "blackness" in the eyes of other blacks.

In the pages that follow, we discuss the current state of research on black political behavior and show how our racialized social constraint framework not only ties together disparate explanations of black political behavior but also helps to fill in the gaps left by earlier attempts to understand black political homogeneity. Building on insights from a range of social science disciplines—political science, sociology, economics, and psychology—our racialized social constraint explanation adds to previous explanations of unity in black political behavior that have focused on the strength of black racial identity as a key explanatory variable. While we do not reject a racial identity framework, our explanation incorporates role expectations and social accountability into a more comprehensive account of how black identity affects black political behavior. We conclude this chapter with a brief discussion of the generalizability of our racialized social constraint explanation and its applicability to other social groupings.

Black Political Decision Making

Since the reincorporation of blacks into the American electorate via passage and enforcement of the 1965 Voting Rights Act, social science research has taken up the question of what might be unique about African American political behavior and decision making (see, for example, Banks, White, and McKenzie 2018; Calhoun-Brown 1996; Cohen and Dawson 1993; Dawson 1994; Gurin, Hatchett, and Jackson 1981; D. R. Harris 1999; Harris-Lacewell 2004; Harris-Perry 2011; Hutchings, Valentino, Philpot, and White 2006; T. Lee 2000; McDaniel 2008; Philpot 2017; Philpot and White 2010; Sigelman and Welch 1991; Shingles 1981; Tate 1991, 1993, 2010; Verba and Nie 1972; Walton 1985; I. K. White 2007; I. K. White, Laird, and Allen 2014). Motivated at first to understand how African Americans would make the transition from political participation centered largely on protest activity to engagement in mainstream politics, initial research attempted to identify the unique features of African American life that might explain blacks' largely unified political views and unique patterns of political participation. What has emerged across nearly fifty years of research since has been a set of explanations for black political behavior that center on identifying the roles that individual-level dispositions related to the strength of black racial group identification play in facilitating black engagement in politics. Here we outline these explanations and how they contribute to our understanding of blacks' ability to engage in unified political behavior. We then consider how our racialized social constraint model helps to fill in important gaps left by this research.

DISCOVERING RACIAL GROUP IDENTIFICATION

For the last fifty years, the dominant frameworks for understanding black Americans' political decisions have focused on the role that the strength of blacks' racial group identification plays in shaping their unique political preferences, beliefs, and patterns of engagement. The frameworks posit that African Americans' experiences with racial injustice in the United States have resulted in a heightened awareness of the political implications of race. This awareness, scholars have suggested, acts as both a resource, much like education, for overcoming the cost associated with political participation, and a belief system, much like liberal-conservative ideologies, for helping structure black political attitudes and decisions. Thus, it has featured in accounts of both political participation decisions and political attitudes and orientations—including partisanship—among black Americans.

One of the earliest empirical manifestations of the racial identity framework can be found in the 1972 work of Sidney Verba and Norman Nie, wherein they argue that a type of black racial identification, called racial group consciousness, is responsible for blacks' ability to out-participate similarly situated whites. Before Verba and Nie's work, it was generally accepted that in addition to the obvious structural impediments to black political participation (i.e., Jim Crow restrictions on political engagement, including voting), socioeconomic differences played a central role in explaining blacks' relatively low levels of engagement in political activities, such as voting, contacting elected officials, and making campaign contributions. Verba and Nie, however, observed that once socioeconomic differences between blacks and whites were taken into account, black Americans actually participated in certain forms of low-cost political activity at noticeably higher rates than similarly situated white Americans. Verba and Nie also observed that those blacks who frequently used race to discuss political issues were more politically active than blacks who did not. Noting the importance of group norms of participation born out of the Civil Rights Movement, Verba and Nie suggested that the heightened salience of race helped to remind blacks of the importance of political engagement to the racial group. Their reasoning was that black Americans had, "over time, developed an awareness of their own status as a deprived group, and this self-consciousness has led them to be more politically active than members of the society who have similar socioeconomic levels but do not share the group identity" (1972, p. 157). Shingles (1981) expanded on this idea, showing that racial group consciousness gains much of its influence through its ability to facilitate political mistrust and heighten blacks' sense of internal efficacy. Although Tate (1991) later found mixed results for the racial group consciousness argument in her examination of data from the 1984 and 1988 presidential elections, Chong and Rogers's (2005) reanalysis of Tate's findings suggests a fairly robust role for racial group consciousness in predicting black participation.

Building on Verba and Nie's racial group consciousness argument, Gurin, Hatchett, and Jackson (1989) introduced the concept of common fate in their discussion of black racial group identity and collective political action. Their logic was that when members of a marginalized group "care about each other, feel themselves bound by a shared culture and a common fate, and develop an ideology concerning the group's position in society they are motivated to take part in collective activities" (p. 75). For Gurin, Hatchett, and Jackson, common fate is made up of two elements that each play an important role in facilitating political engagement. The first is interdependence, which they defined as belief that what happens to blacks as a group generally also affects the individual's own life and that the black rights movement affects one personally. The second is centrality, which concerns how much an individual thinks about being black and what he or she has in common with other blacks. Although Gurin, Hatchett, and Jackson's empirical test of the common fate identified it as predictive of black support of black candidates like Jesse Jackson, they also presented evidence that common fate beliefs, as they operationalized them, were not so widely held within the black population.[2]

LINKED FATE AND THE BLACK UTILITY HEURISTIC

While the initial studies of black political behavior offered important expositions of the relationship between it and racial group identity, Michael Dawson's 1994 book, *Behind the Mule: Race and Class in African-American Politics*, provided a more comprehensive theoretical framework of black unity built around the idea of racial group identification. Dawson relabeled Gurin, Hatchett, and Jackson's (1989) common fate measure, identifying it instead as a measure of what he called linked fate. Dawson argues that this linked fate concept forms the central importance of race to black political decision making, but that it represents not an affective attachment to the group but rather an informational shortcut, or heuristic, to individual blacks' self-interest. In Dawson's telling, given the history of racial discrimination in the United States, when faced with a political decision, it is generally "more efficient for them [African Americans] to use the status of the group, both relative and absolute, as a proxy for individual utility" (p. 10). He further argues that what makes this process especially efficient is that "legislation or a public policy could be analyzed relatively easily for its effect on the race" and that "the information sources available in the black community . . . would all reinforce the political salience of racial interest" (p. 11). According to Dawson, then, much of the political unity we observe in African American political behavior results from African Americans' relying on racial group interest as a proxy for their own individual interests, engaging in a form of bounded or low-information rationality, because the political implications for the group are much more easily identifiable or accessible than individuals' unique utilities are.

Many studies since have employed Dawson's linked fate concept in explanations of African American political behaviors, ranging from policy positions on issues like affirmative action and reparations for slavery to support for black candidates (Dawson and Popoff 2004; Gay, Hochschild, and White 2016; Harris-Lacewell 2004; Tate 2010; I. K. White 2007). Empirically, the common fate measure has been shown to predict blacks' opinions about a range of issues that are explicitly racial, such as affirmative action (Dawson 1994; Tate 1993), and reparations for slavery (Dawson and Popoff 2004). Less evidence exists, however, that indicates that this incarnation of racial group identification consistently matters to blacks' opinions on ostensibly non-racial issues. Tate (1993) for example finds no relationship between racial group identification and blacks' opinions on matters of foreign policy, funding for public schools, or universalistic programs like Medicare. I. K. White (2007) confirms Tate's observational findings but also shows that on ostensibly non-racial issues, political discourse plays a key role in defining the relevance of race to black political decision making. White conducted a series of experiments that manipulated message content to show that the relevance of racial group interest to black political decision making is highly dependent on whether political choices are communicated in a way that makes their implication for the racial group clear and unclouded by subgroup differentiation.

On a theoretical level, while the framework is a sensible tool for understanding black political decision making under conditions of low information, where group interest would appear a reasonable proxy for self-interest, the theory's applicability to understanding decisions where blacks are faced with discernible trade-offs between individual and group interest is less so. Dawson (1994, p.10) himself notes that black Americans' use of racial group interest in political decision making is really just a "proxy for individual

utility," implying that were blacks actually aware of the individual implications of a particular policy or political choice, they would have little use
for group interest maximization. In other words, by relying on bounded
rationality, Dawson's model implies limitations to the "rational" use of group
interest. In particular, the use of group interest as a proxy for self-interest is
only individually "rational" under conditions of low information. This limits
the utility of the model as a general explanation of black political behavior.
Black Americans are frequently faced with social and political decisions that
require them to make explicit and well-understood trade-offs between their
individual preferences and what might be seen as in the best interest of the
racial group. Under such conditions, racial group identification, as defined
in the black utility heuristic model, should offer little guidance for individual
decisions. Indeed, it would seem the group interest ought to have little sway
for such an individual.

A model that speaks to how black Americans realistically weigh group-
and self-interest conflicts seems especially important given that such conflicts are quite common for African Americans in both their social and
their political lives. When evaluating housing options, for example, African
Americans have been shown to express a preference for neighborhoods with
significant numbers of other African Americans (Charles 2000; Krysan and
Farley 2002), as well as an interest in neighborhoods with low crime rates,
good public schools, and quality housing stock (Farley et al. 1993; D. R.
Harris 1999). What happens when these two things conflict, which they
too often do? Similarly, blacks may face conflicts about dating or marrying
outside their race because of the tension such a choice represents between
their individual preferences and their sense of the group interest (Kennedy
2008; Shelby 2005). Similar dilemmas are present in choices about whether
to attend predominantly white colleges and universities or whether to attend
churches with largely white congregations. And these trade-offs are also present in explicitly political choices. Why should middle- and upper-class black
Americans not perceive some tension between their own self-interest and
support for redistributive programs that might disproportionately benefit
blacks as a group? Why should those who strongly favor antiabortion stances
or anti-LGBTQ positions not desire to support Republican candidates who
endorse those positions?

For our purposes, the central shortcoming of the linked fate framework
is its inability to explain blacks' nearly unanimous support for the Democratic Party. Empirically, previous work has found, at best, a weak or conditional relationship between Democratic Party identification and linked

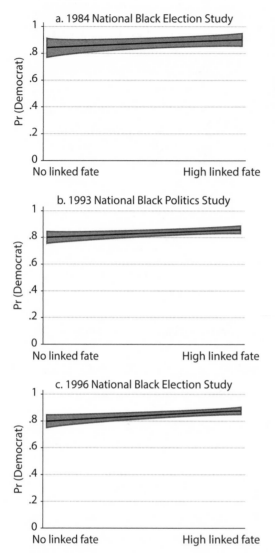

FIGURE 1.1. Relationship between linked fate and Democratic Party identification, 2016 ANES. *Notes:* Results represent the marginal effect of linked fate on Democratic Party identification with 95% confidence intervals. Includes controls for age, sex, education, and liberal or conservative ideology. Bivariate models produce similarly small relationships. Results from the 2012 and 2016 ANES only include data from face-to-face interviews.

fate (Hajnal and Lee 2011; Hutchings and Jefferson 2014; Philpot 2017; Tate 1993). Our own analysis of six different surveys, all probability samples with large samples of black Americans spanning more than thirty years from 1984 to 2016, also finds that the empirical connection between these two concepts is, at best, weak and inconsistent. We summarize the results of that analysis in Figures 1.1a–f by graphing the predicted effect of black linked fate on blacks' willingness to identify as Democrats in each survey. The generally flat shape of the curves illustrates the weak empirical connection. Although

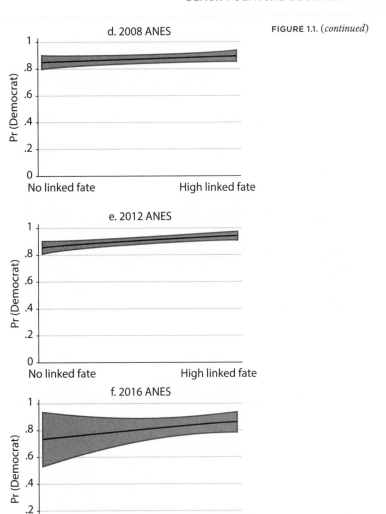

FIGURE 1.1. (*continued*)

higher levels of linked fate do appear to slightly increase the probability that a black respondent will identify as a Democrat, the average effect size of linked fate across all these data sources is only about 4 percentage points. At no point does the probability that those blacks who express the lowest levels of linked fate will identify as Democrats dip below .7. Empirically, then, linked fate just does not seem to significantly differentiate blacks who support the Democratic Party from those who do not (see also Hutchings and Jefferson 2014).

Another read of Dawson's argument might be that linked fate should influence black Democratic Party identification indirectly. Perhaps those blacks whose ideological, class, or other individual interests do not align very well with the Democratic Party's platform nonetheless identify as Democrats because they are constrained by an understanding that the Democratic Party is more likely than the Republican Party to represent the interest of blacks as a group. In other words, instead of identifying a direct connection between linked fate and black Democratic Party identification, we might interpret Dawson's framework to imply that ideology's guidance is contingent on understanding one's own fate to be at least in part driven by what happens to the racial group, leading only those without the group-interest cross-pressure away from Democratic Party identification. Black conservatives who perceive themselves as strongly linked to the group, however, would be constrained by this connection to the group and nonetheless identify as Democrats. This is an argument similar to that forwarded by Philpot (2017), who suggests that racial group consciousness is the "tie that binds" black conservatives to the Democratic Party.

This idea that linked fate works to constrain black ideological defection from the Democratic Party can be evaluated empirically. If those blacks whose ideological interests do not align very well with the Democratic Party's platform will nonetheless identify as Democrats because of the Democratic Party's position on race, then we should observe highly linked black conservatives identifying as Democrats. Using data from the larger-than-normal African American samples collected in the 2008, 2012, and 2016 ANES surveys, we evaluate this proposition. The results of this analysis are presented in Figures 1.2a–c. These chart the probability that a black person identifies as a Democrat by his or her liberal-conservative ideology and level of black linked fate. If linked fate does indeed prevent the defection of black conservatives from the Democratic Party, we should observe among those blacks with high levels of linked fate high levels of Democratic partisanship across the ideological spectrum. Conversely, since low linked fate enables defection, among blacks with low levels of linked fate we should observe a decrease in Democratic partisanship among black conservatives. We find, however, that to the extent ideology explains black Democratic Party identification, it is *not* conditioned by linked fate. Across all years of the ANES data, the relationship between ideology and Democratic partisanship changes very little if at all by level of black linked fate. These results support our suspicion that linked fate is not what leads black conservatives to identify with the Democratic Party.

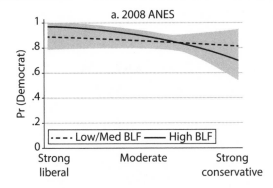

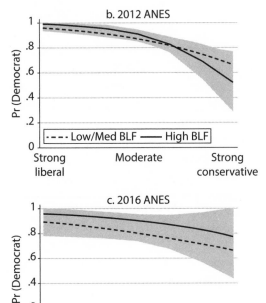

FIGURE 1.2. Black Democratic Party identification by liberal or conservative ideology and levels of black linked fate. *Notes:* Linked fate is a four-point scale that ranges from no linked fate to "a lot." Low/Med BLF (Black Linked Fate) is inclusive of the categories no linked fate, "not very much," and "some." High BLF includes only the "a lot" category.

Theoretically, what is unclear about the explanation for black partisanship that holds that ideology matters, conditional on linked fate, is why black conservatives with true, perceptible ideological reasons to support the Republican Party would not simply rationalize the Republican Party's positions on race to bring it more in line with the partisan identification implied by their own ideological interest. As sociologist Corey Fields's ethnographic (2016) work on black Republicans has documented, there are a variety of reasonings to employ for why it would be in black Americans' interest—both individual and group—to support the Republican Party. Nearly every campaign cycle features Republican arguments about their appeal to black voters. While some question the sincerity of these efforts, they nonetheless exist. Republicans have offered everything from symbolic arguments, such as, "Dr. Martin Luther King Jr. was a Republican," to negative partisanship scripts against the Democratic Party's record, such as, "Democrats today use deception and government handouts to keep blacks from voting for Republicans," or "Democrats have been running black communities for the past 50+ years and turned those communities into economic and social wastelands with their failed socialist policies" (Rice 2015). Black Republican presidential candidate Ben Carson described the Democratic Party as "the party of . . . servitude," suggesting that blacks' dependence on the American "welfare state" keeps them beholden to the Democratic Party (Dinan 2015). Carson would go on to state that he thinks this overreliance on government and lack of understanding of the value of economic empowerment is what really holds black Americans back. In speaking on racial group economic empowerment, Carson once told a group of black voters that "Jewish America understands it. Korean America understands it. Black America, if they could understand it, they could blow everybody else out of the water" (Rice 2015). Given the wide availability of such interpretations, why, then, would not *most* blacks who see supporting the Republican Party as in their individual or ideological interest use the available scripts to resolve any dissonance they experience between their group interest and self-interest?

BELIEFS IN RACIAL GROUP SOLIDARITY

Linked fate, of course, is not the only way that groupness could factor into black decision making. Indeed, one of the ways in which Dawson's linked fate argument has been misunderstood or reconstrued by other researchers is as something akin to a psychological sense of group solidarity or a sort of prosocial disposition through which black Americans exhibit self-sacrificing behavior via beliefs in the importance of the advancement of the group. In their review of the literature on linked fate, Gay, Hochschild, and White (2016) note that, "since the original formulation[,] . . . the connotation of linked fate for many scholars has become 'a sense of belonging or conscious loyalty to the group' [Simien 2005: 529. See also (Meares 1998)]" (p. 11). This is different from Dawson's linked fate. For Dawson, linked fate is a "rational" explanation of black political behavior built on access to information about the group. The group solidarity or loyalty-value explanation implies that black Americans have some sort of principled or affective psychological commitment to the group that impels them to exhibit self-sacrificing behavior toward the advancement of the group.

Black Americans' history of engagement in costly (to the individual) group-based political activities, such as protests, riots, and sit-ins, might tempt a belief that they are somehow uniquely disposed to make individual sacrifices for the good of the group. There are, however, theoretical and empirical reasons to question this conclusion—some of which were articulated long ago by the eminent scholar and practitioner of black politics W.E.B. DuBois. DuBois expressed strong doubts about the idea that black Americans would be uniquely altruistic, even for the sake of a group interest against a society sodden in structural and interpersonal racism. In his discussion of the political philosophy of black group solidarity, philosopher Tommy Shelby (2005, p.87) notes, "He [DuBois] did not expect black people to be altruistic toward one another just because they share a similar fate within the racist society of the United States. Nor did he expect African Americans to be moved solely by their sense of justice, for he recognized that, as laudable as this motive is, it is often compromised or abandoned when it conflicts with one's material interest and thus it alone will be insufficient to the task." If DuBois saw so little promise in the ability of altruistic concern for the group to overcome material interests in a political era defined by open white supremacy, there are reasons to apply his doubts to the expectation of a modern black partisan politics unified by simple feelings of solidarity. The sheer—and increasing—diversity of black opinion and economic interests, as we reviewed in the introduction, presents an ever-higher hurdle for any explanation of black political homogeneity that would rely solely on solidarity dispositions.

There is also little empirical evidence that internalized beliefs in solidarity or psychological dispositions of loyalty to the racial group are a unique feature of black decision making. One line of research that casts particular doubt on the black solidarity hypothesis is the study of behavior inside controlled, incentivized interaction environments, a line of behavioral economics research where study participants play "games" with real monetary incentives or "payouts." Trust games, where players must essentially choose whether to give money to others or keep it for themselves, provide a fairly clean assessment when the race of the players is varied and players are given a choice between keeping money for themselves or giving it to either racial in-group or racial out-group members. Generally, black participants—just like white participants—most often choose to keep the money for themselves and rarely show any in-group preference. This is true for both dictator games, which ask participants (proposers) to split some amount of money between themselves and some other person (receiver), and ultimatum games, which are similar to dictator games but allow the receiver to either accept the offer or reject it, and if the receiver rejects the offer, neither person receives any money (Fong and Luttmer 2009; Griffin, Nickerson, and Wozniak 2012). In one ultimatum game, researchers found black receivers to be *more* sensitive to unfair offers from black proposers (Griffin, Nickerson, and Wozniak 2012), suggesting that while blacks may not themselves feel a need to exhibit an in-group preference, they might expect other blacks to show deference to them. That is, maybe there is a normed expectation of coracial others.

Finding the Social Foundations of Black Political Decisions

Clues to filling in the gaps of the linked fate and group solidarity models' capacity to explain black party unity might be found in rational choice explanations of black political behavior. In his 1991 book *Collective Action and the Civil Rights Movement*, Dennis Chong offers a theoretical model for understanding why individual African Americans would choose to participate in the collective action of the Civil Rights Movement. Chong presents this choice as a dilemma given that individual blacks likely realized that their own participation was not a necessary condition for them to enjoy the benefits of the movement—if any were to actually accrue—but would come with real risks to their personal safety. Chong argues that the collective action problem of the movement was overcome by blacks who were motivated by a number of non-tangible incentives to participate, most centrally social pressure and the desire for in-group status. Chong, in other words, argues that activists during the Civil Rights Movement behaved in ways consistent with group expectations because they were constrained, at least in part, by the reputational consequences of defecting from group expectations for participation.[3]

While the evidence provided by Chong in support of his theory is largely anecdotal, the theoretical insights he offers are quite useful in explicitly outlining possible constraints and motivations underlying blacks' willingness to participate in political action. Most notably, he offers an explanation that centers on the potential of reputational sanctions for constraining black political behavior, even when the behavior in question may come at the risk of significant cost to the individual.[4] Indeed, though Chong does not explicitly evoke them as tools used to constrain black political behavior, notions of punishment with social sanctions by the black community for defection from commonly understood group behavioral norms are tangible enough that terminology for such sanctions is found in political discourse in the form of the epithets such as "Uncle Tom" and "sellout."[5] These phrases are commonly used to describe those blacks who seek personal benefit in supporting the causes of white Americans at the expense of causes that are supported by most other blacks and that are meant to directly benefit all or most members of the racial group.[6] They are linguistic evidence of reputational sanctions for those who engage in what some might call "racial free riding" (see Starkey 2012).

Though Chong's treatment is of the Civil Rights Movement in particular, we have reasons to expect that the threat of reputational sanctions should generally constrain black political behavior and work to prevent defection from the expected group norm of political action, even in the post–civil rights era. Public use of the sellout discourse continues, commonly in expressions of disapproval of blacks who endorse the Republican Party, its candidates, and its issues, and those who reject the social and cultural conventions of the black community. Well-known black Republicans such as Clarence Thomas, Herman Cain, Ben Carson, and Allen West, for example, have all, at one point or another, publicly fallen victim to the "Uncle Tom" or "sellout" characterization (Kennedy 2008; Starkey 2012). Some scholars have argued that the problem with the modern sellout discourse is that defining politically productive and sufficiently inclusive boundaries of blackness can be difficult, and in some cases the expressions appear recklessly overused as ways of punishing any small deviation from group norms (Cohen 1999; Kennedy 2008). Even President Barack Obama acknowledged the tension of in-group concern with the problematic turns that questioning individuals' racial authenticity can take. At a July 2014 event discussing his My Brother's Keeper initiative aimed at addressing challenges to success faced by black boys and young men, Obama said, "Sometimes African-Americans, in communities where I've worked, there's been the notion of 'acting white'—which sometimes is overstated. . . . But there's an element of truth to it, where, OK, if boys are reading too much, then, well, why are you doing that? Or why are you speaking so properly? And the notion that there's some authentic way of being black, that if you're going to be black you have to act a certain way and wear a certain kind of clothes, that has to go. There are many different ways for African-American men to be authentic" (Obama 2014). Despite its potential for problematic implications, that threat of questioning black individuals' racial authenticity or their cultural or political commitment to the racial group can powerfully constrain their behavior (Carter 1991; Cohen 1999; Kennedy 2008; Starkey 2012; Steele 1991).

The enduring power of reputational sanctions to constrain the political behavior of African Americans rests on widely held and historically entrenched expectations within the black community about how blacks are to behave politically and socially. As we describe in more detail later in this chapter and in Chapter 2, while African Americans at times have disagreed about the most effective methods of achieving black empowerment, there has been a long-standing common perception among blacks that *unity* in political efforts is essential to having black political demands recognized (Shelby 2005). Nowhere are expectations of black group unity more clearly seen in modern politics than in partisanship. It is not only well documented but also commonly known that nearly all African American voters will vote for the Democratic candidate in modern presidential elections. In no presidential election in modern times has a Republican candidate received more than 13 percent of the African American popular vote. This "fact" of black political homogeneity also gets reified by media coverage of elections and campaigns, which consistently describe African Americans as the most loyal voting bloc of the Democratic Party (Philpot 2017; Tate 1993). The lack of ambiguity in common knowledge of where "most" blacks stand in party politics is what gives sanctions, including the "Uncle Tom" and "sellout" epithets, their power as tools to constrain partisan behavior. Because the political loyalties and dispositions of the black community are so clear in common understandings, any deviation from the group position, even a small one, could potentially open one up to charges of "selling out" the race.[7]

Not only do black Americans have social tools for sanctioning group members, they also have important social institutions to serve as their conduits. During the Civil Rights Movement, the application of social pressure to encourage black political involvement occurred largely through black institutions, including black churches, colleges, and social and political organizations. Movement leaders' appeals certainly engaged democratic principles such as freedom and equality, but their messages were also constructed to exploit social connections within the black community to place pressure on blacks to participate (see A. D. Morris 1984). Indeed, membership or location in black social institutions has been found to be one of the more consistent predictors of black political behavior (R. K. Brown and Brown 2003; Dawson 1994; D. R. Harris 1999; Harris-Lacewell 2004;

McDaniel 2008; Tate 1993). Typically conceptualized as an organizational resource, membership in black institutions, particularly attendance at black churches, has been shown to be related to greater levels of black political engagement (D. R. Harris 1999; McDaniel 2008; Tate 1993). Research points to the importance of social connections made through these institutions in facilitating political engagement. R. K. Brown and Brown (2003), for example, argue that an important way black institutions—in their work on the black church—help to facilitate greater political engagement is by developing formal and informal social networks that help to "foster trust and feelings of mutual obligation among individuals" (p. 618). Brown and Brown's assessment is also supported by Mckenzie's (2004) work on the black church; when activism is encouraged by the institution, these close social ties help to motivate political engagement among members.

The potential for black social connections and black social institutions to influence black political behavior remains strong today. Racial isolation still structures the American experience for many blacks, and this isolation has helped to maintain many black social and political institutions and foster the creation of new ones. A 2009 Pew study found that nearly 60 percent of African American churchgoers still attend historically black churches, churches that remain predominantly filled with African American members and led by black preachers (Pew Research Center 2009).[8] While the proportion of black college students who attend historically black colleges and universities (HBCUs) has declined over the last forty years, 13 percent of black college graduates still come from HBCUs (Provasnik, Schafer, and Snyder 2004, p. 2).[9] Moreover, many of those blacks who choose to attend non-HBCUs eventually find themselves members of black social and professional organizations within those institutions (Sidanius et al. 2004; Willie 2003).

Unique levels of racial homophily can even be seen in online black social networks. In a study of friendship networks on Facebook, researchers noted that black students were significantly more likely to have same-race social networks than other racial groups (Wimmer and Lewis 2010). Indeed, the increased usage of smartphone technology has opened up social media spaces in which black Americans from all over the nation can interact and hold dialogues about race and the meaning of blackness. The term Black Twitter has been coined to describe the community of black Americans who interact over the Twitter platform. A 2014 Pew Research Center survey found substantial racial difference in the use of Twitter, with 27 percent of blacks who are online reporting that they regularly use Twitter, compared with 21 percent of whites (Duggan et al. 2015). Indeed, many see Black

Twitter as the future of digital racial discourse (Duggan et al. 2015). Thus, despite the legal integration of blacks into mainstream American society, racial isolation still defines the daily interactions of many if not most African Americans. And this segregation—and the investment in black social networks and institutional structures that was born out of it—enables the definition and enforcement of group-based norms of behavior.

Lastly, we note that negative sanctions are not the only tools for inspiring conformity to group expectations of political behavior. Positive social sanctions such as social and material incentives or rewards for conformity to norms of political engagement have also been historically important within the black community. Social incentives for conformity to norms of group behavior can include social approval, praise, reputational status, and leadership roles (P. B. Clark and Wilson 1961). These social rewards for conformity have the potential to increase not only an individual's feelings of belongingness but also his or her sense of social standing within a group. For example, within the black community, individuals who actively participated in the Civil Rights Movement are often revered and frequently referred to as heroes (Chong 1991; Wamble 2018). Positive social sanctioning is a way of conferring reputational status on these individuals for their devotion to the group.

Given the relative deprivation of the black community, material or positive selective incentives for conformity to norms of political engagement are less common. Additionally, because many black political organizations were founded on the principles of inclusiveness that characterized the struggle for civil rights, offering exclusive material incentives to members could be seen as at odds with organizational goals. Yet some black social institutions do at times offer selective incentives to their members. Some black churches provide members with discounted rates on child care or life insurance. Black fraternities and sororities have at times worked with insurance companies to offer discounted life insurance to their members. To the extent that these black social institutions organize around political issues and enforce compliance with norms of black political engagement, these material incentives could indirectly influence black political engagement.

Social Pressure, Norms of Black Racial Identity, and Black Democratic Partisanship

Though not central to the current literature on black politics, the power of social pressure to influence mass political behavior, particularly in the realm of voter turnout, has gained renewed research interest among political scientists in the last decade or so. Building on the ideas of social networks offered by Huckfeldt and colleagues (Huckfeldt, Johnson, and Sprague 2002, 2004; Huckfeldt, Plutzer, and Sprague 1993), recent studies have sought to understand how external social pressure and negative social sanctioning in the form of social shame—a concept similar to the idea of "reputational sanctions," which has permeated understandings of black collective action—can influence an individual's willingness to turn out to vote. In a large-scale get-out-the-vote (GOTV) field experiment, for example, Gerber, Green, and Larimer (2008) demonstrated that threatening to publicize a citizen's turnout record to his or her neighbors could increase turnout by between 2 and 8 percentage points. The conclusion: some people are more likely to conform to norms of participation when they believe that their behavior is likely to be observed by others. This type of effect has been replicated over a number of studies and supports the general idea that "shaming" is an effective tool for shaping political behavior (Gerber, Green, and Larimer 2010; Sinclair 2012).

While this GOTV research identifies the potential for the social pressure of reputational sanctions to influence political behavior, less is known about the process by which shaming influences such behavior. Social psychological research on social pressure and conformity, however, suggests that norm crystallization and norm intensity are both important in determining whether social pressure will result in conformity with the group norm (Bicchieri and Xiao 2008; Jackson 1965). That is, awareness of significant variation in agreement among group members about the importance of the norm to the functioning of the group—lower norm crystallization—decreases the potential for a message of social pressure to lead to compliance with the norm (Cialdini, Reno, and Kallgren 1990). Similarly, some norms are perceived as more or less important to the group than others—to have higher or lower intensity. Concerns about reputational sanctions for violations of less intensely held norms are likely to be discounted, as individuals calculate that their deviations from those norms are likely to go unnoticed or ignored, while violations of more intensely held norms are more likely to deliver reputational costs (Bicchieri and Xiao 2008). If we think about voting within this framework, we might conclude that it would be best characterized by high crystallization and low intensity. That is, while most Americans likely are aware of considerable agreement in society with the notion that voting is an important civic duty (crystallization), most are also aware that not only do many Americans regularly not vote, but the information of who does and does not vote is typically difficult to discover—suggesting that the norm of voting is not a preoccupation of the public (low intensity). Thus, the effectiveness of the shaming GOTV studies appears to hinge on their ability to increase the perception of intensity of the norm of voting. In threatening to publicize a citizen's turnout to his or her neighbors, the message is communicating not newfound information about the desirability of voting but rather the increased chance of reputational costs for not voting.

Another window into how social pressure might affect black political unity is in sociological and psychological work on the concept of role identities. Role identity theory would offer an interpretation of black political behavior that centers not only on the common ground of shared experiences but also on how the shared understanding and mutual expectations that have grown out of these experiences matter for individuals' interactions with each other. For role identity theorists, the individual's sense of self is the outcome of social interactions that define self-value (Mead 1934); the group relates to the self by more than mere psychological connections with a social category, as is the case with linked fate or group consciousness models. In their description of role identities,[10] Hogg, Terry, and White (1995, p. 256) note that what matters is "the self not as an autonomous psychological entity but a multifaceted social construct that emerges from people's roles in society; variation in self-concepts is due to the different roles that people occupy." Feedback from group members about individuals' compliance with group expectations becomes central to an individual's sense of self. As Hogg, Terry, and White (1995, p. 257) articulate, "A role is a set of expectations prescribing behavior that is considered appropriate by others. . . . The perception that one is enacting a role satisfactorily should enhance feelings of self-esteem, whereas perceptions of poor role performance may engender doubts about one's self-worth, and may even produce symptoms of psychological distress. . . . Distress may arise if feedback from others—in the form of reflected appraisals or perceptions of the self suggested by others' behavior—is perceived to be incongruent with one's identity."

Thus, applying role identity theory to understanding black political decision making means moving away from a perspective that necessitates a strict connection between individual and group interest, toward a focus on relational interactions that account for both interpersonal interactions and, importantly, the centrality of intraracial norms and expectations (Brewer 2001) about how one should behave politically as a black person. Applying role identity theory to understanding black partisan constraint centers enforcement of norms and expectations of partisan identification within an individual's dominant racial context. For blacks, primarily socially located as they are in intraracial contexts, that implies that racial in-group social constraint is essential to understanding the maintenance of black political solidarity. Indeed, as the idea of black support for the Democratic Party has become more crystallized in black Americans' understanding of partisan politics, support for the Democratic Party has become closely linked to black identity—so much so that black Americans have come to see black support for the Democratic Party as just something that "black people do." Given the high degree of acceptance of this norm within the black community, the act of publicly supporting the Democratic Party among blacks becomes a racial-identity-confirming behavior that individual blacks perform as a way to obtain social confirmation from other blacks. Having the partisan behavior socially confirmed or rewarded, individuals link the act to racial identity affirmation and thus the behavior is repeated. By the same logic, publicly supporting the Republican Party, which would likely engender negative feedback since it reflects a rejection of the expected group behavior, becomes less self-affirming.

Lastly, additional clues to how race-specific social pressure might work to constrain the partisan political behavior of African Americans appear in research examining the effects of interviewer race on black survey respondents. Researchers have long observed that black respondents to surveys give noticeably different answers to survey questions when interviewed by black as opposed to white interviewers (Hyman 1954). A particularly notable test of race of interviewer effects came from Schuman and Converse (1971), who were able to exert strong causal leverage by using data from the 1968 Detroit Area Study, wherein black and white interviewers were randomly assigned to black survey respondents. They found interviewer race exerted a particularly large causal effect on black respondents' answers to survey questions that dealt with explicitly racial issues. Later studies built on this notion that the reporting of black opinions, particularly on racial issues, is distorted by the race of interviewers. Davis (1997b), for example, finds that blacks' evaluations of white political figures and the predictive power of black group identity measures (Davis 1997a) are both influenced by the race of interviewers. Davis and Silver (2003) even find differences in measurements of political knowledge among black respondents by race of interviewer and surmise that something akin to "stereotype threat" happens among black respondents faced with a white interviewer.

How to interpret the identified effects, however, is not straightforward. Schuman and Converse (1971) attributed the difference they observed to black respondents suppressing their "true" beliefs in the presence of white interviewers. Design limitations within their study and others' mean that empirical leverage on the mechanism behind race-of-interviewer effects is still lacking. Notably, when respondents are interviewed by only black or white interviewers, it is empirically impossible to identify whether white interviewers, black interviewers, or both are influencing black responses to survey questions. The evidence does support the interpretation that blacks have some sense of what is expected of them in these racialized contexts, such that they are offering interviewers answers to questions that they believe are consistent with those interviewers' expectations. Whose expectations they are most sensitive to and how that affects their opinions, particularly on issues that are not explicitly racial, remains largely unanswered by the existing research. In Chapter 4 we offer a research design that helps sort out the causal effect of interviewer race on black partisan beliefs, and we identify the unique effect of black interviewers on blacks' willingness to identify with the Democratic Party.

The Theory of Racialized Social Constraint

Our aim is to integrate the insights we have reviewed on norms and social pressure into a framework for understanding black political decision making that extends beyond existing work on racial group identity and helps us better understand blacks' continuing support for the Democratic Party. Taking seriously the unique social interdependence of black Americans, we argue that racialized social pressure—particularly pressure from in-group members— should be a fundamental element in determining the choices they make and the actions they take in politics.[11] This argument implies that blacks' use of racial considerations in political decision making is more than just the low-information rationality of Dawson's heuristic model of common fate as black utility—though we do not argue that it never functions as such. Instead we argue that many African Americans, even those who are highly racially identi-fied, are regularly confronted with a common social dilemma. They face politi-cal circumstances in which the choice before them involves some *perceptible* conflict between maximizing private or personal benefits and maximizing social benefits that might accrue from behavior consistent with what they and most other blacks see as in the interest of the group. In these circum-stances, rather than weighing how what happens to the group affects them as individuals, blacks are instead weighing the relative costs and benefits of

TABLE 1.1. Social Conditions for Racialized Social Constraint

1. The existence of a well-defined norm of black political behavior	• Norm of collective political behavior • Nearly unanimous Democratic Party support • Widely available information about black support for the Democratic Party
2. Behavior that is either public or verifiable	• Publicly supporting or identifying with the Democratic Party • Turnout
3. Racially homogeneous social networks	• Widespread racial segregation • Exclusively black institutions
4. The potential for social sanctions or rewards	• Concern about non-compliance • Potential for negative social sanctions such as "Uncle Tom" and "sellout" epithets • Potential for heightened social status within networks

siding with their individual interests or beliefs versus conforming to racial group expectations of them. This is the racialized social constraint model.

Social interconnectedness is truly central in this model. The costs of the model rest on the reality of black Americans' social ties—their identification as a black community. These costs of defecting from the understood norms and practices of that group are greater when other members of the in-group might be aware of the defection. And the social benefits, such as social status and praise for publicly conforming to these expectations, depend on the crystallization and intensity of the in-group norms—how widely understood and valued they are across the racial group. In sum, we identify four conditions that shape the potential of racialized social constraint to effectively constrain black political behavior. These conditions, also listed in Table 1.1, are (1) the existence and acceptance of well-defined norms of black political behavior, (2) behavior that is either public or verifiable, (3) racially homogeneous social networks, and (4) individual awareness of social sanctions for defection from and rewards for compliance with group norms. Together these conditions define the unique sociopolitical experience of black Americans, creating an environment in which blacks are compelled to engage in prosocial behavior meant to help the racial group—even when their underlying dispositions or material interests suggest another choice.

Here we offer a general discussion of these conditions. In the chapters that follow, we engage each in greater detail and empirically demonstrate how each characterizes the black social and political experience.

THE IN-GROUP PARTISAN NORM

Throughout this book we highlight the fact that black Americans knowingly face a collective action dilemma in American politics. As they have come to realize that their ability to effectively make demands on government is conditional on their ability to engage in unified political action, they have also come to understand the challenges of maintaining group unity in the face of individual incentives to betray group interest or free ride on the efforts of others. Racialized social constraint, we argue, is an effective means by which black Americans have been able to encourage prosocial political behavior among group members. Essential to racialized social constraint are norms about appropriate group behavior. In the realm of politics, perhaps the most general of these norms is the expectation of working toward and preserving shared interests and common heritage. Dawson (2001, p. 256), for example, notes that the "norm of community still governs black politics even as the norm becomes contested on multiple fronts." In his philosophical rendering of black group solidarity, Tommy Shelby (2015, p. 68) notes that racial group solidarity "entails normative constraints. It is because I feel solidarity with group X that I *ought* to do this or that for or on behalf of fellow members of group X." This common understanding of the necessity of unified in-group behavior can be seen in blacks' responses to survey questions assessing the efficacy of black collective political action. Table 1.2 summarizes relevant items from several surveys. It shows that blacks nearly unanimously agree that it is important for blacks in America to work together to improve the position of their racial group. Only 2 of the 329 black respondents in the 2008 National Politics Study disagreed with the idea that it is important for people to work together to improve the position of their racial group. In the 1996 National Black Election Study, black unity in support of a specific black collective effort, the 1995 Million Man March, approached such a consensus. Nearly 90 percent of all blacks believed it was important to the black community. Perhaps a telling indicator of the primacy of group-defined value is the fact that despite the march organizers' explicit exclusion of black women from the event, a slightly larger percentage of black women (90.3%) than black men (87.7%) described the march as important. The same 1996 survey also shows just how widespread the belief is that collective black efforts are

TABLE 1.2. Black Beliefs about Effectiveness of Racial Group Unity

Survey	Percentage
2008 National Politics Study:	99
It is important for people to work together to improve the position of their racial or ethnic group. (% who agree)	
1996 National Black Election Study:	89
How important do you think the Million Man March was to the Black community? (% who say at least somewhat important)	
1996 National Black Election Study:	88
If enough Blacks vote they can make a difference in who gets elected president. (% who agree)	

effective via a question about the collective power of black voters to decide a presidential election. Nearly 90 percent of blacks conveyed the belief that their racial in-group wielded such potential power.

Although evidence suggests that blacks generally agree that black collective political action is important as a means of improving the overall position of the racial group, there have been important disagreements about how to most effectively develop and employ black political power. In the early twentieth century, W.E.B. DuBois and Booker T. Washington, disagreed about, among other things, the role of formal versus technical education in bringing about black empowerment. During the Civil Rights Movement, Martin Luther King Jr. and Malcolm X disagreed about the efficacy of violent political action in response to white racism. King, a Baptist minister, advocated for non-violent political action, expressing concern that violence had a tendency to spiral out of control and would likely not achieve the goal of racial equality. Malcolm X, however, saw violence as a means of self-defense and thought it might be the only way to deter violence directed at black Americans.

While disagreements about black political strategy still exist today, the successes of the Civil Rights Movement and the role that the Democratic Party played in securing black rights have helped crystallize a specific set of norms for black political behavior centered on support for the Democratic Party. Along with the constraints imposed by the American two-party system and the eventual incorporation of black political leaders into the ranks of the Democratic Party in the 1970s and 1980s, these political history facts provide a basis for the widely held belief among African Americans that black electoral support for the Democratic Party is an effective strategy for black political empowerment. Beliefs about the racial-group-interest commitments of the parties are reflected in how blacks respond to survey questions assessing how hard they believe the Democratic and Republican Parties work on issues blacks care about. In the 1996 National Black Election Study, for example, 70 percent of blacks reported that the Democratic Party works hard on issues blacks care about, while only 17 percent of blacks reported that the Republican Party did the same. Given the value blacks place on electoral politics as a means of racial group empowerment (see Table 1.2) and the limitations placed on electoral choices by the American two-party system, this particular distribution of results points to a strong sense among African Americans that support for Democratic candidates is an especially desirable option for black voters seeking to empower the racial group.

Although sorting out the origins of black norms of partisan political behavior can be difficult in a two-party system, we have reason to believe that black partisan politics is more about support for the Democratic Party than it is about a general opposition to the Republican Party. To understand partisan behavior defined by opposition to an out-party, political scientists Alan Abramowitz and Steven Webster describe what they call negative partisanship. Their idea is that contemporary partisan polarization in American politics is tied to recently emerging "negative feelings about the opposing party and its candidates. This has led to dramatic increases in party loyalty and straight-ticket voting, a steep decline in the advantage of incumbency and growing consistency between the results of presidential elections and the results of House, Senate and even state legislative elections" (Abramowitz and Webster 2016, p. 12). While Abramowitz and Webster certainly have a point about growing partisan conflict in American politics, data from the ANES surveys suggest that "negative partisanship" likely does not explain black Americans' unique partisan political behavior.

Table 1.3 presents a racial breakdown of one of the more common negative partisanship findings. The underlying analysis involves creating a political party impression measure by calculating the difference between Democratic and Republican feeling thermometer scores and summarizing those scores separately for black and white Democratic respondents. We create this party impression measure by rescaling the original 0–100 party feeling thermometer measure to run from −47 to 47.[12] Scores from 1 to 47 suggest that the respondent has a (increasingly) positive impression of that party; scores from −1 to −47 suggest that the respondent has a (increasingly) negative impression of that party; a score of 0 means that the respondent has neither a positive nor a negative impression of the party. If negative

TABLE 1.3. Partisan Impression Scores for Black Democrats and White Democrats, 2000 to 2012 ANES

		Black Democrats	White Democrats	Difference
Democratic Party impression score		30.9	19.6	11.3*
	CI	[30.2, 31.8]	[18.9, 20.2]	
Republican Party impression score		−20.3	−17.8	2.5*
	CI	[−21.4, −19.2]	[−18.6, −17.0]	

Notes: 1 to 47 = positive impression, 0 = neither positive nor negative impression, −1 to −47 = negative impression.
* *p* < .05

partisanship is driving blacks' strong identification with the Democratic Party, we should observe black respondents reporting, on average, more negative evaluations of the Republican Party than positive evaluations of the Democratic Party. If black partisan political behavior is *uniquely* driven by positive support for the Democratic Party, then we might expect to observe black respondents to hold more positive evaluations of the Democratic Party than white Democratic respondents do, but we would not necessarily expect a difference between the two groups in evaluations of the Republican Party.

The results presented in Table 1.3 support the positive partisanship argument. Looking first at the black Democrats column, it is clear that from 2000 to 2012 black Democrats reported having significantly more positive impressions (distance from 0) of the Democratic Party (30.9) than negative impressions of the Republican Party (−20.3); black respondents rank the Democratic Party 10 points more positively than they rank the Republican Party negatively. Turning our attention to the cross-racial comparisons, we can see that while black Democrats interviewed in the 2000 to 2012 ANES were only slightly more likely than white Democrats to express negative feelings toward the Republican Party, they were significantly more likely than white Democrats to express warmer feeling for the Democratic Party.

Similarly, the 2000 to 2012 ANES asked respondents to make the same evaluations of each of the Democratic and Republican candidates for president in the 2000 to 2012 presidential elections. In Table 1.4 we repeat the analysis from Table 1.3 using the candidate impression measures. The results from this analysis essentially replicate what we saw in Table 1.3. In Table 1.4 we see that just as with their impressions of the Democratic Party, black Democratic respondents' positive impressions of the Democratic candidate

TABLE 1.4. Candidate Impression Scores for Black Democrats and White Democrats, 2000 to 2012 ANES

		Black Democrats	White Democrats	Difference
Democratic candidate impression score		35.4	22.1	13.3*
	CI	[34.7, 36.1]	[21.4, 22.9]	
Republican candidate impression score		−18.8	−16.5	2.3*
	CI	[−19.9, −17.7]	[−17.4, −15.6]	

Notes: 1 to 47 = positive impression, 0 = neither positive nor negative impression, −1 to −47 = negative impression.
* $p < .05$

for president are significantly greater (distance from 0) than their negative evaluations of the Republican candidate. Blacks also expressed significantly more positive impressions of the Democratic presidential candidates than white Democrats did.

THE SOCIAL VALUE OF PARTISAN NORM ADHERENCE

The existence and widespread awareness of a norm of Democratic Party support among black Americans, we argue, are not sufficient to constrain political behavior, especially in the face of incentives to do otherwise. As we discuss further in later chapters, African Americans face both ideological and material incentives to defect from the norm of supporting the Democratic Party. Especially as blacks are asked to make political choices that pit their ideological or material self-interest against the well-understood expectations of the racial group, we expect that social pressure from other blacks is necessary to constrain black political behavior. The effectiveness of such pressure derives from several conditions. The structure of American racial segregation implies that black Americans generally have more meaningful social connections with other blacks than they do with whites or other racial minorities. Thus, blacks come to place particular value on their social relationships with other blacks. Chapter 3 covers in detail the structure of black social networks and how variation in the racial makeup of these networks is related to black partisan political beliefs.

Public deviations from in-group norms of political behavior, such as openly opposing the Democratic Party, signal to other black Americans a lack of commitment to the group. That observability conditions the potential for costs to one's standing within these valued social relationships is a rather straightforward but important point. While we consider in later chapters how the internalized value of behaviors associated with performing "good" blackness might exert some constraint over individual choices, it is important to point out here that behavior that invites sanctions from others is tangibly costly. Thus, the more public a political behavior, the more effectively we expect it to be constrained. Similarly, we expect that group-based politics are more effective when the group works to make behaviors more visible than they might otherwise be. In the realm of partisan politics, this means that blacks' unity benefits from political discourse—from a contemporary political environment where partisan loyalties are quite often solicited or encouraged to be expressed in the public domain.

Given both the primacy of social connections with other blacks and the reality that black Americans do not see whites or members of other racial groups as having the capacity to fully understand what it means to be black, we do not expect blacks to regard members of racial out-groups as credible threats to their "blackness." As a consequence, out-group members should possess little capacity to exercise racialized social constraint to hold blacks accountable to norms of black political behavior. Because the racialized social constraint functions uniquely within the black community, as a black person's contact with members of racial out-groups increases, the likelihood that he or she will adhere to norms of black political behavior should fall. Greater social integration with racial out-groups offers blacks outlets for escaping racialized social pressure, making them less accountable to racial group expectations and more susceptible to accepting ideological and material incentives for defection from the racial in-group. Chapters 4, 5, and 6 examine in detail the consequences of in-group versus out-group social interactions for black partisan political behavior. Across a series of experimental and quasi-experimental tests, we indeed find that social monitoring by racial in-group members but not out-group members results in partisan political behavior consistent with the racial group expectations we have outlined.

Lastly, we argue that there are limits on the power of both positive and negative black social pressure. In particular, in line with the social psychological research on group norms, we argue that the effectiveness of black social pressure hinges on the established norms of black political behavior (Cialdini, Reno, and Kallgren 1990). In other words, it should be much more difficult to enlist racialized social pressure to induce blacks to behave in ways counter to well-established norms (to subvert group interest because the group is suddenly saying it is all right) than to enlist racialized social pressure to induce blacks to subvert their own (long-standing or newly found) self-interest. In the conclusion of this book, we examine more broadly the limits of racialized social pressure and the "stickiness" of racialized social norms.

Conclusion

In this chapter, we laid out a framework for understanding the process by which partisan allegiance is maintained among black Americans, which we have called *racialized social constraint*. We outlined how the normalization of Democratic partisanship as an expected black political behavior forms the basis of this process. Expectations created and then reinforced through social sanctioning by the racial in-group, our framework implies, serve as a mechanism that maintains black Americans' nearly unified allegiance to the Democratic Party. Importantly, we argued, this framework can account for continued partisan allegiance even as black America has diversified over recent decades, producing more circumstances in which individual racial group members may have meaningful individual-level incentives to break with the Democratic Party, including ideology and economic status. Continuing racial segregation still marks the typical black American experience, intertwining their interests, yes, but also interweaving their social lives. The ongoing importance of social belonging within the black community—the primacy of other blacks in social ties that bind—provides unique leverage for politics focused on group interest. Blacks are aware of the group's political expectations of Democratic partisan loyalty, and they are incentivized by social rewards and sanctions from the group to prioritize the group-interest norm.

Our task for the rest of this book is to bring evidence to bear on the empirical implications of our theory of the maintenance of black Democratic politics through racialized social constraint. There are a number of crucial questions for us to answer. Is Democratic partisanship an established norm for blacks? Do blacks view this as an expected behavior? In what situations do blacks feel the need to comply with the group norm and conform to the expected political behavior? Are black social networks really racially homogeneous? Can we empirically establish the possibility of reputational sanctions as a cause of norm-conforming political behavior?

In Chapter 2, we begin this task with a historical analysis in which we identify important points at which racialized social constraint has been used to collectively organize black Americans. During the eras of slavery, Reconstruction, Jim Crow, and post–civil rights, blacks not only have found themselves with shared experiences because of their race, including racial isolation and homogeneous social networks, but have also been forced to develop their own means of holding group members accountable. We show how these racially homogeneous social networks have served as spaces that identify the group norm and make coracial members aware of the group's expectations about behavior complying with the norm. We also show how reputational sanctions have been a common tool invoked in black politics exactly when constraining the behavior of group members to work toward the group's interest in racial liberation.

We follow the historical analysis by evaluating Democratic partisanship's capacity to function as a *particularly* effective norm of modern black politics within our racialized social constraint framework. Our focus is on the characteristics of the norm itself that our framework identifies as strengthening the constraint potential: Is Democratic Party support descriptively normal behavior among black Americans, are blacks aware of it as such, and do blacks widely perceive it to be a behavior for which social sanctions are likely to be used by others in order to encourage conformity? Chapter 3 will take up the characteristics of blacks' social environment that our framework identifies as important to the effectiveness of the racialized social constraint process.

2

Norms of Black Political Behavior

To divide and rule could only tear us apart.
—BOB MARLEY, "ZIMBABWE"

To better understand the contemporary norm of Democratic partisanship in black politics, in this chapter we place it in the context of black political history. Using our racialized social constraint framework, we describe how historically the use of well-understood norms of black political behavior and well-understood social costs for defecting from these norms has aided in blacks' ability to offset individual incentives group members might have to either free ride on or actively subvert the group-interest efforts of other blacks. We highlight that across various stages in the black experience in America—slavery, Reconstruction, Jim Crow, and post–civil rights—blacks' ability to clearly define group expectations and incentivize compliance with group norms of political unity using social sanctions has been essential to their ability to effectively organize around issues of social justice and civil rights and to take a consequential place in partisan electoral politics. This historical overview makes clear that the specific norms of black politics change as the needs and goals of the black community do.

In the second part of the chapter, then, we turn to understanding Democratic partisanship as a norm of modern black politics. Our racialized social constraint model offers specific guidance on what shapes the potential effectiveness of such a norm in constraining black political behavior. Such a norm should be widely known in both descriptive (the norm describes how group members do act) and injunctive (it is commonly understood as how group members should act) senses. We take up, empirically, the question of Democratic partisanship as such. Using survey data, we show not only that individual African Americans are aware that most other blacks support the Democratic Party and its candidates but also that they generally understand expectations of Democratic Party support to be common within the black community and are aware that sanctions may be used by racial in-group members to encourage conformity with political behaviors consistent with Democratic partisanship, including supporting its candidates in elections.

The Long History of Political Norms and Black Collective Political Behavior

Blacks' ability to overcome barriers to collective organization in order to act against racial oppression and make unified demands on government has been key to the expansion of their rights and freedoms. Here, we briefly discuss the role that well-understood norms of black behavior and racialized social constraint have played in facilitating black collective organization and how the relative effectiveness of these tools of social and political constraint has evolved over time. We begin by examining the restrictions on blacks' ability to collectively organize under slavery, paying particular attention to how the slave system in America was structured with the specific intent of subverting in-group social accountability as a means of undermining black collective action. We then examine how blacks' concerns about group-based mobilization evolved in the era of freedom. Beginning with Reconstruction-era politics, we demonstrate how norms of black behavior and racialized social constraint aided blacks in maintaining a largely unified voting bloc in the face of threats and material incentives offered by whites seeking to maintain white supremacy. As we move to the era of Jim Crow segregation, we examine the development of black institutions that would remain largely out of white control and how, through these institutions and the social connections that grew out of them, norms of black behavior and racialized social constraint would become even more effective tools of group politics. Notably, these institutions and their ability to constrain defection from group norms would ultimately help facilitate the unparalleled mass mobilization efforts of the Civil Rights Movement in the 1950s and 1960s. Finally, we conclude this section with an overview of racialized social constraint in the post–civil rights era, paying particular attention to how modern social network tools and cultural commitments to blackness may be increasing, for some, the cost of defecting from understood norms of black political behavior.

THE ERA OF SLAVERY

During the era of slavery, enslaved blacks shared a common interest in obtaining any measure of freedom they could, and although white slave owners were afforded enormous control over the lives of the enslaved, enslaved black people often took advantage of any opportunity to gain control over their situations. The historical record gives us accounts of enslaved black people organizing work slowdowns and destroying crops and farm equipment as a means of resistance against their condition (Howard 1982). Enslaved people also made direct claims to their freedom. By some accounts there were as many as two hundred slave rebellions or conspiracies in the United States from the sixteenth century to the end of slavery (Aptheker 1937, 1943). These insurrections were of great concern to whites. In many Southern states, particularly those where the enslaved black population outnumbered the white population, the organization of enslaved blacks was made into an issue of public safety for white residents. Following a number of high-profile slave revolts and the Haitian anti-slavery revolution from 1791 to 1804, many Southern state and local governments passed laws, known as slave codes, expanding the rights of slave owners and giving them even greater control over the people they owned. For example, Virginia and South Carolina each passed laws explicitly restricting the congregation of enslaved black persons without a white person present and regulating the travel of enslaved persons without a white escort.

While slave codes may have helped to reassure the white public, their effect on limiting enslaved blacks' ability to organize remains unclear. Indeed, while many places in the South had strict restrictions on blacks' travel and ability to assemble, the communal nature of plantation slavery made it nearly impossible to fully restrict enslaved people's ability to conspire toward their freedom. Owners came to rely on a system that used slave informants to stay ahead of subversive behavior. As historian Darold Wax (1982, p. 144) points out, "Whites could not readily observe activities within the slave quarters or monitor the social intercourse that was a part of plantation life. The best reporters of the goings-on among blacks were the slaves themselves. Alert to the possibilities of employing blacks as informers, whites did what they could to encourage loyalty among the bondsmen. A divided black community was a goal worth pursuing."[1] To be sure, the use of slave informants was critical to enslavers' ability to stay ahead of subversive behavior. Slave informants were directly responsible for suppressing a number of slave rebellions in the antebellum South. The 1739 Stono Rebellion; Gabriel Prosser's planned insurrection in 1800 outside Richmond, Virginia; and an 1812 rebellion planned by slaves on a plantation outside New Orleans were all suppressed or subverted with information provided by black informants (Kennedy 2008).

Realizing the effectiveness of using such informants as a means of controlling enslaved populations, whites in Southern states sought to formally institutionalize a reward system for slave informants (Dennis 2013). Following the Stono Rebellion, it became the official policy of the state of South Carolina to reward slaves who provided information on potential slave uprisings (Wax 1982). The effectiveness of this strategy was seen ninety years later when Peter Desverneys (also known as Peter Prioleau) informed on Denmark Vesey, a former slave who conspired to organize enslaved and free blacks against whites in Charleston. For his assistance in suppressing the rebellion, Desverneys was manumitted and awarded an annual stipend of fifty dollars from the state (Dennis 2013; Koger 1985). Other accounts detail enslaved people informing on other blacks merely to gain favor with their masters. Whatever the incentives, the informant system stood as a significant barrier to the effective organization of enslaved people toward their freedom.

In response to the informant system, enslaved black communities instituted norms meant to deter servile behavior. Lacking the resources to offer material incentives for loyalty, they often turned to coercion to prevent community members from informing. Ridicule, shunning, and threats of physical violence directed at slave informants loomed large within these often small and tight-knit plantation communities. Historian Norrece Jones (1990, p. 118) points out that "servile blacks who were suspected of collaborating or becoming too familiar with their oppressors were either ostracized, physically accosted or killed." Jones supports this point by quoting text from a petition of manumission for a slave who reported details of a potential insurrection to her owner; the petition reads, "The blacks were very generally excited against her; an evidence of which was the attack made upon her by a negro man named Joe, who was tried for the same and executed" (N. T. Jones 1990, p. 119). Andrea Dennis (2013) notes that because of these threats, it was not uncommon for slave owners to go to great lengths to protect the identities of their informants. Dennis goes on to use the following passage by Frederick Douglass to illustrate the extent to which blacks both on and off plantations would punish informants:

I found the colored people much more spirited than I had supposed they would be. I found among them determination to protect each other from the blood-thirsty kidnapper, at all hazards. Soon after my arrival, I was told of a circumstance which illustrated their spirit. A colored man and a fugitive slave were on unfriendly terms. The former was heard to threaten the latter with informing his master of his whereabouts. Straightaway a meeting was called among the colored people, under the stereotyped notice, "Business of importance!" The betrayer was invited to attend. The people came at the appointed hour, and organized the meeting by appointing a very religious old gentleman as president, who, I believe, made a prayer, after which he addressed the meeting as follows: "Friends, we have got him here, and I would recommend that you young men just take him outside the door, and kill him!" With this, a number of them bolted at him; but they were intercepted by some more timid than themselves, and the betrayer escaped their vengeance, and has not been seen in New Bedford since. I believe there have been no more such threats, and should there be hereafter, I doubt not that death would be the consequence. (Quoted in Dennis 2013, p. 301)

In the era of slavery, then, the need to subvert individual incentives to betray the collective group interest in establishing and maintaining pathways to pursue freedom was ever present. Accounts of retribution against informants, such as the foregoing one, illustrate the extent of group expectations of racial in-group commitment and the lengths to which blacks would go to prevent others from subverting the path to freedom.

THE ERA OF RECONSTRUCTION

Upon emancipation, blacks would, for a short time, be given a voice in electoral politics. They would repurpose the norms of black behavior meant to preserve pathways to freedom in the era of slavery to bring about black unity in electoral politics. In 1870, following the end of Presidential Reconstruction and the enforcement of black electoral rights granted under the recently ratified Fifteenth Amendment, black men in many parts of the South were for the first time allowed to cast ballots in local, state, and federal elections. Based on the belief that the Republican Party sought to ensure the freedom of African Americans, newly enfranchised blacks voted en masse for Republican candidates (Walton 1975). This led not only to Republicans taking control of state and local politics in many parts of the South but also to the election of a number of black Republicans to state and local offices. Over the course of Reconstruction, fifteen black men would be elected to the U.S. House of Representatives and the state of Mississippi would elect two black U.S. senators. Scholars also estimate that during this time nearly two thousand blacks were elected to state and local offices across the South (Foner 1993, p. xiv; Gates 2019).

As black Americans realized the power they could exert through unified exercise of the franchise, small groups nonetheless saw it as in their interest to support Democratic candidates—despite the fact that many Democrats were former Confederate soldiers and slave owners, and that many campaigned on platforms of maintaining white supremacy. Although it is believed that only small, isolated segments of the black population actually supported Democratic candidates, historians have identified a number of elections in which black support for Democratic candidates contributed to Democratic victories (Drago 1999; Walton 1975).[2] Understanding exactly why blacks during Reconstruction would vote for Democratic candidates is complicated. In some cases, black support for Democrats stemmed from outright coercion and threats of violence from whites. Black people still living and working on plantations remained beholden to plantation owners for their livelihoods, giving those plantation owners straightforward means to coerce blacks to vote for Democratic candidates (Foner 1988). In other cases, black people's support for Democrats resulted from loyalty to former masters or from financial benefits promised to them by whites. It was reported, for example, that in the late 1800s, Democrats in Louisiana "opened up a special office in New Orleans to purchase Negro votes at $12.50 per vote" (Uzee 1961, p. 332).

Whatever the reason for the observed instances of black support for the Democratic Party, the black community broadly conceived of Democratic ascendance as a threat to the continued freedom of African Americans, believing that Democrats sought to retrench white supremacy—or perhaps even bring back slavery. A number of well-documented accounts describe black Republicans seeking to rein in black partisan defection by threatening black Democrats with physical violence or shunning those blacks who supported Democratic candidates (Drago 1999). Black Democrats in some parts of the country reported being harassed and physically assaulted by black Republicans and thrown out of their homes by their wives. The concern for retaliation against black Democrats was so great that white Democrats in South Carolina would withhold the names of their black supporters "to protect them against Republican reprisals, especially from blacks" (Drago 1999,

p. 4). White Democrats in Louisiana also vowed to protect their black Democratic supporters from black Republican reprisals. Historian Justin Behrend (2015, p. 168) explains that one group of black Democrats in Louisiana, when confronted by black Republicans, claimed that they would have been killed "on the spot if not for the 'white man' who protected them." The period of Reconstruction thus shows the first use of racialized social constraint as a means of enforcing black in-group norms of partisan and electoral politics. With the end of Reconstruction, black voting rights would be subverted, rendering the partisan behavior norm irrelevant. But the use of racialized social constraint continued as new group norms of politics evolved.

THE ERA OF JIM CROW

With the withdrawal of federal troops from the South during the late 1870s came the end of federal enforcement of black rights and the beginning of Southern Redemption. Blacks were stripped of the franchise, rendering the Reconstruction-era politics of black power through Republican electoral force obsolete. Southern states not only instituted voting restrictions to suppress blacks' electoral participation but also imposed wide-ranging restrictions on social interactions between blacks and whites. By the early twentieth century, state and local governments across the South had enacted strict segregation laws that allowed private citizens to restrict blacks from, among other things, eating at restaurants with whites, using the same bathroom facilities as whites, and even attending the same churches as whites. With the separate-but-equal doctrine established under the Supreme Court's 1896 *Plessy v. Ferguson* decision, however, Southern states found themselves legally obligated to provide blacks with separate, if not equal, public accommodations. Thus developed the system that would be known as Jim Crow.

The Jim Crow system enabled anew the subordination of black Americans, giving new legal tools to white supremacy. It also resulted, however, in the establishment of scores of black social institutions that could become tools for black resistance. Black primary and secondary schools, medical facilities, and colleges and universities grew throughout the South. Historians and sociologists would later demonstrate how this state-sponsored social isolation of black people in the South would be responsible for the creation of exclusively black neighborhoods and the rapid growth of black social and political institutions (Myrdal 1944). As more black Americans began to migrate to the North in the early twentieth century, they faced similar, albeit less formal, restrictions on their ability to interact with whites.

Restrictive covenants, redlining, and social intimidation meant that upon arriving in places like Chicago and New York, blacks had little choice but to move to existing black communities—or to communities that, as a result of white flight, would soon become largely black.

It was within these emerging exclusively black spaces that a significant evolution of the capacity of racialized social constraint to shape black political behavior took place. Through black social institutions, especially, notions of punishment with social sanctions for undermining or free riding on the collective efforts of the racial group would be formally incorporated into black popular culture. Epithets such as "Uncle Tom" and "sellout" emerged from black institutions in the early and mid-twentieth century as linguistic tools for exacting reputational sanctions for those blacks who betrayed the collective goals of the group. Take the "Uncle Tom" epithet, which many believe was born out of George Aiken's dramatic reenactments of Harriet Beecher Stowe's 1852 novel *Uncle Tom's Cabin*. Historian Adena Spingarn (2012, p. 203) notes that many scholars today blame Aiken's plays "for turning Uncle Tom, the heroic Christian martyr of Stowe's novel, into the submissive race traitor his name connotes today." However, according to Spingarn, the popular use of "Uncle Tom" as a derogatory epithet would not catch on until the early 1900s, when writers for what was at the time one of the nation's most popular black newspapers, the *Chicago Defender*, began using it as a means of describing servile behavior among blacks, particularly Southern blacks. Spingarn describes what she believes is one of the paper's earliest uses of the term, in a 1910 story. The story depicts the efforts of a black woman who had migrated to Chicago from Georgia and who wished to start a petition to racially segregate schools in Chicago. Spingarn (2010) quotes the *Chicago Defender* as saying, "When we are in touch with Mrs. Johnson, we will show her the back door to Chicago and have her beat it back to her dear old southern home, where all the Uncle Toms and Topsys should be."

The historical effectiveness of these epithets as tools for social control and racialized social constraint is explored in detail by Randell Kennedy (2008) in his book *Sellout: The Politics of Racial Betrayal*. Kennedy notes that the "Uncle Tom" and "sellout" epithets are useful to the black community because "every social group—from the union to the organized crime family to the nation-state—confronts the challenge of exacting loyalty to the collective in the face of self-interest, hardship, or even danger" (p. 3). As Kennedy and others have described, these epithets are an exertion of social pressure by in-group members on those who seek to deviate from what is

understood as expected group behavior. These epithets also seem to derive
their power from the social investments individual blacks have in both their
own black identities and their social connections with other racial in-group
members. In other words, the fear of being called an Uncle Tom or a sellout
is at base a concern about the individual and social consequences of having
one's commitment to the black community questioned, and the close social
ties that blacks have with one another only serve to enhance the usefulness
of these tools for social and political constraint.

It was the black institutions built under Jim Crow that were at the heart
of the racialized social constraint that encouraged mass participation in the
Civil Rights Movement. By the 1950s black churches, colleges, and social
and political organizations had become so essential to the social lives of
everyday black Americans that they served as far-reaching venues in which
black leaders could communicate black interest and organize the black public toward political action to demand the end of Jim Crow. Through these
organizations, black leaders could directly exploit social connections within
the black community. Such use of social pressure can be seen in Charles
Payne's (2007, p. 260) account of 1960s civil rights efforts in Greenwood,
Mississippi, where, according to Payne, the rallies and meetings organized
by groups such as the NAACP tried "to change the behavior of their members by offering a supportive social environment, public recognition for
living up to group norms, and public pressure to continue doing so. They
create an environment in which you feel that if you stumble, you are letting
down not only yourself but all of your friends. One might be afraid to go to
a particular demonstration or be tired of demonstrations, period, but not
going would mean disappointing those people who were counting on you."
Payne goes on to note how the rather close-knit nature of black communities
in the Jim Crow South facilitated mobilization and recruitment into movement activities. In describing the roles of black women and black churches
in helping to get the Greenwood movement off the ground, Payne (p. 274)
notes, "The situation that SNCC [the Student Nonviolent Coordinating
Committee] usually encountered in the Delta was that while most people
were initially afraid, there were some who were interested right away, and
it seems that given the tightly knit social bonds of rural communities, they
were able to pull others in. If we assume that women tend to be more deeply
invested than men in networks of kin and community, it is not surprising
that more women tended to be drawn in during the early stages."

Perhaps most importantly, black institutions served as venues in which
black community leaders and activists could hold other blacks accountable

to group expectations of behaviorally supporting the movement and prevent free riding. Indeed, free riding was of central concern among black leaders during the Civil Rights Movement. Martin Luther King Jr. observed that one of the biggest obstacles to organization efforts during the movement was the complacency of many blacks who, while they may have believed in the principles of the movement, felt they had too much to lose by actively participating. In King's words, "The sit-in movement is a revolt against the apathy and complacency of adults in the Negro community; against Negros in the middle class who indulge in buying cars and homes instead of taking on the great cause that will really solve their problems" (quoted in Sitkoff and Foner 1993, p. 83).

As the role of black institutions as venues for sanctioning defection and preventing free riding expanded, black leaders and activists strategically used the investments blacks had made in their relationships with other blacks to pressure compliance with movement objectives, even in the face of incentives to do otherwise. Payne (2007) provides a good example of this leadership strategy in his description of an April 1963 speech delivered by national civil rights activist Dick Gregory at a black church in Greenwood. In the speech, Gregory calls out prominent members of the local black community who were slow in expressing their support for the freedom movement demonstrations. Gregory begins by taking on the principal of a local black school, saying, "And your principal you have here [*loud and very sustained applause, shouting*], this guy . . . or whatever his name is. [*Loud applause.*] When this man would ask Negro kids to stop fighting for their rights he is lower than the lowest Negro, lower than the lowest animal that walks the face of the earth. [*Very sustained applause*]" (quoted in Payne 2007, p. 198). Gregory then goes on to attack local black preachers who failed to openly support the protest efforts and calls on parishioners to abandon the churches and pray in the streets instead. He explains that this alternative is "better than worshiping with a man who is less than a man!" (quoted in Payne 2007, p. 198). Indeed, it seems that Gregory's words had some impact. Payne notes that not long after the speech, thirty-one local black ministers issued a joint statement expressing their unwavering support for the freedom movement.

In sum, the Jim Crow era witnessed two important developments in the evolution of black politics through a racialized social constraint process based on in-group norms. First, cut out once again from electoral politics, black people established a new norm of political behavior around active participation in non-electoral collective action. Second, the emergence and proliferation of black social and political institutions during the Jim Crow era provided new tools for social enforcement of this new norm of black political engagement. By heightening the value of blacks' social relationships with other racial in-group members, black social and political institutions would serve as accessible venues in which social accountability to collective political behavior could be enforced. And, importantly, many of those institutions would outlast both Jim Crow and the Civil Rights Movement.

THE POST-CIVIL RIGHTS ERA

With the passage of the 1965 Voting Rights Act and renewed federal government efforts to enforce African Americans' voting rights, the political role of black institutions would shift from facilitating black protest activities to mobilizing black voters in support for the Democratic Party and its candidates. Following the Democratic Party's defeat of Republican segregationist Barry Goldwater in the 1964 presidential election and Democratic efforts to ensure black civil rights and voting rights by pushing for the passage of the 1964 Civil Rights Act and 1965 Voting Rights Act, black Americans firmly aligned their support of the Democratic Party. This consolidation of black Democratic partisan support can be seen in Figure 2.1, which presents the percentage of black and white self-identified Democrats from 1952 to 2012. Before the 1964 presidential election, the percentage of self-identified black and white Democrats was roughly equal, with approximately 55 percent of blacks and 49 percent of whites identifying as Democrats in 1952. By the time of the 1964 presidential election, the racial gap in Democratic partisanship was nearly five times larger than in 1952. By 1970 it was seven times larger, and by 2012 it was nearly ten times what it was in 1952.

The consolidation of normative value among black Americans for the Democratic Party can also be seen in how blacks say they feel about the two major parties. Since 1978, the American National Election Studies (ANES) have measured respondents' ratings of the two major political parties on what is commonly referred to as a feeling thermometer scale, where a score of 0 indicates that the respondent feels very coldly toward the party and a score of 100 means the respondent feels very warmly toward the party. To get a sense of respondents' relative warmth toward the Democratic Party, we subtract each respondent's Democratic Party thermometer score from his or her Republican Party thermometer score to get a difference score. More positive values (1 to 100) mean comparatively warmer feelings toward the Democratic Party, more negative values (−1 to −100) mean comparatively warmer feelings toward the Republican Party, and 0 means the respondent

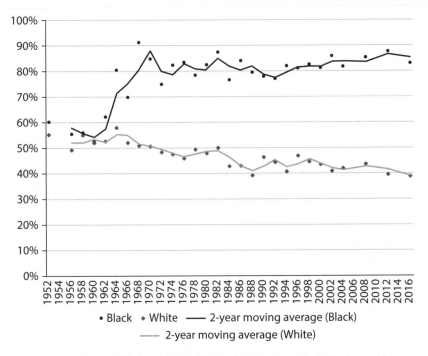

FIGURE 2.1. Percentage of black and white self-identified Democrats (including leaners) by year, ANES cumulative file

sees no difference in the two parties. These difference scores are presented in Figure 2.2, charted separately for black and white Americans across every year of the ANES from 1978 to 2012 when there was a presidential race. Over the course of this time series, black Americans have always felt more warmly toward the Democratic Party. Across all years of the ANES, Democratic Party feeling thermometer scores were, on average, 31 points warmer among blacks than they were for the Republican Party. Consistent with an over-time consolidation of normative value within the group, the difference in affective sentiment for the Democratic Party also appears to be growing over this time period for black Americans. In 1978, the gap between the Democrat and Republican feeling thermometer score averages among blacks was 24 points. By 1988 that gap was 36 points, by 1998 it had grown to 37 points, and by 2016 the gap was 50 points.[3] In comparison, on average, white Americans display little difference in their sentiment about the two major parties. The average difference score for whites across all years of this time series is only 2.1 points—a difference that results not from common agreement among whites about the two parties but from division in how whites feel about the parties.

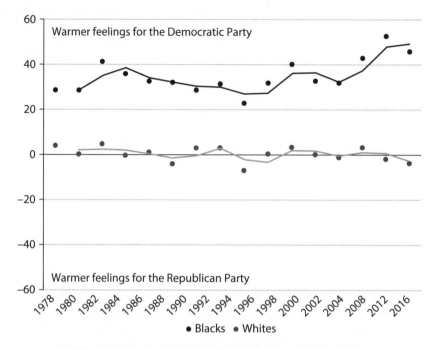

FIGURE 2.2. Difference in Democrat and Republican feeling thermometer score by race and year, ANES cumulative file

Passage of the 1965 Voting Rights Act also resulted in a dramatic increase in black elected officials. For example, in 1965, only five African Americans were in the U.S. Congress. By 2015 there were forty-six, and of these only three were Republicans. According to a 2015 report from the Joint Center for Political and Economic Studies, the number of African American state legislators "rose from under 200 in the late 1960s to well near 700 today" (Brown-Dean et al. 2015, p. 26). The authors of the report also find significant growth in the number of black officials elected at the local level. Blacks went from holding "only 715 local elected offices around the country in 1970 to garnering 5,753 positions by 2002" (p. 28), and again, these officials overwhelmingly identify as Democrats.

We contend that this shift in black support for the Democratic Party and the dramatic increase in black representation that followed have created the conditions necessary for the crystallization of black Democratic Party support as a norm of black political behavior. Once blacks shifted their support solidly behind the Democratic Party, support for the party was then reinforced through black institutions and the social networks formed through them. The result is that institutions established under Jim Crow and once

used as the social basis of the protest mobilization of the Civil Rights Movement evolved into well-known and largely accessible sources for Democratic
voter mobilization. In an interview with Adelle Banks of the Religion News
Service, Bishop Frank Reid III, chair of the Social Action Commission of
one of the nation's oldest African American religious denominations, the
African Methodist Episcopal (AME) Church, noted the importance of the
church's role in getting out the vote. Reid told Banks that the AME Church
is "concerned about voter registration and voter turnout because without
those things we cannot make America fair for the elderly who need afford-
able health care, our children, especially poor children" (Banks 2018). In her
examination of the 1984 and 1988 elections, Katherine Tate (1993) found that
black church attendance and black organizational membership were strong
predictors of black voter turnout. Similarly, Sidney Verba and his colleagues
(1993) identified the black church as having powerful influence on black
political engagement, noting its role in helping blacks gain political skills,
learn about politics, and make social connections.

LOOKING FORWARD: THE EMERGENT SOCIAL BASIS
OF TWENTY-FIRST-CENTURY BLACK POLITICS

Social media is an emerging social space, but one in which it seems that blacks
have already been able to promote and reinforce norms of Democratic Party
support through uniquely racialized networks. A 2014 Pew Research Center
report on technology usage shows that the increased use of smartphones
has helped to diminish the digital divide and increase technology accessibil-
ity for African Americans, with 72 percent of all blacks having access to a
broadband service or a smartphone (A. Smith 2014). The increased usage
of smartphone technology has opened up social media spaces as forums
for discussions about the racial group on a national platform. As discussed
in Chapter 1, the term Black Twitter has been coined to describe one such
space in which this racial dialogue takes place. Indeed, blacks are more likely
than whites to choose the social space of Twitter; Pew's 2014 report (Duggan et al. 2015) found that 27 percent of blacks who are online use Twitter,
compared with 21 percent of whites. Predictable generational differences in
Twitter usage among blacks might mask the potential in-group significance
of the space: fully 40 percent of blacks between the ages of eighteen and
twenty-nine use Twitter (A. Smith 2014).

Scholars of social media and communication indeed argue that we
are observing the creation of a new space for digital racial discourse.

Sanjay Sharma (2013) argues in "Black Twitter? Racial Hashtags, Networks and Contagion" that Black Twitter is a networking space and that #blacktags, racial hashtags, serve as a means to link or create discussions of issues related to race. Sharma (p. 46) asserts that "circulation of these racialized hashtags is analyzed as the transmission of contagious meanings and affects, such as anti/racist humor, sentiment and social commentary. Black tags are instrumental in producing networked subjects which have the capacity to multiply the possibilities of being raced online." Sharma's assessment introduces the notion that the digital space is creating a racialized network for African Americans where explicit discussion about race can take place. Although some have grown concerned with the dissolution of brick-and-mortar black institutions (Dawson 2011), the digital space has become a venue in which group norms can also be defined and maintained, and those that put the group in jeopardy or go against group expectations suffer the consequences of digital shaming or "dragging" by in-group members.[4] We consider it important to keep studying this digital racialized space as one in which norms of Democratic Party support are crystallized and social sanctions are meted out to those who defect from that understood norm.

The example of the 2017 online backlash against Steve Harvey and Chrisette Michele in response to their association with President Donald Trump shows the potential of this new media as a means for using racialized social pressure to enforce group norms and expectations. The decision of Michele, an African American rhythm and blues singer, to perform at Trump's inauguration was in direct contrast with the black partisan norm of Democratic support. Michele's decision found normative derision in a traditional black institution—the black press. Michael Arceneaux (2017) argued in *Essence*, a national African American magazine, that Michele was in a position in which she needed to prioritize the group over her own self-interest. Arceneaux wrote that "when Chrisette Michele was asked to perform for the new president, she had a choice: to stand with the marginalized or to align herself with their orange-tinged oppressor." Despite this clearly communicated community expectation, Michele decided that she would perform.

And then Michele's decision entered the Black Twitterverse. Black Twitter users openly tweeted their disgust with Michele's decision, making her a trending topic on Twitter, with numerous tweets of frustration becoming the top tweets (those tweets that were the most retweeted).[5] In response to the backlash, Michele penned a letter of explanation wherein she claimed that she chose to perform in order to help bridge the divide. She wrote,

My heart is broken for our country, for the hopes of our children, for the fights of those who came before us. I cry at the thought that Black History, American History might be in vain. This country has had great moments. God has shined His light upon us. Today, I hope that Great Moments begin in peaceful & progressive conversation. I am willing to be a bridge. I don't mind "These Stones," if they allow me to be a voice for the voiceless. I am here. Dr. Martin Luther King Jr. once said, "Our lives begin to end, the day we become silent about what matters." I am here, representing you, because this is what matters. (Quoted in Scott 2017)

The letter was not well received by members of the black online community, even with her attempts at racial appeals and quotation of civil rights icon Martin Luther King Jr. One black Twitter user, @Smooth_Orator, argued that "chrisette michele need to cash her check and quit the activist bullshit. Just say you needed the paper. You getting fried either way." This was among the top tweets, with 396 retweets and 549 likes.[6]

Despite narratives that claim that social media does not replicate "real life," the criticisms Michele faced on social media in fact did spill over into her real personal life. In an interview with *Billboard*, she commented on the backlash and said, "I'll say that the backlash, I did personally feel, came from members of my extended family who decided that they didn't want to speak to me anymore or support my family in supporting me" (Gloster 2017). What started as social enforcement in a black social media space also became social enforcement through the more "traditional" means of racially defined kinship networks.

Black talk show host and comedian Steve Harvey suffered a similar dragging in the Black Twitterverse for his decision to meet with Trump before Trump's inauguration. According to reports about the meeting, Harvey visited with Trump to discuss issues related to the inner city and to touch base with the cabinet nominee for Housing and Urban Development, Ben Carson. Harvey publicly commented on the meeting in positive terms, saying, "I walked away feeling like I had just talked with a man who genuinely wants to make a difference in this area. I feel that something really great could come out of this. . . . I would sit with him anytime" (Cowen 2017). As word started to spread about the meeting, "Steve Harvey" became a trending topic on Twitter as the result of African Americans taking to the social medium to openly express their displeasure. Black political analyst Bakari Sellers (2017) questioned Harvey's community commitment, tweeting, "On one side you have @repjohnlewis on the other you have @IAmSteveHarvey and @kanyewest. I'm rocking with the civil rights hero!" (186 retweets and 643 likes). African American screenwriter and producer Lauren Warren (2017) tweeted that Harvey was a sellout and mocked him using lines from his popular game show *Family Feud*: "'Name someone who just sold their soul.' 'OOOH! Steve Harvey!' 'Survey says—'" (2,790 retweets and 5,106 likes). Some users created list of blacks who are publicly behaving in ways that are inconsistent with community expectations. Black Twitter user @darleneturner53 (DKT 2017) tweeted, "Chrisette Michele, Jim Brown, Steve Harvey, Kanye West—Added to the cancelled list" (578 retweets and 777 likes). Attached to her tweet was an image of someone writing notes in a little black book and looking concerned.

Harvey (2017) attempted to respond to the backlash via his morning radio show, providing further commentary and expressing the pain he felt about his criticism: "A lot of y'all hurt me. I didn't expect the backlash to be so fierce. But I also understand that if I'm going to keep getting stabbed at, then at least while you're stabbing me you should understand my intent for even taking the meeting in the first place. I'm from the hood. I've been trying to do my part for years for boys and girls" (Harvey 2017). Harvey's wife, Marjorie Harvey, openly expressed support for her husband's choices on Instagram, writing, "Thank you my love for stepping outside of your comfort zone to do what is right for others. . . . Even in the face of adversity! Doing the right thing sometimes isn't popular but it's ok. . . . You always make me proud! I love you" (quoted in *Inside Edition* 2017). Harvey and his wife both recognized the risk that he took within the black community by meeting with Trump. And although his wife was initially publicly supportive of her husband's choice, Steve Harvey noted days later that he would not be attending Trump's inauguration because his "wife said no" (Golding 2017).

The Michele inauguration situation and Harvey's meeting with Trump are anecdotes about social media creating new venues and tools for racialized social constraint on black politics—but they are ones that suggest the potential effectiveness of racialized social pressure and social sanctions in the digital age. Michele and Harvey clearly violated the norms of black political behavior and suffered the consequences for their decisions in a racialized public space, Black Twitter. Both were reputationally sanctioned for their decisions, which had real social and monetary costs. Michele's decision cost her future opportunities to collaborate with other artists, negatively affected her relationships with her family members, and led to boycotts of her music. In the end, both Michele and Harvey had to learn a significant lesson about defying racial group norms and the power of reputational sanctions.

Democratic Partisanship as a Definitional
Norm of Modern Black Politics

Among the lessons of our brief overview of the long history of political norms and black collective political behavior is that the central norms of black politics have changed over time. Changing political circumstances have redefined what collective aims the group centrally needs to address to make progress toward racial liberation and equality. Structural changes in the political system have also redefined what specific political behaviors are most needed from individuals to advance the group's collective interests. In other words, while group unity has been a constant avenue to greater political power for black Americans, the specific political behaviors that define important and effective political unity have not remained the same. Thus, each era has presented the challenge of establishing the central social norms of black political behavior.

From the racialized social constraint framework we laid out in Chapter 1, we can derive three conditions that define the capacity of a political behavior expectation to function as a *particularly* effective norm of black politics— conditions that help to define the constraint capacity of each era's central norms. First, the constraint potential of an in-group norm depends on awareness of a behavior as descriptively normal for the group—that is, the behavior should be what is commonly termed a descriptive norm. The second condition is a broad in-group awareness that the behavior is generally expected of group members—that it defines an injunctive norm or how group members *should* behave. Third, a norm's capacity to constrain in-group behavior in our framework is shaped by the extent to which group members expect social consequences from others within the group for non-compliance. Norms to which in-group members attach real probability of sanctioning by others are ones to which they anticipate a social need to conform. To be clear, while we are focused here on characteristics of the norm itself, our broader argument implies that the potential of effective racialized social constraint also depends on the social capacity of the group to effectively sanction group members. We cover that dimension of racialized social constraint in modern black politics in the next chapter.

We expect that Democratic partisanship is a norm of modern black politics that satisfies all three of these conditions, making it an in-group norm especially amenable to maintenance through the social sanctioning mechanisms of racialized social constraint. Indeed, we expect that any norm that comes to be viewed as "definitional" for black politics will be one that fulfills all three conditions.[7] What follows are a set of analyses that empirically assess this expectation about the norm of Democratic partisan support. Across the analyses, we operationalize the partisan norm in this broadly defined way—not just as a norm of party identification but as one of behavioral support of the Democratic Party. Such behaviors may include identifying oneself as a partisan, but they also include endorsing, publicly supporting, and voting for the party and its candidates.

BLACK SUPPORT FOR THE DEMOCRATIC PARTY AS A DESCRIPTIVE SOCIAL NORM

Our first task is to assess Democratic support among black Americans as what Bicchieri and Xiao (2008, p. 192) call an empirical norm, which they describe as when individuals expect "the norm to be followed by a majority of people in the appropriate circumstances." Others would term this a descriptive norm. Social pressure to constrain individual group members in the face of motives to defect based on self-interest is more likely to be effective if most blacks have a sense that many black Americans actually do support the Democratic Party in opinion and action. This is, in a basic sense, the "everyone else (you care about) is doing it" condition.

For even the most casual observer of contemporary electoral politics, it would seem quite difficult not to recognize that nearly all African Americans vote for the Democratic Party—and that they have been doing so for some time. Figure 2.3 charts out black support for Democratic candidates, as estimated by exit polls, in the most salient national elections—those for the office of president—from 1976 through 2016. The near-ubiquitous nature of black Democratic voting is clear and enduring. Since 1976 the percentage of blacks who report voting for the Democratic presidential candidate has never dipped below 82 percent, and it climbed north of 90 percent in both the 2008 and 2012 elections.

The 2008 and 2012 elections, of course, were the ones in which black Americans had the opportunity to support a Democratic candidate who would also be the first black president. The Obama candidacy and then presidency indeed elicited a range of ways in which black Americans exhibited especially stark descriptive evidence of support for the Democratic president and his party. In the 2012 election the overwhelming consensus of black voters (93%) in support of the Democratic candidate was striking, but so, too, was the fact that blacks turned out as voters at levels higher than those of other racial groups—despite African Americans as a group lacking many

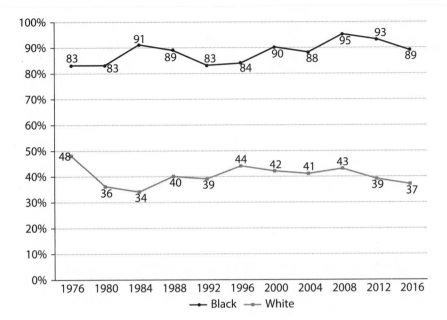

FIGURE 2.3. Democratic presidential vote share by race, exit polls

of the social and economic resources that would facilitate higher turnout (Taylor 2012).

This dedication to the first black Democratic president can also be seen in the intensity of blacks' approval of Obama throughout his two terms as president. As Figure 2.4 shows, while white Democrats' support for Obama began to wane as Obama's first term progressed, perhaps unsurprisingly in the face of criticisms over bailout programs and the president's push for health care reform, blacks as a group remained consistently loyal to the president throughout his entire presidency, averaging close to 90 percent support over its course.[8]

Not only is black support for the Democratic Party easily observed in reports of election exit polls and public opinion polling, but the idea that blacks are loyal Democratic Party supporters is regularly reinforced by news media accounts, which frequently report headlines such as "Can the Democratic Party Retain Its Hold on Black Voters?" (Johnson 2015) and "Four New Southern Senators Owe Victories to Black Vote; Allegiance to Democrats as High as 90%" (Walsh 1986). The idea of unified black Democratic support is also deeply integrated into black popular culture and is regularly reinforced within black entertainment media. For example, in a 2015 episode of the ABC sitcom Black-ish, the lead character, played by Anthony Anderson, states,

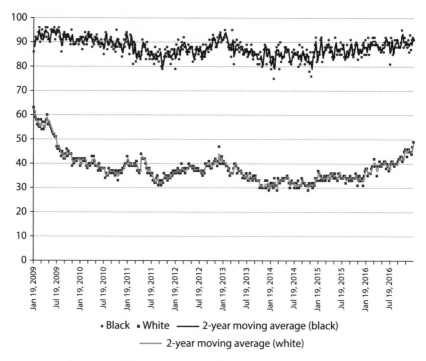

FIGURE 2.4. Obama approval by race. *Source:* Gallup (2017).

"There are certain things in life that are just true. Fact: The Earth revolves around the Sun. Fact: Two times two is four. And fact: Black people aren't Republicans. We just aren't. We vote for Democrats." Anderson's description highlights not only how widespread perceptions of black Democratic support are but also how salient they are within the black community.

Finally, to get a sense of just how aware blacks are that other blacks support the Democratic Party, we conducted an online poll of black and white Americans in 2014 and asked them to estimate the voting preferences of their racial in-group in the 2012 presidential election. A summary of the responses to this question is presented in Table 2.1. Both blacks and whites were able to give us fairly accurate accounts of the percentage of their racial groups that voted for Obama. White respondents estimated that 47 percent of the white vote went to Obama in the 2012 presidential election, which is only 8 percentage points off from the 39 percent estimated via 2012 exit polls. Although black respondents tended to underestimate the percentage of blacks who voted for Obama, their average estimate of 87 percent support among black voters was still a supermajority and just 6 points off from

TABLE 2.1. Respondent's Estimated Percentage of Racial In-Group Voters Who Voted for Democratic Candidate Barack Obama in the 2012 Presidential Election

	Black	White
% of racial in-group support for Democratic candidate (online poll)	87 ($N = 110$)	47 ($N = 735$)
Actual % of in-group supporting Democratic candidate (CNN exit polls)	93	39
Difference	−6	8

Note: Data from non-random sample of online respondents collected through Qualtrics and Mechanical Turk.

exit poll estimates that put the actual level of support among black voters at 93 percent.

Taken together, these pieces of evidence suggest both broad availability and awareness of the information that black Americans as a group consistently support the Democratic Party. That the "fact" of black support for Democrats can be found in both news and popular culture, in particular, shows its level of permeation as a descriptive social norm of black political behavior. That Democratic partisanship is widely understood as a common black political behavior satisfies the first condition of a norm with particular capacity to be enforced through racialized social constraint.[9]

BLACK SUPPORT FOR THE DEMOCRATIC PARTY AS AN INJUNCTIVE SOCIAL NORM

That group members empirically exhibit certain consistent behaviors does not necessarily mean that those behaviors are understood as expected of them by other group members. When individual group members believe that others in their group generally *expect* them to behave a certain way, that expectation is termed an injunctive norm or a normative expectation (Bicchieri 2006). These expectations are generally prescriptive or proscriptive in nature and define behavior in which a person ought (or ought not) to engage.[10] While under certain low-information or low-cost conditions, descriptive norms of political behavior might be sufficient conditions for norm compliance, our racialized social constraint model is meant to explain the trade-offs blacks make between norm compliance and conflicting self- or ideological interest. Under conditions of such conflicts, awareness of consistent group member behavior is less likely to be sufficient for bringing about conformity, as the perceived benefit of self-interest may override lower social benefits of behaving according to the descriptive group behavior (Bicchieri and Xiao 2008).

To evaluate whether individual African Americans are aware of an *expectation* of support for the Democratic Party and its candidates among racial in-group members, we examined the frequency with which blacks (regardless of political affiliation) and white Democrats were asked by their friends and family members to support the Democratic candidate for president in 2012. If a unique expectation of black support for the Democratic Party exists, then black Americans should encounter the expectation more frequently in their social and kinship networks—particularly given the racial homophily that characterizes those networks. We turned to data from a 2012 survey conducted by the Pew Research Center just before the November presidential election. It asked 122 blacks and 798 whites whether any of their family members or friends encouraged them to vote for Barack Obama, Mitt Romney, or both. Respondents were also asked about how this contact was made: whether it was in person, over the telephone, over email, in a text message, or through social networks via Twitter or Facebook. We combined all these methods of contact to create a measure that assesses whether the respondent was contacted and, if so, for whom they were asked to vote: Obama, Romney, or both Romney and Obama. Roughly equal proportions of white Democrats and black respondents reported not being contacted to vote: 40 percent of white Democratic respondents and 39 percent of black respondents. Our analysis only includes those respondents who reported being contacted.

Table 2.2 displays, among those who were contacted by friends and family to vote in the 2012 election, the percentage of blacks and the percentage of white Democrats who were asked only to vote for Obama or only to vote for Romney. Again, if blacks were generally only contacted to vote for Obama, this suggests that the individuals within their social networks have well-defined expectations about how they should behave. Indeed, this is exactly what we found. Nearly 75 percent of those blacks who were contacted by a friend or family member reported only being asked to vote for Obama. In comparison, only 45 percent of white Democrats who were asked by a friend or family member to vote reported only being asked to vote for Obama. That means that over 33 percent of white Democrats were asked either only to vote for Romney or to vote for both Romney and Obama. Only 12 percent of blacks found themselves in that position. Blacks' networks were just far more likely to convey an expectation of Democratic support.

TABLE 2.2. Percentage of Blacks and White Democrats Contacted by Friends and Family to Vote in the 2012 Election Who Were Only Asked to Vote for Barack Obama

	Blacks	White Democrats	Difference
Only asked to vote for Barack Obama	73.9%	44.9%	−29.0%*
Only asked to vote for Mitt Romney	2.4%	10.8%	8.4%*
N	73	138	

Notes: 2012 Pew Survey. "Blacks" is inclusive of all self-identified blacks regardless of political affiliation. Results reflect whether the individual was contacted only to support that candidate across all forms of contact. All other respondents were contacted to support both candidates across any of the forms of contact.
* $p < .05$

These results suggest that the members of the average black person's social network are sending clear and consistent signals about how they expect their friends and family members to behave in electoral politics. Another way to read the results: if you are black, you have a good chance of being told by friends or family that your support ought to go to the Democrat. If you are white and a Democrat, you have a better chance of getting mixed messages or being told by friends or family that your support ought to go to the Republicans than you do of being encouraged only to support the Democrat. That is, given that whites' social networks are politically diverse, even white Democrats are likely to receive mixed signals from members of their social networks about how they should behave politically. For blacks, however, their social networks give a clear and consistent signal that they should support the Democratic Party. Thus, we find support for our second condition of a norm's capacity to produce group behavior via racialized social constraint: that individual African Americans are aware of clear and common expectations from other blacks about how group members should behave politically.

THE EXPECTATION OF SANCTIONS

Thus far we've shown not only that there is a descriptive norm of support for the Democratic Party within the black community—that most blacks are aware that the vast majority of black voters support the Democratic Party and its candidates—but also that the partisan norm is injunctive, with Democratic Party support deemed an expected behavior. While each of these conditions increases the potential of norm conformity under our racialized social constraint framework, in order to counter ideological or material self-interest to defect from these well-defined group expectations, the potential of positive or negative incentives to bring about norm compliance becomes essential. In general, when behavior expectations are clear, norms most effectively constrain group behavior when sanctions (positive or negative) are expected to be used to encourage compliance (Bicchieri and Xiao 2008; Sinclair 2012). The existence of group-based expectations of Democratic Party support suggests that publicly deviating from these expectations could potentially have real social implications and publicly conforming to these behavioral expectations could have real social benefits.

Public displays of sanctioning are one way that expectations of sanctions for defection from group norms of political behavior take hold. Examples of public sanctioning for defecting from the norm of Democratic Party support are not difficult to find in contemporary black politics. Take, for example, the reaction of black Americans to African American actress Stacey Dash when she endorsed Republican Mitt Romney in his 2012 presidential bid. Dash's endorsement drew the ire of many in the black community, who labeled her, among other things, a sellout and an opportunist seeking to revive her acting career. Apparently upset by the social sanctioning, Dash responded publicly, saying in an editorial on TMZ, "Perhaps I publicly endorsed Romney from a slightly naïve place, thinking that I could speak my voice without being criticized in such racially charged and hateful tones" (Dash 2012). The criticism from the black community, however, did not abate. Even Dash's own cousin, hip-hop producer Damon Dash, added to the public criticism after she took a job with the conservative Fox News and became a vocal critic of both the Democratic Party and the black community. In an interview, he stated, "It really isn't the best thing to hear 'Dash' associated with cooning" (*TheGrio* 2016).

To further assess awareness of the social consequences of violating the in-group expectation of supporting the Democratic Party, in a 2014 opt-in internet poll we asked a diverse, national sample of African American and white Obama voters the following question: "Suppose for a moment that you had supported Mitt Romney in 2012, do you think any of your friends and/or family members would have given you a hard time if they found out that you supported Romney over Obama?" A summary of the responses to this question is presented in Table 2.3. Expectations of social sanctioning for supporting a Republican candidate over a Democratic one were nearly ubiquitous among the black respondents. Eighty percent of black Obama supporters expressed concern that either their friends or their family members or both would have given them a hard time if they found out they

TABLE 2.3. Concern for Social Consequences of Supporting Romney among Black and White Obama Supporters

	Black Obama voters	White Obama voters	Difference
Yes, I have friends that would have given me a hard time for supporting Romney over Obama.	19.4%	20.7%	1.3%
Yes, I have family that would have given me a hard time for supporting Romney over Obama.	13.1%	10.4%	−2.7%
Yes, I have both friends and family that would have given me a hard time for supporting Romney over Obama.	47.3%	23.3%	−24.0%*
No, none of my friends or family would have cared if I supported Romney over Obama.	20.0%	45.6%	25.6%*
N	175	775	

Note: Data from a 2014 non-random internet sample collected through Qualtrics.
* $p < .05$

supported Romney. In comparison, only 54 percent of white Obama supporters reported that their friends and family members would have had similar reactions.

This result is replicated by a similar question asked of individuals in a nationally representative survey of white and black Americans conducted in August 2016 by the Joint Center for Political and Economic Studies and Nielsen Scarborough. This time, black and white Obama voters were asked, "If you had voted for Romney/Ryan in 2012, to what extent do you think your friends and/or family members would have supported your decision? Would they have been: Very Supportive, Somewhat Supportive, Not Very Supportive or Not at all Supportive?" Table 2.4 summarizes the responses. Once again, black Obama voters reported that they expected negative social feedback from their friends and family members. Seventy-five percent of black Obama voters reported that their friends and family members would not have been supportive of them if they decided to vote for Romney and Ryan. Again, the expectation of negative social feedback was also more pronounced among blacks than whites. Only 53 percent of white Obama voters expected negative feedback from friends and family over a decision to support the Republican ticket rather than the Democratic one.

Perhaps just as telling about the expectations for social sanctioning for deviating from the norm of supporting the Democratic Party is that even those

TABLE 2.4. Perceived Social Support of Friends and Family for Supporting Romney among Black and White Obama Supporters

	Black Obama voters	White Obama voters	Difference
Very supportive	8.4%	12.6%	4.2%
Somewhat supportive	16.5%	33.8%	17.3%
Not very supportive	29.1%	30.6%	1.5%
Not at all supportive	46.0%	22.8%	−23.2%*
Not supportive	**75.1%**	**53.4%**	**−21.6%***
N	563	411	

Note: Data from the 2016 Joint Center for Political and Economic Studies and Nielsen Scarborough survey. The "not supportive" category is the sum of the "not very supportive" and "not at all supportive" categories.
* $p < .05$

blacks who actually *did* support Romney expected significantly less support for this decision from their friends and family members than white Romney voters did. Table 2.5 summarizes the perceived social support for voting for Romney among black and white Romney voters. Forty-five percent of black Romney voters felt that their friends and family would not be supportive of their decision. This is compared with only 10.6 percent of white Romney voters who said the same. Conversely, while expectations of social disapproval were more common among black Romney voters than among their white counterparts, over half of black Romney voters said their friends and family would support their choice. Stark differences in social feedback expectations across the social networks of most blacks versus the small minority of blacks who chose to vote for the Republican candidate suggest that social network differences helped enable that choice. Black Romney voters were decidedly less likely to anticipate that their networks would disapprove of that choice.

This same basic pattern of expected social support holds for the 2016 election between Hillary Clinton and Donald Trump. The results in Table 2.6 are from data we collected through the Lucid Technologies online panel. Unlike in the 2016 Joint Center for Political and Economic Studies and Nielsen Scarborough survey, these data are not a probability sample but rather are an opt-in sample of black and white Americans that roughly reflects the social and political diversity of the United States. There is a difference of roughly 11 percentage points between black and white perceived supportiveness among black and white Hillary voters. Although the racial differences are somewhat smaller than for the Romney-Obama contest, this seems to

TABLE 2.5. Perceived Social Support of Friends and Family for Supporting Romney among Black and White Romney Supporters

	Black Romney voters	White Romney voters	Difference
Very supportive	30.0%	59.0%	29.0%
Somewhat supportive	25.0%	30.4%	5.4%
Not very supportive	30.0%	8.5%	−21.5%
Not at all supportive	15.0%	2.1%	−12.9%*
Not supportive	**45.0%**	**10.6%**	**−34.4%***
N	20	293	

Note: Data from the 2016 Joint Center for Political and Economic Studies and Nielsen Scarborough survey. The "not supportive" category is the sum of the "not very supportive" and "not at all supportive" categories.
* $p < .05$

reflect more the polarization of whites around the 2016 election than it does a decrease in blacks' perception that there would be social consequences for supporting the Republican presidential candidate. Indeed, the percentage of black Hillary voters who reported that their friends and family members would not have been supportive of them if they decided to vote for Trump and Pence (76.9%) is almost identical to the percentage of black Obama voters who reported that their friends and family members would not have been supportive of them if they decided to vote for Romney and Ryan (75.1%).

These results support our third condition of norm compliance: that individual African Americans believe that social sanctions could well be used by racial in-group members to encourage compliance with Democratic Party support. Individual blacks are well aware of real social consequences for defecting from the expectation of black support for the Democratic Party. This concern about social punishment for non-Democratic choices is racially unique—it is more widespread among black Americans as a group than among white Democrats. These salient partisan behavior expectations and the widespread awareness of the social repercussions of violating them, along with the constraints of the American two-party system, help us to understand why African Americans of all ideological and economic backgrounds have continued to actively and openly support the Democratic Party and its candidates for over fifty years. Supporting Democratic candidates and policies is understood to advance the racial group's interests, and to defect from that choice will likely not only hurt the group but also incur significant reputational costs to the individual, too.

TABLE 2.6. Perceived Social Support of Friends and Family for Supporting Trump among Black and White Hillary Clinton Supporters

	Black Clinton voters	White Clinton voters	Difference
Very supportive	11.0%	13.9%	2.9%
Somewhat supportive	12.0%	20.2%	8.2%*
Not very supportive	21.0%	26.1%	5.1%*
Not at all supportive	55.9%	39.8%	−16.1%*
Not supportive	**76.9%**	**65.9%**	**−11.0%***
N	540	732	

Note: Data is from an online survey collected by the authors. The "not supportive" category is the sum of the "not very supportive" and "not at all supportive" categories.
* $p < .05$

Conclusion

Our brief overview of black American political history in this chapter highlighted both consistency and change in black politics. Consistently across quite different political eras, we observed a black politics characterized by in-group norms and the effectiveness of racialized social constraint in producing black political behavior consistent with those norms even in the face of cross-pressuring self-interests. Change came in the creation of new black political norms, ones fitted to the unique challenges blacks faced and the unique possibilities for racial group progress in that era.

We showed that during the antebellum period in the Southern United States, to quell slave resistance, whites provided incentives like manumission and money to entice slaves to become informants about efforts to escape and potential uprisings and rebellions. Slaves responded to the informant system by using, among other methods, social coercion to keep other slaves from reporting on resistance efforts. During the era of Reconstruction, many blacks felt a loyalty to the Republican Party for its efforts to end slavery, but some in the black community actively supported the Democratic Party and its candidates because of allegiance to former masters, coercive efforts by whites, or attempts by Democrats to simply buy black votes. Recognizing the political power of the black voting bloc, black Republicans pushed back against the efforts of black Democrats by questioning their place within the black community and in some cases threatening them with physical violence. The creation of Jim Crow laws following the end of Reconstruction further segregated blacks according to race, resulting in the emergence of black social and political institutions and an even stronger reliance on black social ties. In the post–civil rights era, the racial politics of the Southern Strategy tarnished the relationship between Republicans and blacks. Over time and in response to changing commitments from the Democratic Party, black Democratic Party support became normalized. In the twenty-first century, new social institutions like Black Twitter have emerged, offering new and developing in-group social tools for reinforcement of the now well-established Democratic partisan norm.

In the latter part of this chapter, we took up exactly how well established this norm currently is and how well it fits the three conditions that increase the constraint capacity of norms identified by our racialized social constraint framework. We found support for the Democratic Party to be well understood as both a descriptive and an injunctive norm of black political behavior. We showed not only that there is a strong awareness that most black Americans do indeed support the Democratic Party but also that when asked, black Americans are able to fairly accurately describe the extent of racial in-group support for Democratic presidential candidates. We also showed that blacks do have a sense that other blacks expect them to support the Democratic Party. Blacks, we showed, were likely to have members of their social and kinship networks tell them to support the Democratic candidate—and only the Democratic one. Finally, we found expectations among black Americans of being socially sanctioned for violations of the Democratic norm to be commonplace. In short, the norm of support for the Democratic Party is not just well established but also well equipped for employment in the process of racialized social constraint, making it one quite capable of defining black politics in the modern era.

Exactly when this norm factors into the political decisions of blacks remains unanswered. When are blacks considering the social consequences of their political decisions? In which types of contexts are we more likely to see norm conformity? What are the consequences of norm conformity for black partisan political decisions? In Chapter 3 we begin to answer these questions by assessing the conditions of social location that define the potential for racialized social constraint. Racial homophily in black social networks, we will see, creates political homogeneity and heightens the social consequences for norm defection for blacks. This will deepen our understanding of black partisan loyalty as a fundamentally social phenomenon.

3

The Political Consequences of Black Social Networks

In 1967, following two weeks of violent racial unrest in Detroit, Michigan, and Newark, New Jersey, which left nearly forty people dead and more than one thousand wounded, President Lyndon B. Johnson commissioned a study to examine the social and political origins of racial discontent in American cities. After several months examining black life in American cities, the commission, called the Kerner Commission after its chair, Otto Kerner Jr., released a 426-page report that concluded that racial inequality stemming from racial segregation was at the heart of the unrest and that government needed to act decisively in alleviating racial divisions, or American cities would once again boil over into violence and destruction. The commission concluded that the nation was "moving toward two societies, one black, one white—separate and unequal," and that "discrimination and segregation . . . threaten the future of every American" (National Advisory Commission on Civil Disorders 1968, p. 1).

The commission's recommendations that the government act decisively to address racial segregation, discrimination, and racial inequality proved even more urgent when, in the months following the release of the report, rioting once again erupted in cities across the country, this time in response to the assassination of Martin Luther King Jr. This second wave of racial unrest seemed to indicate that the United States was even more racially bifurcated than the commission's report suggested, and instead of moving toward two societies, perhaps the country was already irreversibly divided along racial lines. Indeed, for African Americans, American life had for the last four hundred years been characterized by little more than racial discrimination and segregation. In fact, even today the day-to-day experiences of most African Americans continue to be largely divided along racial lines. While many of the more explicit practices of racial segregation have legally ended, years of both institutionalized and de facto segregation have produced neighborhoods, communities, and schools in which black populations are heavily concentrated and largely isolated from their fellow Americans. Today, the most obvious social consequence of this racial isolation is that black and white Americans are afforded few if any opportunities for meaningful cross-racial social interaction because spatial segregation and racial discrimination limit social contact to members of an individual's own racial in-group. It is this homogeneity, along with well-understood expectations of black political behavior, that we argue facilitates racialized social constraint.

In this chapter, we will explore in detail the role that racial segregation plays in facilitating racialized social constraint and ultimately leading to partisan unity among African Americans. We argue that black social networks are essential to holding blacks accountable to norms of black political behavior; the "blacker" an individual's social network, the more likely that individual is to conform to norms of black political behavior such as identifying with and supporting the Democratic Party. As discussed in the previous chapters, accountability to norms of black political behavior is ensured through the threat of social sanctions for those individuals who defect from racial group norms and the promise of rewards for those individuals who comply with these norms. Close spatial proximity to in-group members enables the implementation of these rewards and sanctions. Conversely, we believe that the more integrated a black person is into white society, the more likely he or she is to act on incentives to violate norms of black political behavior, as social distance from the black community will limit accountability and allow greater opportunities for norm-inconsistent behavior. Furthermore, we show that racialized social constraint works primarily through its ability to prevent blacks who hold conservative ideological beliefs from identifying as anything other than Democrats. We conclude this chapter with a discussion of the uniqueness of blackness as an institutionalized social identity that has meaningful implications for black political beliefs.

Racialized Social Context and Its Implications

In the wake of the unrest following the August 9, 2014, shooting of unarmed black teenager Michael Brown in Ferguson, Missouri, the *Atlantic* magazine ran a story entitled "Self-Segregation: Why It's So Hard for Whites to Understand Ferguson." The author, Robert P. Jones, argues that one of the reasons that whites and blacks have such starkly different interpretations of the events surrounding Brown's death is that white Americans have such little day-to-day contact with African Americans. Building on observations made nearly fifty years earlier by the Kerner Commission, Jones (2014) notes that "the chief obstacle to having an intelligent, or even intelligible, conversation across the racial divide is that on average white Americans live in communities that face far fewer problems and talk mostly to other white people." Jones then turns to survey data, the American Values Survey conducted in 2013 by the Public Religion Research Institute (PRRI), to support his racial isolation argument. He shows that not only do white Americans see their communities as faced with different problems from those of African Americans, and fewer of them, but they also have very little meaningful day-to-day interaction with African Americans. Jones presents data on the self-reported social networks of white Americans that show that white social networks are, indeed, almost exclusively white. Jones reports that according to data from the PRRI survey, the average white American's social network is 91 percent white, 1 percent black, 1 percent Asian or Pacific Islander, 1 percent Hispanic, 1 percent mixed race, and 1 percent "other race." Jones infers from this that were white Americans to have more social contact with African Americans, there could, at the very least, be a dialogue about race in America, but without such contact, dialogue—and consequently racial progress—will remain out of reach.

While Jones is certainly correct in his description of the enormous gap in black-white social contact, the effect of increased interracial contact on the behavior of black and white Americans remains widely debated. Early efforts to systematically understand the effects of social contact on intergroup relations can be traced to the 1954 work of Gordon Allport. Allport proposed an explanation of intergroup relations that he called the "contact hypothesis," which sought to identify the role of interpersonal contact in reducing prejudice between majority- and minority-group members. Introduced as a general explanation of out-group prejudice, the contact hypothesis suggested that increased contact under certain conditions could effectively reduce out-group prejudice. In the years following its introduction, the contact hypothesis was frequently applied to attempts to understand black-white race relations. Seeing whites as the agents of racial discord in the United States, researchers have used the contact hypothesis to better understand how interventions meant to increase white Americans' interactions with African Americans might alter their attitudes about blacks.

While over the last fifty years a number of studies have found that interracial contact can indeed have the effect of reducing white racial prejudice (Cook 1984; Harrington and Miller 1992; Jackson 1993; Pettigrew 1998), the effects of interracial contact remain largely conditional on context and have been found to come with significant costs for minority populations. For example, scholars argue that one of the primary effects of contact is learning about out-groups, so as groups such as whites have more exposure to blacks, they have the opportunity to learn about blacks in a way that helps them move beyond their stereotypes and existing prejudice. Researchers have come to recognize, however, that if the interactions between groups such as whites and blacks are characterized by unequal status, which they nearly always are, then it is just as likely that contact will result in the reinforcement of existing prejudices (Amir 1976). Similarly, Amir (1998) shows that for minority-group members, contact with higher-status out-group members under conditions of inequality can lead to increased feelings of inferiority and diminished regard for one's own group. Thus, while the overall effect of contact may be improved intergroup relations, the cost may be disproportionately borne by minority groups who conform to out-group expectations out of a diminished view of their own in-group.

Important questions have also been raised about the efficacy of increased contact under conditions of heightened conflict or competition. Political scientists, for example, have found very little support for the contact hypothesis. Conceptualizing contact as the geographic distance between black and white Americans, these researchers have found that an increase in opportunities for interracial contact typically leads to greater conflict and increased white animosity. In studying the relationship between changes in the black population and conflict over political power, Blalock (1967) found that whites' hostility toward African Americans increased significantly as their social distance from blacks decreased. Originally introduced by V. O. Key in 1949, the "power-threat hypothesis" has become a widely cited explanation of whites' animosity toward African Americans. It suggests that as the proportion of blacks in the local population increases, the potential for conflict increases as whites see growing minority populations as a threat to the social, economic, and political status quo. While power-threat research offered an interesting examination of the spatial dynamics of racial politics in America, it became clear that, despite its compelling findings, it suffered from many of the same problems as the contact hypothesis, in particular its inability to identify the exact process by which a shift in racial context results in attitudinal or behavioral change. Unanswered questions such as "How big does the black population need to be to trigger white animosity?" and "Why are some white populations more affected by racial context than others?" continue to cast doubt on power-threat explanations of political behavior (see Oliver and Mendelberg 2000).

While we have learned a great deal about how interracial contact affects the attitudes of white Americans, the fact remains that little is known about how these theories might inform our understanding of African American political behavior. Because African Americans are not seen as the antagonist in racial conflict, much of this work has focused on understanding the behavior of white Americans, but there are good reasons to believe that interracial contact (and the lack thereof) may have profound consequences for the behavior of African Americans. In one of the few studies on the topic, Bledsoe et al. (1995) identify a strong link between the proportion of African Americans in a neighborhood and blacks' beliefs in black social, economic, and political solidarity. Analyzing data from a survey of black residents in the Detroit area, Bledsoe et al. find that blacks who live in mixed-race neighborhoods report having less of a sense of racial group solidarity than those blacks who live in more heavily black neighborhoods. The authors attribute this diminished solidarity to the effects of racial contact. Blacks who live in mixed neighborhoods are more likely to have contact with whites and are more likely to be exposed to the group-based norms of these communities. Racially mixed communities also place less value on engaging in collective action on the part of any one racial group.

Gay (2004) builds on Bledsoe et al.'s (1995) idea about black social context by examining the roles of neighborhood quality and neighborhood socioeconomic composition in conditioning the effects of social context on blacks' political beliefs. Gay finds that for blacks, an inverse relationship exists between neighborhood quality and black group solidarity. Specifically, as neighborhood quality increases, blacks' belief in black group solidarity decreases. While Bledsoe et al. and Gay add considerably to our understanding of the role that social context might play in shaping blacks' views on group solidarity, much remains to be understood about the scope of these effects. In particular, while racialized social context certainly seems to be related to black perceptions of group solidarity, does this relationship extend to other forms of black political behavior, such as blacks' unified support for the Democratic Party? Additionally, while both Bledsoe et al. and Gay examine racialized social context using geographic indicators as proxies for racialized social contact—typically at the metropolitan, neighborhood, or block level—others have found these sorts of measures problematic, as individuals' understandings of neighborhood boundaries exhibit a great deal of heterogeneity, resulting in measures that may not capture the *type* of meaningful inter- and intraracial contact researchers suspect (Wong, Wang, and Kangasharju 2012).

The racialized social constraint argument offered in this book centers on how the meaningful social contact blacks have with other blacks can influence black political behavior. Our argument, however, differs from both the contact and the group-threat explanations in that instead of focusing exclusively on how social contact might increase or decrease competition with or learning about racial out-groups, we see inter- and intraracial contact as a means of facilitating or constraining individual political behavior through the encouragement and enforcement of norms of political behavior. The normalization of black support for the Democratic Party within black popular culture, along with the spatial isolation of black Americans in the United States, has resulted in a set of dynamics that greatly constrain black political behavior. Specifically, we argue that the dynamics of spatial segregation by race essentially force blacks into racially exclusive social relationships with other blacks. As a result, these black individuals then find themselves compelled to either accept the dominant political beliefs of the racial group or risk loss of status within these largely black social networks. Thus, we see increased intraracial contact as causing increased homogeneity in black political preferences because blacks hold one another accountable to group norms of political behavior. Blacks with more racially diverse social relationships, in particular those with more whites in their social networks, will likely engage in political behavior that more closely reflects their individual interests, because spatial and social distance from other blacks insulates them from racial in-group expectations. In other words, because the political positions of white Americans are more politically heterogeneous, blacks who have more whites in their social networks will likely have more outlets for the expression of diverse political beliefs and fewer sources of constraint.

The next sections of this chapter will examine the relationship between the racial composition of black and white individuals' social networks and their political beliefs. One of the central assumptions of the racialized social constraint model is that black Americans are invested in same-race social relationships. In the following section, we will describe the consequences of racial segregation for black political dispositions by first demonstrating the large degree of racial homophily present within both black and white social networks. Next, we will connect this racial homophily to our earlier observation that well-understood norms of Democratic Party support exist within the black community and show that more exclusively black social relationships are strongly related to adherence to these norms of black political behavior. Additionally, we will show that black social networks most powerfully constrain the behavior of those blacks who have ideological reasons to defect from the group norm of supporting the Democratic Party, black conservatives.

Social Networks and Racial Homophily

RACIAL HOMOPHILY AND SOCIAL INSTITUTIONS

Black and white Americans are remarkably isolated from one another in their daily lives. At home, school, work, church, and even the hair salon or the grocery store, the daily social interactions of blacks and whites are defined almost exclusively by interactions with other racial in-group members. Indeed, researchers examining measures of racial homogeneity in cities and metropolitan areas across the United States have found that opportunities for interracial interaction are greatly constrained by the spatial distribution of black and white households (Massey and Denton 1993). Examining the average racial composition of the neighborhoods in which black and white Americans live, these researchers have found strong evidence suggesting that the spatial isolation of black and white populations is likely an important factor in limiting opportunities for cross-racial social interactions (Charles 2003; Massey and Denton 1993).

The extent to which this racial isolation defines black Americans' daily social interactions can be seen in Table 3.1. Presented here are segregation scores for the ten U.S. cities with the largest black populations. Together these ten cities contain 56 percent of the black population in the United States. The scores presented here are two of the most widely used measures of racial isolation: the exposure index and the dissimilarity index. In the first column of Table 3.1 is the Black-Black Exposure Index, which measures the degree of potential contact blacks in a given city are likely to have with other blacks, or the probability that a given black person in that city will meet or interact with another member of his or her racial in-group. In other words, a score of, say, 75 on the Black-Black Exposure Index would mean

TABLE 3.1. Dissimilarity and Exposure Indices for the Ten U.S. Cities with the Largest Black Population, 2000 Census

	Black-Black Exposure Index score	White-Black Dissimilarity Index score
Chicago, IL	85.8	87.3
New York, NY	62.4	85.3
Washington, DC	83.5	81.5
Philadelphia, PA	78.7	80.6
Houston, TX	60.2	75.5
Baltimore, MD	84.7	75.2
Los Angeles, CA	37.2	74.0
Dallas, TX	59.5	71.5
Memphis, TN	81.4	68.6
Detroit, MI	89.8	63.3

Source: CensusScope (n.d.).

that seventy-five of every one hundred people a black person from this city interacts with would also be black. Thus, high values suggest greater racial isolation. As we can see, the probability of a black person interacting with members of his or her own racial group is generally very high. These scores suggest that for the average black person living in, for example, Detroit, Chicago, Memphis, Baltimore, or Washington, DC, eight out of every ten people the black person is likely to come in contact with will also be black. Only in Los Angeles does the likelihood of black-black interaction decrease below 50 percent, as blacks appear to be more evenly distributed across neighborhoods there (W.A.V. Clark et al. 2015). Measures of neighborhood racial dissimilarity suggest a similar pattern of racial isolation. The White-Black Dissimilarity Index, presented in the second column of Table 3.1, measures the number of white Americans who would have to move to another neighborhood in their city to make whites and blacks evenly distributed. As we can see, in Chicago, New York, Washington, DC, and Philadelphia, more than 80 percent of the white population would have to move to another neighborhood for whites and blacks to be evenly distributed within these cities.

The spatial isolation of blacks can also be seen in blacks' own descriptions of their daily life experiences. Table 3.2 summarizes data from surveys of blacks and whites in the Detroit and Houston areas. The Detroit data are from the 1996 Detroit Area Study, which is a probability sample of

TABLE 3.2. Percentage of Blacks and Whites Who Report Being in Various Social Contexts with Mostly or Exclusively Racial In-Group Members

	Doctor (DAS)	Grocery (DAS)	Barber or Salon (DAS)	Neighborhood (DAS)	Neighborhood (HAS)	Work (DAS)	Church (DAS)	Church (HAS)
Black	37	38	98	79	35	34	89	85
White	73	73	95	90	63	68	93	68

Note: Data from the 1996 Detroit Area Study (DAS) and the 2003 and 2010 Kinder Houston Area Survey (HAS).

residents in the Detroit metro area. The Houston data are from the 2003 and 2010 Kinder Houston Area Survey. These surveys are ideal for our purposes because not only do they include a relatively large number of African American respondents,[1] but they also include a number of questions measuring the respondents' self-described daily interactions with members of other racial groups. These surveys measured, among other things, the proportion of blacks and whites who report interacting with mostly racial in-group members daily in different social environments, such as work, church, the grocery store, or doctors' offices. We see that both blacks and whites describe their neighborhood, work, and church environments as largely segregated by race. For example, in the Detroit area, as many as 89 percent of blacks and 93 percent of whites describe the church they attend as composed mostly or exclusively of racial in-group members. Similarly, blacks and whites each describe their barber and beauty salons as essentially racial in-group spaces. Blacks' work environments appear to be the least racially segregated, with around 34 percent of blacks in these metro areas saying that the people they worked with were mostly or all black. White Americans describe more racially isolated workplaces, with about 68 percent of whites describing their workplaces as mostly or all white.[2]

While the lack of interracial contact in daily social interactions is certainly one way of measuring racial isolation, such social interactions may not reflect the kind of *meaningful* personal connections that would likely constrain political behavior. Racial segregation greatly limits the potential for interracial friendships and other associations that might help build the interracial trust and cooperation necessary for collective political action. Thus, to measure the frequency of meaningful interracial interactions, we turn to survey data that assess black and white respondents' descriptions of their close social connections, such as the people they consider close

TABLE 3.3. Social Network Question Wording

A. CLOSE FRIEND QUESTION

2015 Pew survey of multiracial Americans	How many of your CLOSE FRIENDS are . . ." black, white. Answer Choices: All, Most, Some, None
Social Capital Community Survey, January 2006–August 2006	Do you have a personal friend who is: black, white . . . Answer Choices: Yes/No

B. LIST QUESTION

2013 PRRI American Values Survey	From time to time, most people discuss important matters with other people. Looking back over the last six months, I'd like to know the people you talked with about matters that are important to you. Max number of discussion partners = 7 Number of African American respondents = 220
1992 Cross-National Election Studies: United States Study	From time to time, most people discuss important matters with other people. Looking back over the last six months, I'd like to know the people you talked with about matters that are important to you. Max number of discussion partners = 5 Number of African American respondents = 111
1985 and 2004 GSS	From time to time, most people discuss important matters with other people. Looking back over the last six months— who are the people with whom you discussed matters important to you? Just tell me their first names or initials. Max number of discussion partners = 5 Number of African American respondents = 237

Note: All questions subsequently ask the race of these friends or discussion partners.

friends or the people with whom they regularly discuss important issues. We examine two sets of questions. The first set simply asks respondents whether they have close personal friends who are either black or white. These questions are described in the first part of Table 3.3. The second social network measure we examine asks respondents to first list either all the people they consider close personal friends or the individuals with whom they regularly discuss important matters. Once each of these sets of individuals is listed, the survey then asks the respondent to report the race of each individual. Over the last twenty or so years, a number of surveys have used this approach to assess individual-level social networks. This measure appears to have been adopted from Edward Laumann (1973), who assessed individual social networks by asking respondents to name five people with whom they regularly discuss important matters. This measure also appeared within the 1985 and 2004 General Social Survey (GSS), which additionally asked respondents to describe a set of demographic and behavioral or attitudinal characteristics of their discussion partners by answering a series of questions that assesses each discussion partner's race, gender, and, in some cases, political behavior. These measures have become the foundation of survey-based research on social networks, serving as the basis for understanding how social networks affect social and political attitudes and behavior (see Huckfeldt and Sprague 1995; Sinclair 2012). The second part of Table 3.3 describes how this measure was presented in the 2013 PRRI American Values Survey, the 1992 Cross-National Election Studies: United States Study, and the 1985 and 2004 GSS.

In Tables 3.4 and 3.5 we use these measures to get a sense of the proportion of black and white associates that form the social networks of the black and white respondents in these surveys. Unfortunately, most of these surveys have very few African American respondents; thus, our ability to replicate our findings across these different data sources will be key to ensuring confidence in our observations.

We begin our analysis of black social networks by examining the measures of close friendships from the 2015 Pew survey of multiracial Americans and the 2006 Social Capital Community Survey. This measure simply asks black respondents how many of their close friends are black and asks white respondents how many of their close friends are white. We see that most black and white Americans maintain close friendships primarily with people of their own race. In both data sources, about 65 percent of blacks stated that their close friendships were with other blacks. White Americans were more likely to have same-race friendships: between 76 percent and 89 percent of whites said that their close friendships were with other whites. The problem with this measure, however, is that given its presentation, respondents are susceptible to the pressure of describing diverse social networks and thus are likely to overestimate the percentage of racial out-group friends and underestimate the percentage of racial in-group friends.

Our second social network measure is somewhat less susceptible to this bias. By asking respondents to first list their friends or discussion partners,

TABLE 3.4. Percentage of Black and White Americans with All or Most Close Friends of the Same Race

	Pew, 2015		Social Capital Community Survey, 2006	
	Black	White	Black	White
% same race close friends	65.8	76.1	65.0	89.1

TABLE 3.5. Social Network Racial Homophily among Black and White Americans

	PRRI American Values Survey, 2013		Cross-National Election Studies, 1992		GSS, 1985 and 2004	
	In social network		In social network		In social network	
	% black	% white	% black	% white	% black	% white
Black	84	9	84	13	86	10
White	1	94	1	96	1	93

respondents are more likely to list individuals whom they actually have meaningful contact with and thus are less likely to overstate the diversity of their social networks. Turning to the results of this measure presented in Table 3.5, we can see, consistent with the data on daily social interactions, that both black and white Americans report relatively few interracial acquaintances. The average white American's social network is almost exclusively white. We see that whites form about 93 percent of the average white American's close social connections. Although black Americans appear to describe more racially diverse social networks, they still associate largely with other blacks. Whites form only about 10 percent of the average black American's social networks, while racial in-group members make up roughly 85 percent of those networks.

Figure 3.1 further highlights this distinction. Assuming each respondent in the 2013 PRRI American Values Survey had ten people in his or her social network with whom the respondent regularly discussed important matters, then according to these data, the average black person would have only one white person in his or her social network and the average white person would have no black people in his or her social network. The contrasts between black and white social networks presented here highlight just how starkly different the day-to-day social interactions of black and white Americans are,

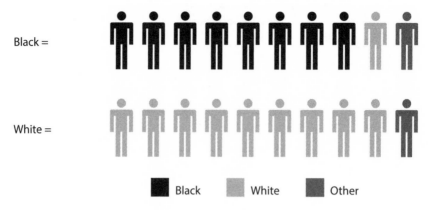

Black =

White =

| | Black | | White | | Other |

FIGURE 3.1. Racial makeup of black and white social networks

as well as how the lack of interracial associations greatly limits potential for meaningful cross-racial social interaction between the two racial groups.

RACIAL TO POLITICAL HOMOPHILY

Having demonstrated that racial segregation restricts both the day-to-day social interactions of black and white Americans and their close personal relationships, we now turn to understanding how this social isolation might be connected to the unified partisan political behavior of black Americans. Specifically, if racialized social constraint is indeed behind increased black support for the Democratic Party, then we should be able to observe that the greater the proportion of black Americans in a black person's social network, the more likely that person will be to support the Democratic Party. Again, we see the process underlying this relationship as resulting from the habitual imposition of social pressure by racial in-group members to elicit conformity to norms of black political behavior. Conversely, given that no such norm currently exists among white Americans, since whites are fairly evenly split in partisanship nationally, we expect that having a greater proportion of whites in one's social network will lead those blacks who have incentives to defect from this norm to feel freer to identify as something other than Democrats. In other words, we see the establishment of social relationships with whites as offering meaningful social outlets for blacks, particularly conservative blacks, to express divergent political views.

We begin our examination of this idea by first investigating the relationship between our measures of close friendships and Democratic Party identification from the 2015 Pew survey of multiracial Americans and the 2006

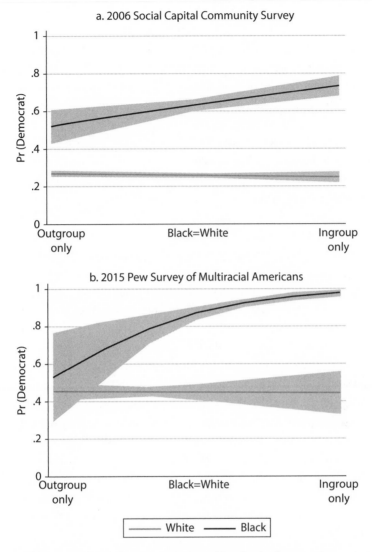

FIGURE 3.2. Black and white Democratic Party identification by proportion of black associates. *Note:* The 2006 Social Capital Community Survey data do not distinguish leaning partisans. This likely explains the overall lower rates of Democratic Party identification for both blacks and whites.

Social Capital Community Survey. We examine how the rate of Democratic Party identification among our black and white respondents changes as a function of whether the respondent had more close friendships with racial in-group members or racial out-group members. The results of this analysis are presented in Figures 3.2a–b. On the *x* axis is a simple difference score of the number of close friendships with racial in-group members subtracted from the number of close friendships with out-group members.[3] A score of 0 means that the respondent described himself or herself as having an equal number of racial in-group as out-group close friends. The y axis represents the probability that the respondent identifies as a Democrat. According to our racialized social constraint model, we would expect that as black Americans' close friendships become more exclusively black, they will be more likely to identify as Democrats. We also expect that because no such norms exist governing white partisan behavior, there should be no relationship between the racial makeup of white Americans' friendship networks and their party identification.

As we can see in Figures 3.2a–b, for black Americans a strong relationship exists between Democratic Party identification and the racial composition of their friendship networks. Blacks who describe their friendship networks as mostly made of other black Americans are much more likely to identify as Democrats, while blacks who have more non-black friends are significantly more likely to identify as something other than Democrats. In the Pew data, for example, we can see that there exists a particularly strong relationship between the racial makeup of black social networks and Democratic Party identification. We see that having all black friends nearly perfectly predicts black Democratic Party identification; the probability of Democratic Party identification among blacks who describe themselves as having only racial in-group friends is .98. For blacks whose close friends are primarily from the racial out-group, the probability of Democratic Party identification drops significantly, to about .50. In other words, while this model predicts that nearly all blacks who have exclusively black friendship networks will identify as Democrats, there is only a fifty-fifty chance of Democratic Party identification among blacks who describe their friendship networks as being exclusively non-black.

For whites, the pattern of results is very different. The relationship between the racial makeup of white social connections and party identification is essentially zero, suggesting that having exclusively white or non-white friends or associates does very little to encourage white Americans to identify as Democrats. This perhaps should not come as a surprise given that although white social networks are also racially homogeneous, they lack the norms of partisanship that characterize the black political experience.

We are also able to replicate these results using the traditional social network measure from 2013 PRRI American Values Survey and the 1985 and 2004 GSS. We create a similar difference score reflecting the proportion of

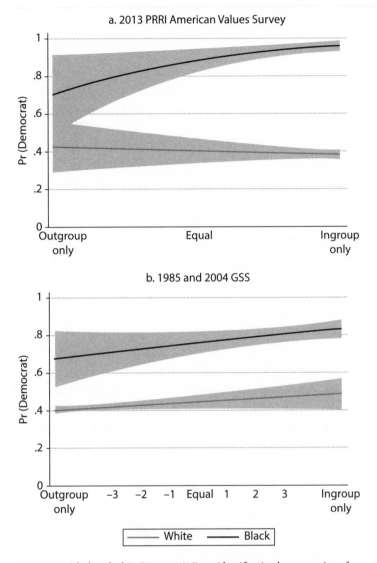

FIGURE 3.3. Black and white Democratic Party identification by proportion of black associates

black discussion partners identified by the respondent in response to the social network question. In Figures 3.3a–b we present the probability of identifying as a Democrat given the racial makeup of one's discussion partners. Looking first at the 2013 PRRI data, which included 193 valid black respondents and 1,528 valid white respondents, we see that having exclusively black associates once again nearly perfectly explains black Democratic Party identification. The probability of identifying as a Democrat for those blacks whose social networks are made up exclusively of other blacks is about .96. Keep in mind that blacks who have exclusively black social networks make up over 73 percent of the African American sample in these data. On the other hand, for those blacks who described themselves as having no black associates (6%), the probability of identifying as a Democrat dips to .71, a 25-percentage-point decrease in Democratic Party identification. Indeed, given that the overall rate of black Democratic Party identification typically is somewhere between 80 and 90 percent, it seems clear that blacks with few black associates appear to behave very differently from the typical African American.[4] In fact, in both of these analyses, blacks with few black associates appear to behave more like white Americans in their Democratic Party identifications than they do the average black person. As we can see, white Democratic partisanship changes little as a function of the racial makeup of their social networks. The probability of a white person identifying as a Democrat in these data ranges from .39 to .44, a very modest change compared with the 25-percentage-point decrease observed among black Americans.

The same basic pattern appears to hold for the 1985 and 2004 GSS data. The probability of identifying as a Democrat decreases from about .85 among blacks with all black discussion partners to about .61 among blacks with no black associates. As in the 2013 PRRI data, the racial makeup of white social connections matters little to whites' party identification. It seems that black friends or associates likely play an important role in preventing blacks from acting on whatever interest they might have to identify as something other than Democrats.

———

If blacks' social connections with other blacks are the mechanism by which norms of political behavior within the black community are enforced, then not only would we expect black social networks to powerfully influence attitudes about Democratic Party identification, but these norms should also influence other black partisan political behaviors. In Figures 3.4a–b we examine the probability that an individual will vote for the Democratic presidential candidate given the difference in the proportion of black associates relative to non-black associates using the 2013 PRRI data and the 1985 and 2004 GSS data.[5] Looking first at the 2013 PRRI data, we can see that the probability of voting for Barack Obama in the 2012 presidential election varies for both black and white respondents as a function of the percentage of discussion partners who are from the respondent's racial

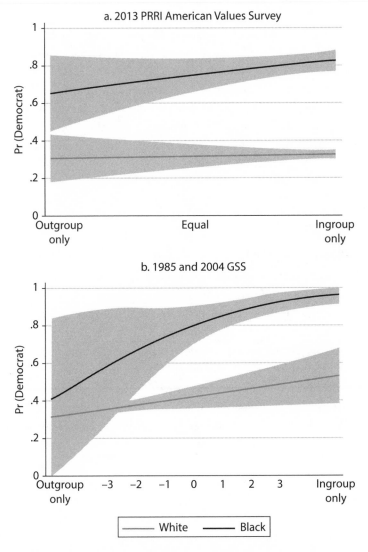

FIGURE 3.4. Black and white 2012 Democratic presidential candidate vote by percentage of black friends

in-group. Once again the evidence suggests that the presence of more blacks in a black person's social network appears to be related to constrained political behavior on the part of black respondents. For example, based on the data of the 2013 PRRI American Values Survey, we estimate that the probability of a black person with no black associates voting for Obama in 2012 is about .61, while the probability that a black person whose social network is made up only of other blacks will vote for Obama is about .81, a 20-percentage-point increase. This result is also replicated in the GSS data. Here we see a nearly 60-percentage-point increase in the probability of voting for the Democratic presidential candidate as we move from blacks who have no black associates to blacks whose social networks comprise only other African Americans. The results for whites are, once again, mixed. Although there is a negative relationship between the proportion of black and white associates and the probability of voting for Democratic candidates in the GSS data, this relationship was not replicated in the 2013 PRRI survey.

BLACK SOCIAL NETWORKS AND IDEOLOGICAL CONSTRAINT

If social connections to other blacks do, indeed, have the effect of constraining black political behavior, then we should be able to observe this constraint working to curtail the defection of those individuals who actually have good reasons to defect from the norm of black political behavior. While this norm revolves around support for the Democratic Party, black conservatives have a clear ideological interest in not conforming to it. As discussed earlier, strong support exists within the black community for certain conservative ideological positions, particularly socially conservative positions such as those in favor of prayer in school and repression of LGBTQ rights. Yet as we saw in Chapter 1, we seldom observe black ideological conservatism translating into opposition to the Democratic Party or Democratic candidates. We have offered the theory of racialized social constraint as an explanation of this puzzle, suggesting that blacks' social connections with other blacks help to constrain defection from normalized group behavior. Indeed, we have certainly seen evidence for this point; blacks with particularly close social ties to the black community exhibit significantly more norm-consistent behavior than those without these connections. In this section, we will examine how these social ties to other blacks help to prevent ideological defection from the group norm of political behavior, particularly among self-identified black conservatives.

To test the proposition that black conservatives are constrained in their support for the Democratic Party by their associations with other blacks, we examine how blacks' social connections with other racial in-group members might condition the relationship between liberal or conservative ideology and Democratic Party or candidate support. To do this, we examine how the relationship between ideology and Democratic support changes as a function of having a social network composed of greater than 50 percent

African Americans. Ideology is perhaps the strongest predictor of party support; thus, what we are looking for is how this relationship changes as black social networks move from being made up of mostly non-blacks (who here are mostly white) to being mostly black. If we are right, then we should see a reduction in the size of the relationship between ideology and party support among those blacks with social networks made up of mostly racial in-group members. We expect that black conservatives with largely black social networks are more likely to realize the social benefits of conforming to the group norm and the social cost of defecting from the political expectation. Consequently, they will identify with the Democratic Party. Conversely, we would expect that party identification for blacks with social networks made up of mostly non-blacks (or evenly split between blacks and non-blacks) should more accurately reflect the individual's ideological tastes, since connections with whites (or non-blacks) offer opportunity for black conservatives to act on their ideological interests.

The results of this analysis are presented in Figures 3.5a–c. Here we return to the 2013 PRRI American Values Survey, the 2006 Social Capital Community Survey, and the 2015 Pew survey of multiracial Americans to examine how the relationship between black Democratic Party identification and black liberal or conservative ideology changes as a function of the racial composition of black social connections. The results of this analysis are once again consistent with our argument that black social connections with other blacks are associated with greater unity in partisan preferences. Looking first at the results from the 2013 PRRI data, we see that for blacks whose discussion partners were less than 51 percent black, the relationship between Democratic Party identification and ideology is the typical relationship that one might assume would exist between party identification and ideology. We see an extremely high probability of black liberals identifying as Democrats and a significant decline in the probability of Democratic Party identification among black conservatives. The probability of strongly identified black liberals identifying as Democrats is about .98, while the probably of black conservatives identifying as Democrats is about .40. This relationship is replicated in the 2015 Pew survey data. In the Pew data, we see that the probability of strongly identified black conservatives identifying as Democrats is about .50, while the model predicts a nearly 100 percent chance that black liberals will identify as Democrats. As we move to examining blacks whose social networks are greater than 50 percent black, we see that this relationship changes dramatically. Among this group of African Americans, the probability of identifying as a Democrat appears to vary

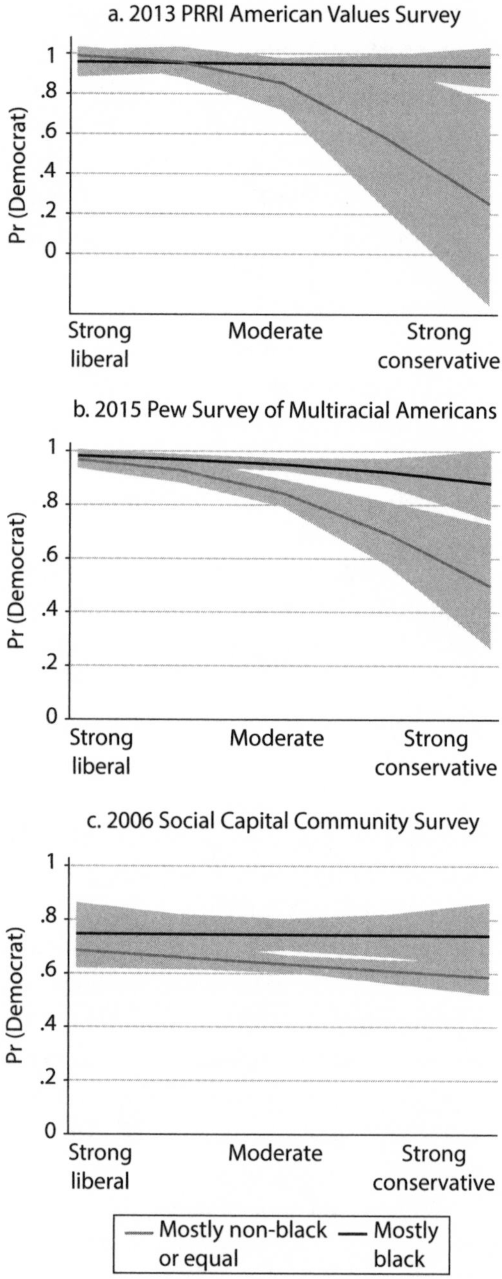

a. 2013 PRRI American Values Survey

FIGURE 3.5. Black Democratic Party identification by percentage of black associates or friends and ideology

b. 2015 Pew Survey of Multiracial Americans

c. 2006 Social Capital Community Survey

—— Mostly non-black or equal —— Mostly black

little by the strength of the respondents' liberal or conservative ideological beliefs. Across both surveys we see essentially no relationship between ideology and Democratic Party identification among blacks who have social connections mostly with other blacks. This result suggests that the presence of meaningful social connections with other blacks does indeed constrain blacks' partisan political behavior. The results for the 2006 Social Capital Community Survey are less dramatic, yet we still observe more constraint among blacks who have close friendships with mostly in-group members. It is also important to keep in mind that the 2006 Social Capital Community Survey does not differentiate leaning partisans; thus, many leaning black Democrats are coded here as non-Democrats, and this likely distorts the relationship between ideology and Democratic Party identification.

The ability of blacks' social connections with other blacks to constrain partisan defection among black conservatives also applies to principled conservatives. In Figures 3.6a–c we examine the ability of black social networks to constrain partisan defection that might result from disagreements with Democrats about moral beliefs such as those regarding gay marriage, gun control, and abortion. It is well recognized that a sizable portion of the black population opposes both gay marriage and certain elements of abortion rights. According to the 2013 PRRI American Values Survey, 40 percent of African Americans express opposition to gay marriage and nearly 30 percent express support for further restrictions on abortion rights. For many whites, social stances such as opposition to gay marriage, gun control, and abortion represent the foundation of their support for the Republican Party, but as we saw in the introduction of this book, for black Americans these issue positions seldom translate into Republican Party support. As we can see from Figures 3.6a–c, the disconnect between these issues and black partisan beliefs is largely isolated to those blacks who have social networks made up largely of other blacks. In fact, among those blacks whose social networks are made up mostly of racial out-group members, quite a strong relationship exists between these social or moral issues and Democratic partisanship. Take, for example, the relationship between blacks' support for gun control and their Democratic Party identification. As we can see in Figure 3.6a, for blacks with mostly non-black social connections, moving from having a liberal position on gun control to having a conservative position on this issue results in about an 80-percentage-point decrease in Democratic partisanship. For those blacks who have mostly black friends, the change is essentially zero as we move from those supporting gun control to those opposing it. While the results are less dramatic for abortion, the difference for gay rights is essentially

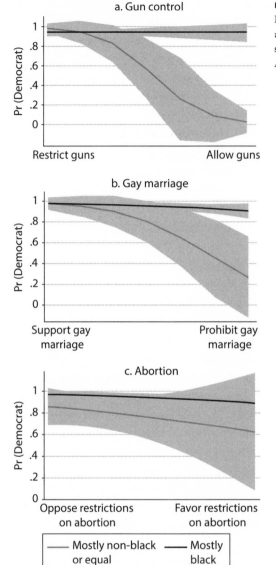

FIGURE 3.6. Black Democratic Party identification by percentage of black associates and social issue ideology, 2013 PRRI American Values Survey

the same as that for gun control, suggesting that black social connections to other blacks are especially constraining for moral issues.

Lastly, we examine how black social networks might condition the relationship between blacks' economic conservatism and their support for the Democratic Party. Again, examining data from the 2013 PRRI American Values Survey, we test whether blacks' beliefs about increasing taxes as opposed to increasing spending as a means of growing the American

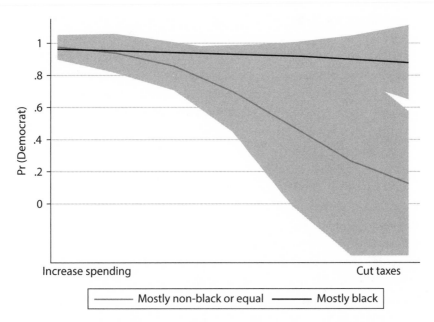

FIGURE 3.7. Black Democratic Party identification by percentage of black friends and tax or spend ideology, 2013 PRRI American Values Survey

economy, expanding jobs, or providing better health care are related to blacks' Democratic Party support. As we can see in Figure 3.7, the results for this analysis again mirror what we saw with liberal or conservative ideology and social or moral issue beliefs. While we can see that beliefs about taxing and spending are related in the expected direction to black support for the Democratic Party among those individuals with fewer blacks in their social networks, no such relationship exists between these beliefs and Democratic support among those blacks whose social networks are composed primarily of other African Americans. This suggests again that black social networks are effective tools for constraining black partisan defection and imposing compliance with norms of black political behavior.

Conclusion

The contention by Robert P. Jones discussed at the beginning of this chapter was that increased social contact would lead to a better understanding of different racial experiences. While the implications of close social ties for interracial cooperation are still being debated among scholars, what is clear from the evidence presented in this chapter is that, although racial diversity has its virtues, the ability of black Americans to constrain partisan defection within the group appears to be tied to racial and political homogeneity in social networks. In other words, we find strong support for the most basic empirical expectation of our racialized social constraint model: that the greater the proportion of racial in-group members in a black person's social network, the more likely it is that that individual will identify as a Democrat.

This observation has important implications. In particular, it seems to suggest that blacks' desire for integration is at odds with their ability to engage as a collective in partisan politics. The greater the social distance blacks have from the black community, the less accountable they are to group members and, thus, the freer they are to act on their individual interests. In the chapters that follow, we will explore further this tension between integration and black collective political engagement and discuss what options, if any, blacks have for maintaining collective political engagement in the era of integration.

Lastly, although the results presented here are consistent with our racialized social constraint argument, their descriptive nature does not provide much evidence to support any strong *causal* claim about the role that social interactions with other blacks play in increasing black support for the Democratic Party. Since this chapter relies on survey data, we cannot be sure of the precise causal mechanism underlying this correlation between racially homogeneous social networks and Democratic Party identification. We grapple with the question of causality in Chapter 4, leveraging the interracial constraints on black political beliefs created through the assignment of black and white interviewers to black respondents during the face-to-face survey interviews in the American National Election Studies and the GSS. There we demonstrate the *process* by which black party unity is maintained through racialized social pressure to comply with black role expectations.

4

The Process of Racialized Social Constraint

In Chapter 3, we were able to establish a strong link between the racial homogeneity of black social networks and black political homogeneity. We observed that for black Americans, the proportion of racial in-group members within an individual's social network is directly related to a greater adherence to norms of political behavior that characterize the racial group, specifically Democratic Party identification and support for Democratic candidates. While the findings offered in Chapter 3 are consistent with our racialized social constraint argument, the descriptive nature of these results do not necessarily support any *causal* claim about the role that social interactions with other blacks actually play in maintaining black support for the Democratic Party.

In this chapter, we offer our first attempt at elucidating the process by which social connections with other blacks result in conformity to norms of black political behavior. Building on research that draws a distinction between group identities as purely psychological dispositions and research that conceives of identities as a set of social role expectations that define group member behavior, we argue that the mere presence of another black person, even a complete stranger, can encourage conformity to norms of black political behavior. By leveraging the racialized social context created through face-to-face survey interviews and the quasi-experimental nature of how black and white interviewers are assigned to respondents, we are able to get one step closer to identifying the *causal* effect of race-specific expectations of black political behavior. We demonstrate how widespread knowledge of black political norms can lead to conformity with the norm of Democratic Party identification and support for Democratic candidates when blacks are asked to reveal their political preferences in the presence of black interviewers, because black respondents in national surveys consider the social consequences of deviating from racial group norms. We also demonstrate that the social context created by the presence of a black interviewer can effectively constrain ideological defection as well. These results further highlight the power of racialized social constraint as we demonstrate that race and the norms associated with black identity have the ability to personalize social interactions in a way that ultimately influences political behavior and drives black party unity.

Role Identity

While our racialized social constraint argument represents a larger set of processes that ultimately lead to unified partisan support among blacks, key to this explanation is identifying the psychological mechanism by which individual political preferences are constrained by group expectations. Research on role identities (Hogg, Terry, and White 1995; Stryker 1980; Turner 1978) offers a useful sociological framework for understanding how social and psychological factors interact to constrain black political preferences. While the racial group consciousness or shared fate model of black political unity has sought to understand the connection between the shared experience of African Americans as a group and ideological or individual interest, an explanation based on role identity theory (sometimes known as identity theory; see Hogg, Terry, and White 1995) offers an interpretation of black political behavior that would center on the internalization not only of shared experiences but also of the shared understandings and expectations that have grown out of these experiences. As a sociological concept, role identity moves beyond simple psychological connections with a social category to consider one's sense of self to be the outcome of the individual's interactions with others and the expectations in-group members have for how that person should behave. In many ways, role identities are similar to Bicchieri's (2006) normative expectations and Cialdini, Reno, and Kallgren's (1990) injunctive normative perceptions, as each relies heavily on an understanding of the expectations of others as key to defining behavioral expectations. Thus, while a person's sense of racial identification represents a psychological connection with the racial group, that person's role identity centers on the extent to which he or she demonstrates behaviors typically associated with being a "black" person. These behaviors are then subject to evaluation from other group members, who may judge whether the behavior is appropriate. For some, the idea that there exist behaviors that might convey blackness can come across as troubling, since these can evoke recollections of a time when blacks had little or no control over their societal roles. However, as discussed in Chapter 2, these same historical constraints on black choices, slavery and segregation, created an interdependence among black Americans that ultimately empowered them with the ability to exert control over the meaning of blackness and define for themselves what it means to be a black person in America. In other words, it is important to recognize that our sense of self is formed through our knowledge of our memberships in social groups and that "it is through our public selves that we are able to simplify the world around us by using categorizations to infer our similarities and differences to other people" (Andriot and Owens 2014).

A focus on role identity and the normative expectations framework discussed in Chapter 2 allows us to explain black political unity in a way that centers on expected racial group behavior and the consequences of complying with or failing to comply with these expectations. In other words, a role identity explanation would suggest that social connections to the group are what is most important to shaping behavior, not merely a psychological connection. Applying this to attempts to understand black political behavior, this explanation would suggest that even those individuals who might lack a psychological connection to the group would feel constrained because the social cost of violating well-accepted group expectations would potentially outweigh other ideological or personal incentives to behave otherwise.

In Chapter 2 we saw evidence that black Americans view support for the Democratic Party as a normalized form of black political behavior, and as a consequence, they face a unique set of expectations (or norms) of political behavior that they understand as likely to be enforced through close social ties with other blacks. These expectations, we argue, have led to an understanding within the black community that supporting the Democratic Party is "just something that black people do." The widespread reinforcement of this norm, through repeated observation that most blacks do in fact support the Democratic Party, means that the act of publicly supporting the Democratic Party among blacks, we believe, is a racial-identity-confirming behavior that individual blacks perform in an attempt to obtain social confirmation or status from other blacks. Once this behavior is confirmed or rewarded, individual blacks then come to see these acts as linked to identity affirmation, and thus they have incentives to repeat the behavior. Likewise, publicly supporting the Republican Party would likely be viewed as an antisocial or antigroup behavior, as it reflects a rejection of the expected group behavior and would likely be met with pushback from other blacks.

Design

To evaluate this claim that black party unity is maintained through racialized social pressure to comply with black expectations of political behavior, we leverage the intraracial constraints on black political beliefs created by black interviewers in the face-to-face interviews[1] of the cumulative American National Election Studies (ANES) surveys from 1988 to 2012,[2] the 2004 to 2014 General Social Survey (GSS), and the 2012 ANES Time Series Study. The 2012 ANES Time Series Study is particularly useful as it has a nationally representative oversample of black respondents, which allows for nuanced analysis of black political behavior at the national level. Using these data, we examine the effects of black and non-black interviewers (the vast majority of whom are white) on how blacks respond to survey questions that measure partisanship. We think the effect of interviewer race on the expression of partisanship is an ideal means of testing the ability of racialized social pressure to constrain black partisan defection. Despite the fact that much political science research considers partisanship a stable disposition (Campbell et al. 1960), we argue that the social expectations among blacks are so strong that they can actually alter the distribution of blacks' (expressed) party identification and candidate support. The interaction of black interviewers with black respondents represents a special type of controlled social interaction that, when compared with non-black interviewers' interactions with black respondents, allows us to be reasonably confident that differences in respondent choices are likely the result of compliance with expected racial behavior. Additionally, the 2012 ANES not only included face-to-face interviews but also conducted simultaneous interviews online. The use of the data from the online interview sample will give something approximating a control group, allowing us to compare how blacks would respond to identical questions *without* the biases associated with an interviewer's presence.

One limitation of this design, however, is that black and non-black interviewers in face-to-face surveys are not typically randomly assigned to respondents. Our correspondence with ANES officials suggests that while interviewers are certainly not able to select respondents (or vice versa), interviewers do tend to come from areas proximate to the respondent. While we have no reason to believe this would bias blacks' responses to the party identification question or candidate support questions, we nonetheless think it prudent to account for possible confounders that may emerge from this assignment strategy. We account for the lack of random assignment in two ways. First, we attempt to ensure the reliability of the results by replicating the analyses in multiple years of the ANES and GSS cumulative data files that contain data about the race of the interviewer. This includes the 1988, 1992, 1996, 2008, and 2012 ANES surveys and the 2004, 2006, 2008, 2010, 2012, and 2014 surveys for the GSS.[3] Assuming that any biases that exist are not likely to manifest in the same way across all years of both the ANES and the GSS, our ability to replicate the effects across time and study should increase confidence that any relationships we observe are not likely the result of systematic bias in interviewer assignment.[4] Second, we also employ multiple adjustment procedures to account for possible confounders. We adjust for pretreatment covariates using logistic regression and propensity score matching. This allows us to essentially approximate random assignment and compare individuals who are as similarly situated as possible across interviewer type.

Lastly, we replicate many of our findings in a set of large-N telephone surveys. Since telephone surveys do not assign interviewers based on residential proximity (telephone interviews are typically conducted from centralized call centers), we can be more confident that the matching of interviewee to respondent resembles a random assignment. Similarly, compared with face-to-face interviews, telephone surveys offer a conservative test of our explanation, as the degree of possible discomfort experienced in a telephone interview is not as strong (Davis 1997a).

Hypotheses

We have the following set of expectations for the relationship between interviewer race and partisanship and candidate support. First, because of the strength of the expectations that exist within the black community of identification with and support of the Democratic Party, we expect that those black respondents who are interviewed by coracial interviewers will be more likely than those interviewed by non-black interviewers to identify with the Democratic Party than with either independents or Republicans (H1a) and will also express greater levels of support for Democratic presidential candidates (H1b).

Second, we expect that in absence of a black interviewer, black respondents will *not* feel pressure to conform to racial group norms. Instead, respondents interviewed by non-black interviewers or who complete the online questionnaire will not experience social pressure to conform to group norms but will instead report partisanship and candidate preferences that more accurately reflect their individual ideological preferences. Thus, they will report partisanship that is significantly less Democratic than the partisanship expressed by those individuals interviewed by black interviewers (H2a and H2b). These expectations (H1 and H2) are supported by previous scholarship that shows the effect of social interaction on partisan attitudes. Klar (2014) demonstrates that social context has a significant effect on partisan-based motivated reasoning. Klar compares the policy attitudes of individuals based on their interactions with varying types of partisans with attitudes not based on social interaction. Engaging in social interactions (policy dialogue) with homogeneous partisan groupings resulted in heightened levels of partisan-motivated reasoning for individuals of the same party identification as the group. Interaction with heterogeneous partisan networks resulted in ambivalent policy positions for both strong and weak partisans. Similarly, Levitan and Visser (2009) find that individuals in attitudinally diverse social networks have a propensity for more ambivalence in their policy attitudes relative to those individuals in attitudinally congruent networks.

Third, we expect (H3) that interviewer race should condition self-reported Democratic partisanship in the context of telephone surveys. While we certainly expect this effect to be much smaller in the context of the telephone survey compared with face-to-face social interaction, where a greater potential exists for ridicule and derision, we nonetheless expect black interviewers to constrain blacks' expressions of Democratic partisanship.

Lastly, we expect that the race of the interviewer will condition the effect of liberal or conservative ideology on black partisanship and candidate support (H4a and H4b). Previous research has demonstrated a strong connection between partisanship and ideology where more conservative individuals are likely to identify as Republican and more liberal individuals are likely to identify as Democrats (Campbell et al. 1960). While this is one of the more consistent relationships in American political behavior research, it is also driven largely by the behavior of non-black Americans. As Figures 4.1a–b show, while Democratic Party identification among both

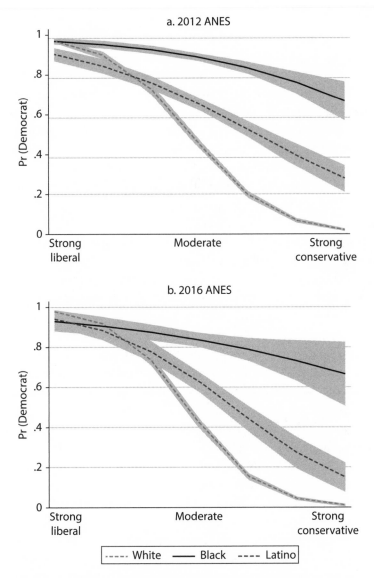

FIGURE 4.1. Probability of identifying as a Democrat by ideology and race, 95% confidence intervals. *Notes:* Results are marginal effects of the bivariate relationship between ideology and Democratic Party identification. These results are only for respondents interviewed in face-to-face ANES interviews.

whites and Hispanics is strongly related to their liberal or conservative ideology, among black Americans the connection between liberal or conservative ideology and Democratic partisan identification is much weaker (see Philpot 2017). Compared with whites and Hispanics, significantly larger proportions of self-identified black conservatives identify as Democrats.[5] In the 2016 ANES, only 27 percent of white conservatives identified as Democrats, compared with 83 percent of black conservatives. While other researchers have offered explanations for this discrepancy that focus on racial identity and the historical experiences of blacks (see Dawson 1994; Philpot 2017), we seek to identify the role that racialized social constraint plays in moderating the relationship between ideology and party (and candidate support) for blacks. We expect that this relationship will be strongest in the presence of a non-black interviewer or no interviewer. In other words, in these contexts we expect that more conservative blacks will be *less* likely to identify as Democrats. On the other hand, we believe that in the presence of a black interviewer, blacks will exercise more constraint and suppress their ideological preferences. Thus, we expect that when blacks are interviewed by a black interviewer, liberal or conservative ideology will have no meaningful relationship with black Democratic Party identification. In this context, black conservatives and black liberals should be equally likely to identify as Democrats.

Democratic Partisanship

To test our initial expectation (H1a) that in the presence of another black person, black Americans will experience social pressure to conform to the norm of identifying with the Democratic Party, we begin by examining whether the percentage of blacks who identify as Democrats varies as a function of the race of the interviewer in face-to-face surveys of black Americans. In Table 4.1 we analyze data on the distribution of black partisanship and the race of interviewers from two of the nation's highest-quality national public opinion surveys, the cumulative ANES and the cumulative GSS.[6] We analyze the results for Democrats and Republicans with those for leaners and true independents. We focus on Democratic leaners for a couple of reasons. First, a great deal of research suggests that leaners are actually partisans and behave much more like partisans than like true independents (Keith et al. 1986; Keith et al. 1992; Wattenberg 2009). Second, given the branching nature of the party identification question, we expect that at each level of questioning, racialized social pressure exerts increased influence on black party identification.

TABLE 4.1. Distribution of Black Party Identification by Race of Interviewer, ANES Cumulative File and the GSS Cumulative File (Face-to-Face Surveys)

	ANES			GSS		
	Non-black interviewer	Black interviewer	Difference	Non-black interviewer	Black interviewer	Difference
Republican	7.4	2.5	−4.9*	8.6	5.3	−3.3*
(incl. leaners)	[6.0, 8.8]	[1.1, 3.9]		[7.3, 9.9]	[3.8, 6.8]	
Independent	12.1	4.2	−7.9*	15.9	13.1	−2.8*
	[10.3, 13.8]	[2.3, 5.9]		[14.2, 17.7]	[10.8, 15.3]	
Democrat	80.5	93.3	12.8*	74.1	81.2	7.1*
(incl. leaners)	[78.4, 82.5]	[91.1, 95.5]		[72.0, 76.1]	[78.6, 83.8]	
N	1,357	479		1,724	848	

Note: The 95% CI is in brackets.
*$p < .05$

The results presented in Table 4.1 support our expectation that racialized social pressure increases blacks' willingness to identify with the Democratic Party. Looking at the second-to-last row of Table 4.1, we see that black respondents appear to express greater levels of Democratic partisanship in the presence of a black interviewer. In both the cumulative ANES and the cumulative GSS, we observe greater reported Democratic partisanship when respondents are interviewed by black interviewers than when they are interviewed by non-black interviewers. In the ANES the Democratic Party identification gap between blacks interviewed by black interviewers and those interviewed by non-black interviewers is 12.8 percentage points, moving the percentage of blacks who identify as Democrats from about 80 percent in the presence of a non-black interviewer to well over 90 percent when blacks are asked about partisanship by a black interviewer. While the Democratic Party identification gap resulting from having a black interviewer is smaller in the GSS, 7.1 percentage points, it is still substantively large and statistically significant. In both data sources, the presence of a black interviewer appears to be encouraging a number of black respondents to identify as Democrats, while if these same individuals were interviewed by a non-black interviewer, many of them would likely identify as either Republican or independent.

Although the results presented in Table 4.1 suggest that the race of the interviewer present during face-to-face surveys can strongly influence blacks' willingness to identify as Democrats, we should keep in mind that this is not a true experimental design since neither the ANES nor the GSS survey randomly assigns interviewers to respondents. While we can be confident that interviewers are not explicitly selecting respondents based on their partisanship, we nonetheless think it is important to account for, as best we can, any preexisting differences that might exist between respondents interviewed by black interviewers and those interviewed by non-black interviewers. To ensure that these two groups of respondents are as similar as possible, we adjust for pretreatment respondent characteristics (sex, age, Southern region), pretreatment interviewer characteristics (interviewer gender),[7] and pretreatment survey characteristics (year of survey).[8] We adjust for these possible confounders using both matching estimators and logistic regression models. Once the observed differences in confounders between the treatment and control groups have been taken into account, we then reestimate the effects of interviewer race on Democratic Party identification (including leaners). The results from this analysis are presented in Table 4.2a and 4.2b. In both parts of this table, the first row presents the raw, unadjusted percentages of black Democratic partisanship by race of interviewer pooled across all years of the survey (the ANES in Table 4.2a and the GSS in Table 4.2b) for which we have data about the race of the interviewer (same as the second-to-last row of Table 4.1); the second row presents the results of race-of-interviewer effects, adjusting for pretreatment characteristics using logistic regression; and the last row presents race-of-interviewer effects on Democratic partisanship, adjusting for pretreatment characteristics using propensity score matching. Comparing these different adjustment strategies, we see that while the adjustments for pretreatment covariates at times reduce the effect of the black interviewer on black Democratic Party identification, the effect remains large and statistically significant in both data sources. These results should add to our confidence that what we are observing is in fact the result of black Americans altering their self-reported Democratic partisanship in response to the race of the person interviewing them and not any preexisting difference in the type of respondents interviewed by black interviewers. This change in partisan affiliation supports our racialized social constraint claim that when black Americans' roles as group members have the potential to be challenged or subject to negative sanctions from other racial in-group members, they alter their behavior to appear more in line with the established group norm.

To further ensure that this relationship is not simply a design artifact of face-to-face surveys, we also test for this effect in the context of telephone surveys. Again, one concern with face-to-face surveys such as the

TABLE 4.2. Percentage of Self-Identified Black Democrats (Including Leaners) by Race of Interviewer, ANES and GSS Cumulative Files

A. ANES

	Non-black interviewer	Black interviewer	Difference
Unadjusted			
95% CI	80.5	93.3	12.8*
	[78.4, 82.5]	[91.1, 95.5]	
Adjusted			
Logistic regression	81.2	91.9	10.7*
95% CI	[79.1, 83.2]	[89.2, 94.7]	
Propensity score matching (ATE)			7.3*

Notes: Pretreatment adjustments for year of survey, age, sex, South, married, and interviewer gender. The 95% CI is in brackets.

* $p < .05$

B. GSS

	Non-black interviewer	Black interviewer	Difference
Unadjusted			
95% CI	74.1	81.2	7.1*
	[72.0, 76.1]	[78.6, 83.8]	
Adjusted			
Logistic regression	74.2	81.4	7.2*
95% CI	[71.1, 77.2]	[77.6, 85.2]	
Propensity score matching (ATE)			9.5*

Note: Pretreatment adjustments for year of survey, age, sex, and South.

* $p < .05$

ANES is that they tend to assign interviewers from areas proximate to the respondent. As a result, black interviewers may be more likely to interview a certain type of black person who may for whatever reason be more predisposed to identify as a Democrat. Although we are confident that the adjustment procedures just presented account for much of this difference, to be more confident that what we are observing is in fact the result of racialized context, we replicate our analysis in the context of a phone survey. As previously mentioned, phone surveys generally operate from centralized call centers. To the extent that no explicit attempts are made to match interviewers by some criteria related to the race or background of the respondent, telephone surveys may better meet the "as if random" criteria of a good quasi-experimental design by ensuring more equivalent groupings.

There are, however, drawbacks to using telephone surveys to test this question. In particular, the social distance between interviewer and respondent during phone surveys can greatly reduce our ability to observe a treatment effect. Although phone surveys do not eliminate the potential threat posed by the interviewer, interviewer behaviors such as facial gestures and body language cannot be conveyed over the phone. As a result, we cannot expect the effect of interviewer race on Democratic Party identification to be as large as that observed in the face-to-face context. Similarly, given the ambiguity present in determining a person's racial background via voice recognition, we would expect significantly more variation in individual responses to the treatment (interviewer race). In sum, while we certainly expect black interviewers to heighten black Democratic Party identification, we also expect this effect to be considerably smaller than that observed in face-to-face interviews since phone surveys represent a somewhat less direct test of our theory.

To test this, we examine public opinion data from the widely available Pew Research Center (2008–2010) data archives and Gallup News Service polls. These data are useful because both are publicly available data sources that consistently report interviewer race: Pew after 2007, and Gallup after the middle of 2011. They also have measures of party identification and identify leaning Democrats and Republicans. Because we expect small effects in response to interviewer race over the phone and because the average survey from these sources has only about 150 black respondents, we pooled over one hundred randomly selected surveys from Pew's U.S. Politics & Policy data archive from 2008 to 2014 and more than fifty Gallup News Service polls from the middle of 2011 to the middle of 2015. The result is a data set with 13,138 black respondents from the Pew data and 4,648 black respondents from the Gallup data, with corresponding race-of-interviewer and party-identification data.[9]

The results of this analysis are presented in Table 4.3. We see that in the Pew data, on average, 2.1 percent more blacks identify as Democrats when they are interviewed by black interviewers, and in the Gallup data that number increases to 4.8 percent. These results are, as we expected, smaller than what we observed in the face-to-face studies, but not only are they statistically significant ($p = .00$), they are also substantively meaningful in that they replicate the findings of the face-to-face studies while at the same time offering a more conservative test of our theory of racialized social pressure.

TABLE 4.3. Distribution (%) of Black Party Identification by Race of Interviewer, Pew and Gallup Cumulative File (Telephone Survey)

	Pew (2008–2014)			Gallup (2011–2015)		
	Non-black interviewer	Black interviewer	Difference	Non-black interviewer	Black interviewer	Difference
Republican (incl. leaners)	9.5 [8.8, 10.2]	7.9 [7.3, 8.5]	−1.6*	15.5 [14.4, 16.6]	13.9 [10.9, 17.0]	−1.6
Independent	8.9 [8.2, 9.7]	8.4 [7.8, 9.1]	−0.5	10.8 [9.8, 11.7]	7.6 [5.2, 9.9]	−3.2*
Democrat (incl. leaners)	81.6 [80.6, 82.5]	83.7 [82.8, 84.5]	2.1*	73.7 [72.4, 75.1]	78.5 [74.8, 82.1]	4.8*
N	5,851	7,287		4,160	488	

Notes: Non-black only includes white. The 95% CI is in brackets.
* $p < .05$

Baseline Party Identification

To this point we have seen strong evidence for our racialized social constraint argument, observing a strong connection between interviewer race and reporting of Democratic Party identification among black respondents in face-to-face and telephone surveys. When black respondents are interviewed by black interviewers, they appear to express significantly greater levels of Democratic Party identification. We have also seen that this relationship remains quite strong even when controlling for pretreatment characteristics of the respondent and survey context. While we certainly see these results as compelling, the nature of this relationship is still somewhat unclear. For example, instead of adhering to norms of black political behavior, when interviewed by a black interviewer, blacks may instead be responding to the white interviewer. Davis (1997a, p. 320) posits that when interviewed by a white individual, black respondents are more likely to respond in counterstereotypic ways to distance themselves from other blacks. Because the nature of white partisanship is more heterogeneous than it is for blacks, when interviewed by a white person, black respondents who are unsure of the interviewer's partisan leaning may simply desire to portray themselves as less stereotypical. In the results presented thus far, we have only compared the effects of black interviewers with those of non-black interviewers. What we still do not know is *what blacks' partisanship would be in the absence of*

TABLE 4.4. Distribution of Black Party Identification by Race of Interviewer and Online Mode, 2012 ANES (Face to Face and Online)

	Online (control)	Non-black interviewer	Black interviewer	Difference	
	(A)	(B)	(C)	(B−A)	(C−A)
Republican (incl. leaders)	5.1	7.2	1.9	2.1	−3.2*
	[3.2, 6.9]	[3.9, 10.5]	[0.2, 3.7]		
Independent	9.9	8.9	1.6	−1.0	−8.3*
	[7.4, 12.4]	[5.2, 12.5]	[0.0, 3.1]		
Democrat (incl. leaders)	85.0	83.9	96.4	−1.1	11.4*
	[82.0,87.9]	[79.2, 88.6]	[94.2, 98.7]		
N	554	237	255		

Note: The 95% CI is in brackets.
* $p < .05$

any interviewer. Without a comparison group (control), we cannot confidently say whether what we are observing is the effect of a black interviewer encouraging blacks to identify as Democrats, white or non-black interviewers encouraging blacks to report *less* Democratic identification, or both. Indeed, this is a problem that characterizes much of the existing research on race-of-interviewer effects (see Rhodes 1994).

To get around this problem, we turn to the 2012 ANES. In addition to having results for those who participated in face-to-face interviews with non-black and black interviewers, the 2012 ANES also featured an online component that was conducted at roughly the same time as the face-to-face survey and asked identical questions but was completely self-administered. This offers us a unique opportunity to estimate the percentage of blacks who likely would have identified as Democrats in the absence of an interviewer. The effect of interviewer race by mode of survey on Democratic partisanship from the 2012 ANES is presented in Table 4.4. The results presented reveal that in the presence of a non-black interviewer, 83.9 percent of blacks identified as Democrats, but in the presence of a black interviewer, that percentage increases by 12.5 percentage points, to 96.4 percent.[10] When we compare these results with the results from respondents who completed the online questionnaire, we see that the percentage of blacks who identify as Democrats in our online control group is 85 percent, which is essentially indistinguishable from the reported Democratic partisanship of those blacks interviewed by non-black interviewers (1.1-percentage-point difference)

TABLE 4.5. Adjusted Distribution of Black Party Identification by Race of Interviewer and
Online Mode, 2012 ANES (Face to Face and Online)

	Online (control)	Non-black interviewer	Black interviewer	Difference	
	(A)	(B)	(C)	(B−A)	(C−A)
Logistic regression	83.3	86.4	96.8	3.1	13.5*
95% CI	[80.1, 86.5]	[82.4, 90.5]	[94.7, 98.8]		
N	551	232	250		

* $p < .05$

and more than 11 percentage points less than that of blacks interviewed by
black interviewers.

The lack of random assignment to the interviewer conditions and to
the online questionnaire suggests that we should once again adjust for pretreatment characteristics. Because the online mode had no interviewers,
we will not be able to adjust for interviewer characteristics, but we do have
respondent characteristics that were not likely affected by the treatment:
gender, age, and living in the South. The results of this analysis appear in
Table 4.5. Once again we see that the results of our adjustments appear to do
very little to alter the relationship between interviewer race and Democratic
Party identification. Large and statistically significant increases in predicted
Democratic Party identification continue to exist despite our adjustments.
Even with these adjustments, the presence of a black interviewer appears
to increase reported Democratic partisanship among blacks by somewhere
between 10.4 and 13.5 percentage points, compared to the presence of a
non-black interviewer and our control.

The results presented in Tables 4.4 and 4.5 confirm our expectations
(H2a) that black interviewers have a unique effect on how black respondents
report partisanship during surveys. Returning to our role identity argument,
these results show that social interactions that might result in negative or
positive sanctions relating to one's group status can significantly affect a
black individual's reported affiliation with the Democratic Party.

Who Is Constrained?

To this point we have seen a great deal of evidence to suggest that role identities are central to shaping the public expression of black political beliefs.
The presence of a black interviewer clearly creates a unique social context

in which blacks appear to feel compelled to conform to racial group expectations (i.e., identifying as a Democrat). We now turn to examining who exactly is being constrained by this racialized interaction. As discussed earlier, given the widespread awareness of the norm of identifying as a Democrat within the black community, we believe that those individuals who have ideological reasons for behaving in ways inconsistent with the racial group norm, in particular black conservatives, will be the most likely to be constrained in the presence of a black interviewer (H4). Absent this social interaction with a coracial interviewer, we believe that blacks who identify as ideological conservatives will *be less likely* to identify as Democrats because there will be no social pressure to conform to group expectations. However, because black conservatives are very much aware of the social consequences of defecting from the norm of Democratic partisanship that exists within the black community, when questioned about their partisanship by a black interviewer, they will feel constrained by these social expectations and instead choose to behave in a way inconsistent with their own ideological interest and identify as Democrats to avoid jeopardizing their standing in the eyes of a fellow racial group member.

Figures 4.2a–f summarize the effect of the interviewer's race on blacks' self-reported seven-point party identification and two-point Democratic partisanship by the respondent's liberal or conservative ideology in the 1988–2012 cumulative ANES, the 2004–2016 GSS, and the 2012 ANES.[11] Beginning with those blacks interviewed by non-black interviewers, we see across all three data sources that the probability of a black person identifying as a Democrat declines sharply as that person becomes more conservative. In the 1988–2012 cumulative ANES (Figure 4.2b), we see that the probability of a black person identifying as Democrat decreases by more than 20 percentage points, from around .90 among blacks who are strong liberals to about .60 for blacks who are strong conservatives. Not only is this decrease statistically significant ($p < .05$), but it is also of roughly the same magnitude as the decrease in the GSS surveys (Figure 4.2d). In the 2012 ANES (Figure 4.2f), the difference is even greater, with the model predicting .97 probability of identifying as a Democrat among strong liberals interviewed by non-black interviewers and a .56 probability of identifying as a Democrat among self-identified strong conservative blacks, a 41-point decrease ($p < .00$) in the probably of identifying as a Democrat.

A similar pattern exists for black respondents who answered the 2012 online survey. Free of the constraints that an interviewer might impose, the model predicts a roughly .96 probability of black liberals in the online portion of the ANES identifying as Democrats and only a .49 probability of black conservatives in the online 2012 ANES identifying as Democrats. This represents a 47-point decrease ($p < .00$) in the probably of identifying as a Democrat; this pattern is consistent with standard accounts of how liberal or conservative ideology should relate to party identification.

Turning our attention to the black interviewer condition, we see that this well-recognized relationship between party and ideology is broken when blacks are asked about their partisanship by a black interviewer. Consistent with our expectations, it appears that when interviewed by a black interviewer, black Americans, regardless of ideology, express a strong and largely undifferentiated willingness to identify as Democrats. As we can see in the ANES analysis, while it is not surprising that nearly all liberals in the black interviewer conditions identify as Democrats, in neither the cumulative ANES nor the 2012 ANES does the probability of black conservatives identifying as Democrats ever dip below .90 when a black interviewer is present. While black interviewers less effectively constrain black respondents in the GSS data, little change occurs in predicted party identification across ideology measures for either the seven-point party identification measure or the dichotomous Democratic Party identification measure. In fact, in the interactive models testing the ability of black interviewers to condition the effects of ideology on both the seven-point party identification measure and the Democratic Party identification measure, we observe a statistically significant ($p < .05$) interaction effect for all of the seven-point party identification models and for the two-point Democratic Party identification model in the cumulative ANES ($p < .05$) and cumulative GSS ($p < .10$).[12] These results suggest that the presence of a black interviewer almost completely constrains black conservatives, largely eliminating the link between ideology and partisanship for blacks.

Lastly, if we are correct that the effect of black interviewers on black Democratic partisanship is the result of black interviewers holding black conservatives accountable to the norms of black political behavior, then we should also be able to observe this effect across other measures of conservatism. Therefore, we examine the ability of black interviewers to condition the relationship between the expression of Democratic partisanship and two distinct forms of conservatism: economic or free market conservatism and moral or traditionalist conservatism. Free market conservatism has its basis in the belief that government should play only a very limited role in regulating the U.S. economy. We measure this concept with two questions from the 2012 ANES that assess blacks' opinions about how much government regulation of business is good for society and whether the free market

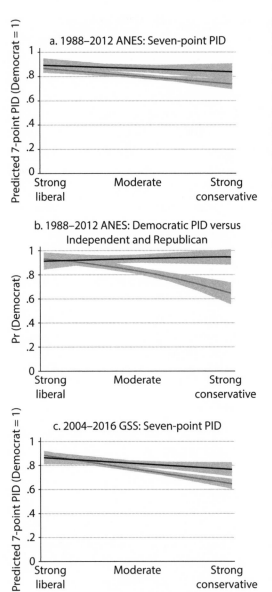

FIGURE 4.2. Black Democratic Party identification (PID) by liberal or conservative ideology and race of interviewer, 95% confidence intervals. *Notes:* For a–d: Marginal effect of liberal or conservative ideology on probability of identifying as Democrat. Includes controls for sex, age, South, interviewer sex, and study year fixed effects. For e–f: Marginal effect of liberal or conservative ideology on probability of identifying as Democrat. Includes controls for sex, age, and South.

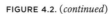
FIGURE 4.2. (*continued*)

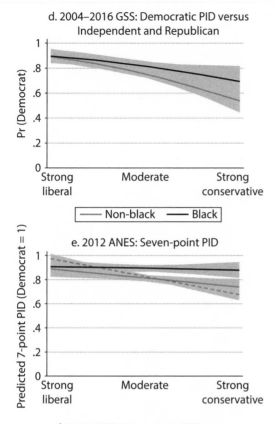

d. 2004–2016 GSS: Democratic PID versus Independent and Republican

Pr (Democrat)

Strong liberal — Moderate — Strong conservative

—— Non-black ——— Black

e. 2012 ANES: Seven-point PID

Predicted 7-point PID (Democrat = 1)

Strong liberal — Moderate — Strong conservative

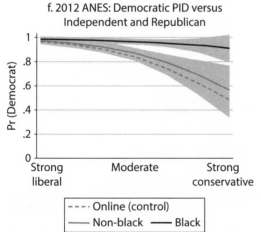

f. 2012 ANES: Democratic PID versus Independent and Republican

Pr (Democrat)

Strong liberal — Moderate — Strong conservative

---- Online (control)
—— Non-black ——— Black

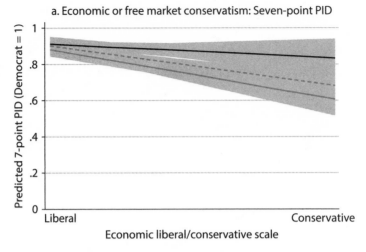

a. Economic or free market conservatism: Seven-point PID

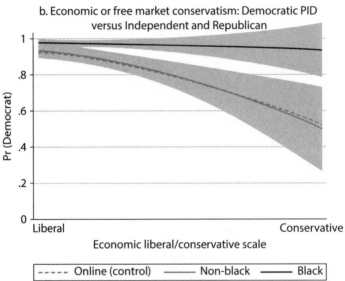

b. Economic or free market conservatism: Democratic PID
versus Independent and Republican

----- Online (control) ——— Non-black ——— Black

FIGURE 4.3. Economic or free market and moral or traditionalist conservatism
by black Democratic PID and race of interviewer or mode, 2012 ANES, 95%
confidence intervals

or government is better equipped to handle today's complicated problems.
Conservative responses to these questions prioritize free market solutions
and downplay government intervention. We measure moral or traditionalist
conservatism with four measures that assess belief in the need to preserve
traditional lifestyles, such as "Do you think newer lifestyles are contributing
to the breakdown of society?" and "How tolerant should society be of people

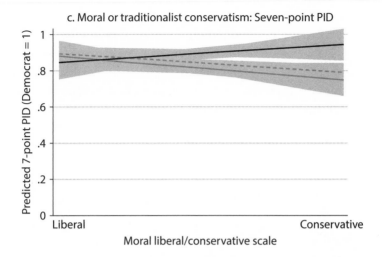

c. Moral or traditionalist conservatism: Seven-point PID

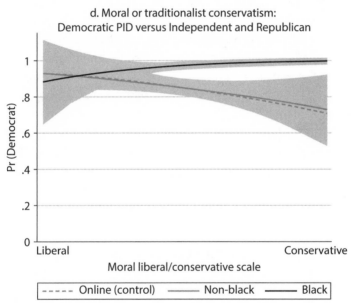

d. Moral or traditionalist conservatism:
Democratic PID versus Independent and Republican

```
----- Online (control)    ——— Non-black    ——— Black
```

FIGURE 4.3. (*continued*)

who have different moral standards?" Conservative responses to these questions prioritize the need to preserve traditional values and ways of living.

Figures 4.3a–d summarize the results of this analysis. We see that generally both the free market and moral or traditionalist results seem to mirror the
liberal or conservative ideology results presented in Figure 4.2. For blacks in
the non-black interviewer and online conditions, the more conservative the

respondent, the less likely he or she is to identify as a Democrat; for blacks in the black interviewer condition, the relationship between these ideological values and Democratic partisanship is once again essentially zero. Interestingly, there appears to be a slight increase in Democratic partisanship among morally conservative blacks interviewed by a black interviewer. This, we think, highlights the interesting confluence of black moral conservativism and black Democratic partisanship that exists among religious blacks and the black church (McDaniel 2008).

Partisan Candidate Support

Having demonstrated that black interviewers can indeed induce racialized social constraint among black respondents, which results in increased levels of Democratic Party identification, we now turn to examining whether interviewer race can also shape blacks' expressed support for Democratic candidates. Here we will examine the ability of racialized social constraint, as induced by black interviewers, to alter black support for Democratic presidential candidates relative to Republican presidential candidates. We examine a couple of different measures of candidate support, beginning with blacks' assessment of whether they think Democratic candidates for president are more likely than Republican candidates to advocate for government efforts to help blacks as a group, differences in blacks' feeling thermometer ratings of the Democratic and Republican presidential candidates, and blacks' stated intention to vote for the Democratic presidential candidate in the months before the election.

GOVERNMENT EFFORTS TO HELP AFRICAN AMERICANS

We begin our examination of how racialized social constraint shapes black candidate support by examining whether the presence of a black interviewer can alter blacks' assessment of whether Democratic candidates for president are more likely than Republican candidates to advocate for government efforts to help blacks as a group. Since the 1970s the ANES has asked respondents a series of questions that require them to place where they think the Republican and Democratic presidential candidates stand on the issue of government assistance directed specifically at black Americans. The question reads, "Some people feel that the government in Washington should make every effort to improve the social and economic position of blacks.

(Suppose these people are at one end of a scale, at point 1.) Others feel that the government should not make any special effort to help blacks because they should help themselves. (Suppose these people are at the other end, at point 7.) And, of course, some other people have opinions somewhere in between, at points 2, 3, 4, 5, or 6."

Respondents are then asked where they would place the Republican and Democratic presidential candidates on this scale. As mentioned earlier, many have attributed blacks' continued support for the Democratic Party to a belief that the Democratic Party is simply more likely than the Republican Party to substantively represent the interest of blacks as group. While we are sure that substantive policy positions do at times play a role in shaping black party support, blacks' interpretations of the political parties' substantive policy positions may actually have their origins in the very norms that we believe underlie black political behavior. If our racialized social constraint argument is correct, then we would expect that blacks interviewed by black interviewers would be more likely to conform to the norm of believing that the Democratic Party and its candidates more strongly support black interests. As discussed in Chapter 1, this is exactly the argument espoused by Corey Fields (2016), who argued that black Republicans in particular have a tendency to rationalize their party's position on race to bring it more in line with their own belief in Republican or conservative principles. In this case we see the norm of black interest as captured by expressions of support for the belief that the Democratic candidate for president would be more likely than the Republican candidate to advocate for government efforts to improve the economic positions of blacks as a group.

Figures 4.4a–b presents the average difference scores of black respondents to the measure assessing the placement of the Democratic candidate on the "aid to blacks" measure minus their placement of the Republican candidate on the "aid to blacks" measure. The figure shows data from the cumulative ANES 1988 to 2012 and the 2012 ANES. A score of 1 on this measure means that the respondent thinks that the Democratic candidate is much more likely to support assisting blacks economically, while a score of −1 means that the respondent thinks that the Republican candidate is much more likely to support assisting blacks economically. As we can see, the race of the interviewer present when this question is asked conditions blacks' assessment of which candidate they think is more likely to assist in improving the economic position of blacks as a group. Looking first at the results for the cumulative ANES, we see that going from having a

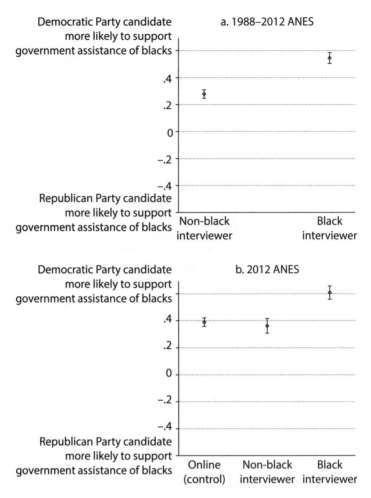

FIGURE 4.4. Blacks' evaluation of presidential candidate difference on aid to blacks by race of interviewer, 95% confidence intervals

non-black interviewer to having a black interviewer results in a more than 20-point increase in the extent to which black respondents' see the Democratic presidential candidate as being more likely to support assisting blacks economically. In other words, blacks interviewed by black interviewers see significantly more difference between the Democratic and Republican candidates in their willingness to support government efforts to assist blacks economically. We observe similar differences in the 2012 ANES. Even when we compare respondents who were interviewed by a black interviewer with our online (control) respondents, we once again observe approximately a 20-precentage-point increase in the extent to which blacks are willing to report that the Democratic presidential candidate is more likely to support assisting blacks economically, moving from the online condition to the black interviewer condition.

Next, we turn to examining whether the effect of racialized social constraint on candidate support works by constraining the ability of black conservatives to defect from the expected group behavior—in this case believing that Democrats more strongly support black interest. Figures 4.5a–b displays black respondents' predicted score on the same measure of presidential candidate aid to blacks by race of interviewer and liberal or conservative ideology. We expect, just as we did for party identification, to observe no relationship between liberal or conservative ideology and blacks' difference scores for presidential candidate aid to blacks when the respondent is interviewed by a black interviewer but a strong and statistically significant relationship between liberal or conservative ideology and the candidate difference scores when black respondents are interviewed by a non-black interviewer or when the survey is conducted online. As we can see in Figure 4.5, the results for this expectation are somewhat mixed. As predicted, ideology has no effect on blacks' responses to the measure of presidential candidate aid to blacks in the presence of a black interviewer. In both data sources the effect of liberal or conservative ideology on the difference scores for presidential candidate aid to blacks is essentially zero when the question is asked by a black interviewer.

The effect of liberal or conservative ideology for respondents who answered the survey in the presence of a non-black interviewer or online is somewhat mixed across the different surveys. Consistent with our expectations, the cumulative ANES shows a rather strong relationship between liberal or conservative ideology and blacks' responses to the difference measure of presidential candidate aid to blacks. We see that black liberals who are interviewed by non-black interviewers express a rather strong belief that the Democratic candidate is more likely to support providing economic aid to blacks. However, as we move to black conservatives interviewed by non-black interviewers, we see their average responses approach little or no difference in how they see the candidates with regard to support for assisting blacks economically. Turning to the 2012 ANES, we see that while this relationship appears to replicate for those blacks interviewed by black interviewers, the relationship between liberal/conservative ideology and how blacks see the candidates with regard to support for assisting blacks economically appears to be significantly weaker than what we saw in the cumulative ANES.[13]

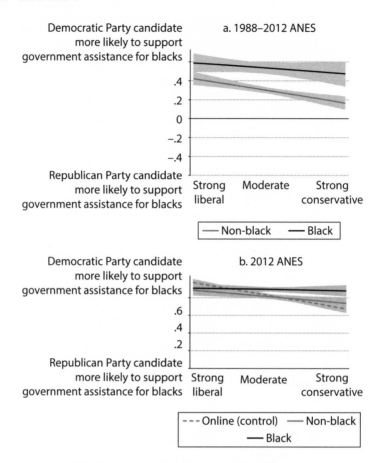

FIGURE 4.5. Blacks' evaluation of presidential candidate difference on aid to blacks by race of interviewer and ideology, 95% confidence intervals

In sum, this set of analyses suggests that even the perception of how well the parties represent the interest of blacks can be influenced by racialized social pressure. Although at no point do we see the majority of black respondents believing that the Republican presidential candidate will be more likely than the Democratic candidate to support assisting blacks economically, the mere fact that racialized social constraint can alter blacks' perceptions of how well the parties and their candidates represent the interest of blacks is telling about the power of racialized social constraint to influence black political behavior. Indeed, even if black party unity has its basis in the perception that the Democratic Party does a better job of representing the interest of blacks, that perception itself appears to be influenced by racialized social constraint.

CANDIDATE AFFECT

Next, we turn to examining how racialized social constraint, as induced by black interviewers, can alter blacks' affective responses to Democratic and Republican presidential candidates. We examine how blacks' candidate feeling thermometer scores vary by the race of the interviewer asking the question. In this analysis, we take the difference in the Democratic and Republican presidential candidates' feeling thermometer scores and examine how blacks' responses to this measure vary by the race the interviewer and, in the case of the 2012 ANES, the mode of the interview (online vs. face to face). The average feeling thermometer difference scores by interviewer race or mode for the cumulative ANES and the 2012 ANES are presented in Figures 4.6a–b. Here we see that, once again, the presence of a black interviewer appears to lead to heighten support for Democratic candidates. Beginning with the cumulative ANES, we see about a 20-percentage-point increase in blacks' feelings of warmth toward the Democratic candidate relative to the Republican candidate as we move from having a non-black interviewer to having a black interviewer. In other words, in the presence of a black interviewer, black respondents exhibit a greater difference in their feelings toward the Democratic and Republican candidates. This same basic result appears to hold up in the 2012 ANES, although the differences are somewhat smaller. We observe that, moving from having a non-black interviewer to having a black interviewer, there is about a 10-percentage-point increase in the relative warmth blacks feel for the Democratic candidate over the Republican candidate. This difference decreases to about 5 percentage points when we compare having a black interviewer with completing the survey online, yet the difference remains statistically significant.

In turning to how interviewer race might condition the effect of ideology on the presidential candidate feeling thermometer difference scores, we see once again somewhat mixed results (Figures 4.7a–b). Consistent with our expectations, we see that across both the 1988–2012 ANES and the 2012 ANES, the presence of a black interviewer largely mutes the effect of ideology on black candidate feeling thermometer difference scores. This is especially true in the 2012 ANES, where the estimated feeling thermometer difference remains essentially the same as we move from liberal (67) to conservative (69). For those blacks interviewed by non-blacks or who completed the survey online in the 2012 ANES, we see that the relationship between ideology and the presidential candidate feeling thermometer

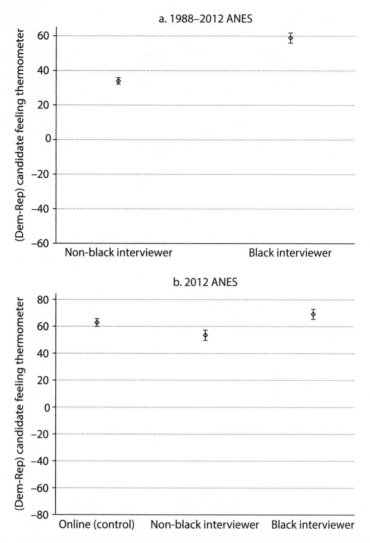

FIGURE 4.6. Presidential candidate feeling thermometer difference scores by race of interviewer for black respondents, 95% confidence intervals

difference scores grows slightly stronger, suggesting that blacks in these groups are relying slightly more on ideology to make their candidate evaluations. However, the strength of this relationship is not as strong as we would have expected, leaving open the possibility that non-black interviewers are encouraging some other means of affectively evaluating presidential candidates.

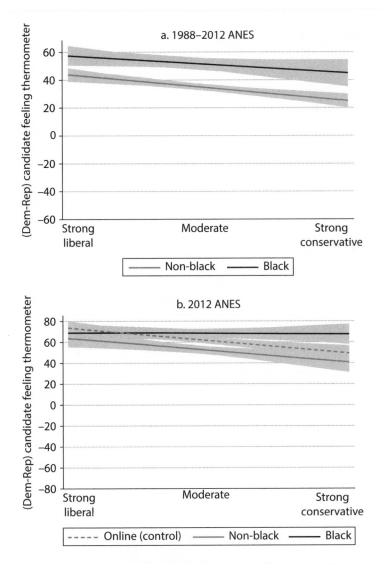

FIGURE 4.7. Presidential candidate feeling thermometer difference scores by race of interviewer and ideology, 95% confidence intervals

VOTE INTENT

Now we turn to examining the effect of black interviewers on blacks' intent to support Democratic candidates in the November presidential election. We measure intent by examining the percentage of blacks who state in the pre-election ANES survey that they will turn out and vote for the Democratic candidate in the upcoming election. We expect that if our racialized social constraint argument is correct, the presence of a black interviewer will cause black respondents to report greater intention to turn out and vote for the Democratic candidate. Table 4.6 presents the percentage of black respondents in the cumulative ANES who stated an intention to vote for the Democratic candidate by the race of the person who interviewed them.[14] In each of the relevant years of the ANES, the percentage of blacks who say they will vote for the Democratic candidate for president is greater in the presence of a black interviewer than when a non-black interviewer is present. While we can see that in some years this effect is not statistically significant, in most of the early ANES studies, this lack of significance is due in part to the small number of black interviewers and black respondents in those years. Generally, however, the effects we observe are substantively large, ranging from a 7-percentage-point difference in 1988 to a 14-percentage-point difference in 1996. Similarly, when we pool the results (effectively increasing the number of respondents and interviewers), we see a large statistically significant increase in the percentage of blacks who say they intend to vote for the Democratic candidate for president when we move from having a non-black interviewer to having a black interviewer.

Once again, we are able to replicate this general result in the 2012 ANES (Table 4.7), which gives us the added advantage of having an online sample that we can use to obtain a baseline estimate of black respondents' intention to support the Democratic candidate for president. While we do see that the percentage of blacks who intend to vote for the Democratic candidate in the black interviewer condition is 96.3 percent and 93.2 percent in the online

TABLE 4.6. Percentage of Blacks Who Intend to Turnout and Vote for the Democratic Candidate by Race of Interviewer, Cumulative ANES, 1988 to 2012

	Black interviewer	Non-black interviewer	Difference
1988	69.2%	61.9%	−7.3%
1992	75.5%	64.2%	−11.3%
1996	91.3%	77.0%	−14.3%
2008	94.5%	85.2%	−9.3%*
2012	95.5%	88.7%	−6.8%*
Total	90.9%	75.1%	−15.8%*
N	361	1,385	

Note: Results are the percentage of all black respondents who stated an intention to both turn out and vote for the Democratic candidate for president.

* $p < .05$

TABLE 4.7. Percentage of Blacks Who Intend to Turnout and Vote for the Democratic Candidate by Race of Interviewer and Online Mode, 2012 ANES (Face to Face and Online), 95% CI

	Online (control)	Non-black interviewer	Black interviewer	Difference		
	(A)	(B)	(C)	(B − A)	(C − A)	(C − B)
	93.2%	86.1%	96.3%	−7.1%*	3.1%[a]	10.2%*
N	470	253	244			

Notes: Results are the percentage of all black respondents who stated an intention to both turn out and vote for the Democratic candidate for president. There exist slight differences in how respondent race is coded across the 2012 ANES and 1988–2012 ANES.

[a] $p < .1$

* $p < .05$

condition, this difference is smaller than the one we observed between the black and non-black conditions. There nonetheless exists a marginally significant 3.1-percentage-point increase in blacks' intention to vote for the Democratic candidate for president when we move from the online (control) condition to the black interviewer condition. The ability of black interviewers to constrain the stated vote intention of black respondents further supports our racialized social constraint argument and highlights the primacy of norms of Democratic Party support in black social context. In the next chapter, we will build on this finding by examining in more detail the ability of racialized social constraint to influence blacks' willingness to engage in costly political action in support of the Democratic Party.

Conclusion

The main goal of this chapter was to elucidate the causal process underlying racialized social constraint. We accomplished this by first defining the mechanism underlying basic constraints on black partisan political behavior. As part of our racialized social constraint argument, we offered role identity theory as an alternative process for understanding the maintenance of black Democratic Party identification. Its focus on behavior considered appropriate by other group members and the positive and negative social sanctions used to encourage compliance with such behavior offers a concise explanation of black decision making that not only is more consistent with the patterns of homogeneous partisan political behavior exhibited by blacks over the last fifty years than the linked fate explanation but also accounts for the sorts of trade-offs that black Americans are faced with when making political decisions.

We then moved to empirically demonstrating the causal process under-lying racialized social constraint. Leveraging the quasi-experimental nature of social interactions that occur within face-to-face survey interviews of black respondents, we observed that when in the presence of other blacks, black respondents expressed significantly greater identification with the Democratic Party. Here we observed the effect of racialized social pressure exerted by non-black and same-race interviewers on blacks' willingness to identify as Democrats when asked the party identification question in these surveys. We found that blacks reported higher levels of support for the Democratic Party (about a 12-percentage-point increase) when they were speaking to a black interviewer relative to a non-black interviewer. We were able to replicate these results across a number of different data sources, and we also found them to be robust to different adjustment strategies meant to account for the lack of random assignment of interviewers to respondents. We even found these effects in telephone interviews of African Americans. In aggregated Pew and Gallup telephone surveys, we saw a significant increase in Democratic partisanship with a black interviewer, ranging from 2 to 5 percent. We also utilized the online survey component of the 2012 ANES as a baseline comparison group, allowing us to observe black party identification absent any interviewer. The results showed that Democratic partisan support was roughly the same between non-black interviewers and the online survey (85% and 83%, respectively). These results allowed us to confidently conclude that there is some direct causal link between black survey interviewers and black respondents' reporting of Democratic Party identification.

We also observed that those who had an ideological interest in deviating from the partisan norm, black conservatives, were the most constrained by racial group pressure and expectations. For example, in the absence of a black interviewer, we saw that black conservatives reported partisanship that was more line with their ideological preferences, but when interviewed by a black interviewer, black conservatives expressed levels of Democratic partisanship that were indistinguishable from those of black liberals: nearly unanimously Democratic. We also tested variations on conservative ide-ology by examining different conceptualizations of it that go beyond our conventional seven-point liberal-conservative scale. Specifically, we exam-ined how the race of the interviewer conditioned the effects of moral or traditional perspectives and attitudes about free market economics on black partisan beliefs. We found that, once again, black conservatives were the most constrained in behavior by black interviewers, reporting levels of

Democratic partisan support that are comparable to those reported by black liberals.

In sum, the discussion and results presented in this chapter further substantiate our claim that the normalization of Democratic partisanship and the social incentives that govern the intraracial interactions of black Americans can powerfully constrain black partisan defection. In the next chapter, we will delve deeper into how these norms and social pressures might constrain black political behavior. Specifically, we will move beyond examining how these norms might influence the simple expression of political beliefs to examine how they might shape black respondents' intentions to engage in political action, willingness to overreport certain political behaviors, and engagement in costly political action. While in this chapter we examined how racialized social constraint prevented ideological defection from group norms of political behavior, in Chapter 5 we turn to engaging the question of how individuals navigate conflicts between their material self-interest and racial group expectations of political behavior. Chapter 5 will delve further into this question as we show how concerns about immediate sanctions from in-group members constrain blacks' political behavior even when they have an opposing a monetary incentive.

5

Self-Interest versus Group Interest and "Racialized" Social Constraint

In the previous chapter, we demonstrated that racialized social constraint has the ability to prevent blacks from defecting from the Democratic Party, at least publicly. We showed that when party preferences are expressed in the presence of another black person, many blacks who embrace ideological conservatism feel the need to identify as Democrats in an effort to conform to the well-understood expectations of political behavior set forth by the black community. We were also able to identify this effect as particular to the black social context by showing that no such behavioral constraint exists in the presence of a white person or when blacks' political beliefs are expressed in relative privacy. Although these findings provide compelling evidence of the effectiveness of norms of black political behavior and racialized social constraint as means of constraining black Americans' expressions of Democratic partisanship, these results demonstrate constraint of only a narrow range of relatively low-cost political behaviors. In this chapter, we take the first steps toward demonstrating the power of racialized social constraint to inspire individual blacks to engage in political action to support the Democratic Party and its candidates that has direct and obvious costs to the individual.

Building on the results presented in Chapter 4, we begin by showing that the mere presence of other blacks, even complete strangers, not only can lead blacks to express an increased desire to act in support of Democratic candidates before an election but can also affect blacks' willingness to overstate their actual involvement in campaign activities following the election. We then experimentally demonstrate the process of racialized social constraint using two lab-in-the-field experiments, which allow us to directly observe the effects of racialized social pressure on blacks' willingness to engage in political action even when that behavior has costs to the individual. In the first experiment, we are able to test the effects of racialized social pressure on the willingness of African Americans to contribute to Barack Obama's 2012 presidential campaign. Using the behavior of contributions to the Obama campaign as a behavior consistent with the black group norm, and using personal monetary incentives to defect from contributing to induce a self-interest conflict, we are able to examine the effects of social pressure, exerted by either racial in-group members (blacks) or racial out-group members (whites), on constraining self-interested behavior. We find that it is only social pressure from other blacks that reduces self-interested behavior and results in group-norm-consistent political behavior. In the second experiment, we test the limits of racialized social pressure by showing that social pressure from other blacks cannot encourage defection from well-established group norms of political behavior.

The Individual Cost of Political Behavior

Engaging in certain forms of political action can come at significant cost to the individual (Downs 1957). Voting, for example, requires not only the time and effort needed to travel to the polling place but also the ability and time to research candidates and their positions. Other forms of political engagement are even more costly. Contacting elected officials, attending protests, and campaigning all require significant time commitments, while contributing to campaigns involves real monetary cost to the individual. With these real and identifiable costs to political engagement and the vague and often non-existent benefits that accrue from these efforts, scholars have noted the irrationality of engagement in certain forms of political action. In his classic analysis of the economics of voting, Anthony Downs (1957) points out that given the cost in time and energy required to vote, along with the extremely small chance that any individual's vote will determine the outcome of an election, turning out to vote makes little economic sense. Following this logic, Downs then notes the "paradox" that is revealed by the observation that in modern democracies, most citizens nonetheless do turn out to vote in national elections. In the United States, for example, more than 50 percent of the eligible voting-age population regularly turns out to vote in presidential elections.

Faced with this "paradox" of political participation, researchers have explored ways that individuals might overcome the costs associated with political engagement. In particular, these researchers have focused on the role that material and psychological resources play in supplementing the cost of political engagement (Riker and Ordeshook 1968; Verba and Nie 1972; Verba, Schlozman, and Brady 1995). Important here is the work of Verba and Nie (1972), who argue that individual-level socioeconomic status (SES) factors such as education and income are essential to facilitating increased political engagement. They find that SES is strongly related to voting, working for a campaign, contacting an elected official, and engaging in civic activism.

Despite these significant observations, one of Verba and Nie's (1972) most interesting findings relates to racial differences in political engagement. As discussed in Chapter 1, Verba and Nie observed that despite a general lack of socioeconomic resources, African Americans in the 1960s frequently out-participated whites of similar SES. To explain this result, they argued that essential to African Americans' greater political engagement was a sense of racial group consciousness. While Verba and Nie (1972) and later Shingles (1981) would find strong support for the idea that racial group consciousness worked as an important psychological resource for African Americans in the mid-twentieth century, researchers have struggled to find much support for the racial group consciousness explanation of black political engagement in the modern era (see Bobo and Gilliam 1990). For example, in her comprehensive examination of blacks' involvement in electoral politics, Tate (1991) finds only weak support for the racial group consciousness explanation of black political participation in the 1984 and 1988 presidential elections. Even Verba and Nie, in their 1993 work with Kay Schlozman and Henry Brady examining civic participation (Verba, Schlozman, Brady, and Nie 1993), appear to step back from the group consciousness claim and suggest that racial differences in political participation likely have their origins in the relative distribution of resources across the racial groups. Leighley and Vedlitz (1999) also find no support for the group consciousness explanation of black political behavior, instead noting the importance of SES for facilitating black political engagement. Thus, while it seems that group consciousness was essential to black political behavior in the 1960s, socioeconomic resources appear to have supplanted its importance as a predictor of black political engagement today.

The failure of the group consciousness model to explain black political participation has left us once again trying to understand how blacks, despite their relative lack of socioeconomic resources, continue to engage in certain forms of political action at rates equal to or at times greater than those of whites. Take voting, for example. In the last four presidential elections, blacks as a group have turned out to vote at rates roughly equal to those of whites. Given that blacks have on average less education and lower incomes than whites, something else must be motivating black political engagement beyond SES. Again, we offer racialized social constraint as an alternative explanation for how black Americans are able to overcome the costs associated with political engagement. We contend that the social pressure resulting from blacks' interactions with other blacks and the well-defined expectations of political behavior that characterize these interactions can motivate black political engagement—that it can constrain political behavior, as well as political beliefs. In the previous chapter, we were able to show that racialized social constraint effectively prevented defection from the norm of Democratic Party identification and candidate support in the context of a survey interview. However, public expressions of political beliefs in a survey require little of the respondent and may not translate into meaningful political action outside the context of the survey interview. In other words, changing one's political beliefs in the context of a survey interview is a fairly low-cost action; the effect of racialized social constraint in this context may be exaggerated. A good illustration of this concern can be found in a 1992 paper by D. P. Green and Cowden, who show that while whites directly affected by busing were no more likely to oppose busing than those who were not affected, they were more likely to engage in antibusing activism. Green and Cowden (1992, p. 476) explain this relationship by stating that "people tend not to reflect on their personal interests when making political decisions in the context of a survey interview, but are stimulated to think about their interests when faced with the choice of whether to take action. The more costly the act, the greater the influence of self-interest, as individuals are prompted to consider the relationship between their personal circumstances and the political question at issue." We believe the same process likely characterizes black political engagement. In other words, it is possible that the reason contemporary scholars have found only a weak connection between black political engagement and black groupcentric beliefs is that, when it comes to participation, the individual costs associated with this type of political engagement are so clear that group interest becomes secondary to individual interest. As stated earlier, groupcentric explanations, such as Dawson's linked fate, posit that group interest is only a proxy for self-interest, so that when faced with the choice of whether to participate in costly political action, the individual costs associated with such action are made salient, which reduces the influence of group interest. It is in these conditions that racialized social constraint is especially useful. Unlike linked fate, racialized social constraint can work to counter self-interest since it imposes its own (social) costs and benefits on the individual. Thus, when deciding whether to engage in costly political action that might help the racial group, individual blacks are faced with weighing the social costs and benefits of defecting from expected group behavior against the individual costs and benefits that might result from non-compliance.

In the pages that follow, we examine the ability of racialized social constraint to inspire individual blacks to engage in *costly* political action to support the Democratic Party. We do this by showing that the presence of other blacks can lead black respondents in a survey to overstate their actual involvement in campaign activities following the election. Because these behaviors represent actions that can be verified, lying about or misreporting a past behavior comes at a greater cost to the individual than simply changing one's expressed beliefs or intentions. In other words, lying about political action subjects the respondent to the potential of being caught in the lie either through additional questioning or through actual verification (i.e., voter validation). This represents a significantly more stringent test of our racialized social constraint explanation that moves it beyond simply constraining expressed beliefs to also constraining behavior.

We then offer an even more direct test of the ability of racialized social constraint to constrain black political behavior using a lab-in-the-field experiment that allows us to directly observe the effects of racialized social pressure on blacks' willingness to engage in costly political action. This experiment is meant to replicate the conditions under which racialized social pressure might affect blacks' willingness to contribute to Democratic candidates. We use the behavior of contributions to the Obama campaign to examine the effects of social pressure, exerted by either racial in-group members or racial out-group members, on constraining self-interested behavior. Lastly, we examine the limits of racialized social pressure, demonstrating that social pressure from other blacks must work in conjunction with well-established group norms of political behavior and cannot encourage defection from group expectations. Together these tests offer a persuasive examination of the ability of racialized social constraint to constrain blacks' willingness to engage in costly political action in support of the Democratic Party.

Design

To test our expectation that racialized social constraint can lead blacks to express a heightened intent to engage in costly political action to support the Democratic Party, we begin by examining how the intraracial social interactions present during the face-to-face survey interview can influence the extent to which blacks overreport their own engagement in political action in support of the Democratic Party. Again, we think of overreporting as costly political behavior because it involves some degree of misrepresentation of behavior that could potentially be verified. Because we have no reason to believe that blacks interviewed by black interviewers are fundamentally different from those interviewed by non-black interviewers, we would expect that any reporting of greater campaign engagement in postelection surveys is likely due to the social pressure created by the presence of the black interviewer. Again, we take steps to ensure that these groups are in fact comparable by adjusting for pretreatment respondent and interviewer characteristics and validating certain campaign activities.

We once again utilize data from the cumulative American National Election Studies (ANES) surveys from 1988 to 2012 and the 2012 ANES to test whether the presence of other blacks, even complete strangers, can lead black respondents to overstate their actual involvement in campaign activities in postelection ANES surveys.[1] In our first set of analyses, we test the ability of racialized social constraint to lead black Americans to overstate their actual engagement in political campaign activities meant to support the Democratic candidate for president. We begin by examining whether the presence of a black interviewer in postelection ANES surveys leads black respondents to overreport that they both turned out and voted for the Democratic candidate for president. To verify that what we are observing is actually over- or underreporting in response to a black interviewer and not that blacks interviewed by black interviewers are *actually* more or less likely to engage in these behaviors, we then turn to the 2012 ANES. Not only does the 2012 ANES have a relatively large sample of black respondents, but it also validated turnout in the 2012 presidential election, which allows us to have a measure of actual black voter turnout that we can then use to assess whether those blacks interviewed by black interviewers are actually more likely to overreport their turnout in the 2012 presidential election. If we are correct in our expectations about the power of racialized social constraint, we should observe a greater number of validated non-voting blacks telling black interviewers, as opposed to non-black interviewers, that they voted when they actually did not.

We also test whether black interviewers can lead blacks to overreport the number of campaign activities that the respondent engaged in during the campaign period, as well as to understate the degree to which they engaged in split-ticket voting. Under a racialized social constraint model, in the presence of a black interviewer, we should observe blacks reporting greater support for the Democratic Party and greater involvement in campaign activities compared with those blacks interviewed by non-black interviewers.

Results

Having seen in Chapter 4 that black interviewers can alter blacks' stated intention to turn out and vote for Democratic candidates, we now turn to examining whether we might see the same effect in blacks' reporting of whether they turned out to vote for the Democratic candidate for president after the election. Again, this represents a somewhat harder test of the racialized social constraint argument since respondents are less likely to alter the reporting of behavior that they may or may not have actually engaged in. Yet we nonetheless suspect that the power of racialized social constraint is such that the pressure put on black respondents to say they voted for the Democratic candidate will alter the reporting of their behavior, causing them to overstate the degree to which they actually acted in support for the Democratic candidate for president. Looking once again at data from the cumulative ANES postelection survey, we see in Table 5.1 that having a black interviewer does indeed seem to increase the likelihood that a black person will say that he or she voted for the Democratic candidate for president in that year's election when compared with blacks interviewed by non-black interviewers. In every year for which we have data, we see that reported turnout for the Democratic candidate for president is greatest in the presence of a black interviewer. Although this difference is only statistically significant in 2012, when we combine all years, we nonetheless observe a large, statistically significant 16-point difference in the percentage of blacks who report turning out to vote for the Democratic candidate for president.

What also appears obvious from these results is that much of the difference we observe in reported support for the Democratic Party appears to

TABLE 5.1. Percentage of Blacks Who Report Voting for the Democratic Candidate by Race of Interviewer, Cumulative ANES, 1992 to 2012

		Black interviewer	Non-black interviewer	Difference
1992	Dem.	60.5	51.1	−9.4
	Rep.	4.6	2.6	−2.0
	Other/did not vote	34.8	46.2	11.4
1996	Dem.	56.5	48.7	−7.8
	Rep.	0.0	0.6	0.6
	Other/did not vote	43.4	50.6	7.2
2008	Dem.	76.5	71.2	−5.3
	Rep.	0.0	0.4	0.4
	Other/did not vote	23.4	28.3	4.9
2012	Dem.	80.0	67.9	−12.1*
	Rep.	1.2	1.5	0.3
	Other/did not vote	18.7	30.5	11.8*
Total	Dem.	73.9	57.7	−16.2*
	Rep.	1.0	1.9	0.9
	Other/did not vote	25.0	39.6	14.6*

Note: Includes non-voters.
* $p < .05$

come from higher turnout reported in the presence of a black interviewer. In other words, in the presence of a black interviewer, more blacks are claiming to have turned out to vote. This is not surprising given that the turnout question is asked before the vote choice question and if one felt pressure to overstate support for the Democratic candidate, he or she would first have to overreport turnout. Fortunately for us, the ANES has at times validated whether the respondent actually turned out to vote in the November presidential election, allowing us the ability to test whether overreporting of turnout is in fact greatest in the presence of a black interviewer. Using validated turnout as a measure of an individual's *actual* turnout, we can test whether those blacks who we know did not vote in the election were more likely to report that they did vote when asked the turnout question by a black person in a face-to-face interview.

We begin our assessment of this expectation by first testing whether blacks interviewed by a black interviewer are more likely to overreport voting in other years of the ANES. Table 5.2 shows the percentage of blacks who reported turning out in that year's presidential election by the race of the interviewer who interviewed them in the face-to-face interview. We

TABLE 5.2. Black Turnout by Race of Interviewer, Cumulative ANES, 1990–2012 (in Person Only)

	Black interviewer	Non-black interviewer	Difference
1992	79.4%	62.8%	−16.6%*
1996	77.7%	66.1%	−11.6%
2008	85.7%	81.6%	−4.1%
2012	88.0%	75.0%	−13.0%*
Total	84.5%	71.4%	−13.1%*
N	433	1,090	

Notes: Interviewer data pre-1988 is not available in the ANES cumulative data file. The 2004 ANES only recorded interviewer race as white or non-white. The 2000 and 2002 ANES surveys had no black face-to-face interviewers.
* $p < .05$

see that in every year of the face-to-face ANES, having a black interviewer leads to higher levels of reported black voter turnout. This difference ranges from 4 percentage points in 2008 to 16 percentage points in 1996.[2] Overall, when we pool all the years of the ANES, we see a statistically significant 13-percentage-point gap in black self-reported turnout resulting from having a black interviewer. While these data identify a strong relationship between the interviewer's race and self-reported turnout, much like in the earlier analysis, we still cannot be sure that the black interviewer is altering the reporting of turnout or whether those black respondents interviewed by black interviewers are just more likely to actually turn out and vote than those interviewed by non-black interviewers.

The fact that black voters are more likely to report turning out in the presence of a black interviewer suggests one of two possibilities: first, that the mere presence of a black interviewer is, as we have suggested, encouraging black respondents to report higher levels of turnout more consistent with their perceptions of the interviewers' expectations than with their actual political engagement, or second, that those black respondents interviewed by black interviewers actually did turn out at higher levels than those interviewed by non-black interviewers. To get at the causal effect of black interviewers on vote overreporting, we turn to the validated vote data from the 2012 ANES and narrow our analysis down to the only group of individuals who are capable of overreporting their vote: validated non-voters. We then examine whether the percentage of black validated non-voters who reported to the ANES interviewer that they voted in the 2012 presidential election changes as a function of the race of the interviewer. Table 5.3 presents

TABLE 5.3. Percentage of Validated Non-Voters Who Reported Having Voted by Race and Race of Interviewer, 2012 ANES

	Same-race interviewer	Different-race interviewer	Difference	P-value	N
Black	69.7%	43.3%	26.4%*	.02	86
White	31.5%	31.0%	0.5%	.96	175

* $p < .05$

self-reported turnout among black and white validated non-voters. Having a black interviewer seems to strongly encourage black non-voters to say that they voted when they actually did not, and this effect is largely isolated to black respondents. Validated black non-voters who were interviewed by a black interviewer reported that they voted at a rate of 69.7 percent, whereas only 43.3 percent of black non-voters who were interviewed by a non-black interviewer reported voting in the election. This produces a rather large difference of 26.4 percentage points in the rate of overreporting of turnout between black respondents interviewed by an African American interviewer and those interviewed by a white interviewer. This difference is both substantively large and statistically significant ($p < .02$). The substantive difference is particularly notable when compared with the differences in overreporting by race of interviewer for whites. White non-voters interviewed by a white interviewer reported voting at a rate of 31.5 percent, whereas 31.0 percent interviewed by a non-white interviewer reported turning out to vote. In other words, there are no interviewer effects. Thus, the pattern of overreporting based on the race of the interviewer appears to only hold for African American respondents. This would also suggest that, as our racialized social constraint theory would predict, there is a unique social norm within the African American community regarding political participation that is activated when in the presence of another African American, resulting in social pressure to conform that leads to overreporting by black respondents faced with black interviewers.

Having seen that black interviewers can lead to both the overreporting of turnout and the overreporting of voting for the Democratic candidate, we now turn to an examination of split-ticket voting. We examine whether the presence of a black interviewer can constrain blacks' willingness to state that they voted for at least one non-Democratic candidate in the presidential, House, or Senate race. Table 5.4 presents the percentage of blacks who revealed to the interviewer that they voted for at least one non-Democratic candidate in the presidential, House, or Senate race for

TABLE 5.4. Percentage of All Blacks Who Split-Ticket Vote by Race of Interviewer, Cumulative
ANES, 1988 to 2012

	Black interviewer	Non-black interviewer	Difference
1992	8.6%	23.6%	15%
1996	8.0%	17.9%	9.9%
2008	3.7%	22.2%	18.5%*
2012	6.5%	8.3%	1.8%*
Total	5.5%	18.8%	13.3%*
N	288	564	

$p < .05$

the 1988, 1992, 2008, or 2012 election. We see that blacks are generally
more likely to indicate that they voted for at least one non-Democratic
candidate in the presence of a non-black interviewer than in the presence
of a black interviewer. The difference in split-ticket voting by the race of
the interviewer is statistically significant in two of the four years of the
ANES data, with the difference in 2008 reaching 18 percentage points. The
pooled results show a 13-percentage-point difference ($p < .05$), with blacks
reporting significantly higher levels of split-ticket voting in the presence of a
non-black interviewer relative to a black interviewer. Given the consistency
of these results with the many other race-of-interviewer results we have
seen, we can confidently conclude that the mere presence of other blacks
can greatly influence a black person's willingness to overreport his or her
loyalty to the Democratic Party.

We now turn to examining whether the reporting of the overall number of
campaign activities engaged in by the respondent is affected by the racialized
social constraint induced by having a black interviewer. Table 5.5 presents the
average number of campaign activities, out of six, reported by the respondent
for that year in the postelection interview of the cumulative ANES. Again, if
our racialized social constraint argument is correct, then we should observe
a greater overall increase in the number of reported activities in the presence
of a black interviewer. We see that in every election except for that of 1992,
black respondents interviewed by black interviewers reported higher rates
of campaign activism. Again, earlier years of the survey featured significantly
fewer black interviewers, which is partly responsible for the lack of statistically
significant differences. Nonetheless, when we pool all years, we see that blacks
who are interviewed by black interviewers report being engaged in about one-
fifth of an activity more than those interviewed by non-black interviewers.

TABLE 5.5. Mean Number of Campaign Activities by Race of Interviewer, Cumulative ANES, 1988–2012

	Black interviewer	Non-black interviewer	Difference
1992	1.41	1.47	0.06
1996	1.50	1.35	−0.15
2008	2.20	1.97	−0.23[a]
2012	2.01	1.77	−0.24*
Total	2.00	1.80	−0.20*
N	433	1,090	

Notes: Respondents could choose 0-6 activities in which they could participate. The table above reflects the average number of activities in which they participated.
[a] $p < .1$
* $p < .05$

The results presented thus far in this chapter confirm our suspicions that racialized social constraint can powerfully influence blacks' willingness to overreport actual engagement in a broad range of electoral activities. While interesting, however, these results are limited not only in their ability to assess how racialized social constraint leads to actual political behavior but also in their ability to speak to how racialized social constraint conditions black political behavior in the face of identifiable costs associated with engaging in norm-consistent political action in support of the Democratic Party. In the section that follows, we will discuss the results of a lab-in-the-field experiment that we designed to allow us to observe racialized social constraint in action. We test the ability of racialized social constraint to lead to norm-consistent behavior in the face of direct benefits to an individual's material self-interest.

Experiment 1: Self-Interest versus Group Expectations

We have pointed out throughout this book that one of the most basic social dilemmas that black Americans face is how to maintain group unity in the face of incentives to free ride on the efforts of others. Thus far, we have observed the ability of racialized social constraint to enforce compliance with racial group norms of political behavior in the face of ideological incentives to defect. We have, however, yet to fully examine the effectiveness of racialized social constraint at bringing about norm compliance in the face of material incentives to do otherwise. Material incentives such as direct cash payouts appeal directly to an individual's private self-interest and have the potential to reduce the effectiveness of racialized social constraint. To understand how black Americans make trade-offs between material incentives and racialized social constraint, we designed an experiment that pits direct cash payouts against the enforcement of racial group norms as assessed by the expectations of behavior resulting from social monitoring by another black person.

The experiment was conducted from October 11 to October 20, 2012, and involved 106 black students recruited from a predominantly white university in the Midwest. Subjects were randomly assigned to one of three conditions: a control or one of two treatments. Across all of the conditions, subjects were asked to fill out a short pretest questionnaire and were then instructed that they were going to participate in a brief interview about the current presidential campaign. Subjects then entered a hallway, where they approached an interviewer at a table outside a classroom, as shown in Figure 5.1. Once subjects reached the interviewer location, they were given information on the decision-making task. During the course of the interview, participants were told that the researchers conducting the study were awarded a grant from an organization called the Voter Turnout Project and that the funds from this grant were to be used to provide young people with the opportunity to contribute to campaigns. Each subject was then given ten dollars in one-dollar bills and instructed to enter the classroom (the private contribution room), where there were two contribution boxes—one labeled "Obama" and the other labeled "Romney." These boxes were sitting side by side on a table in the classroom. Subjects were told that if they would like to make a contribution to the campaign of either of the candidates, they could do so by putting money into its contribution box. Finally, they were told that they were in no way obligated to contribute; if they wanted to keep the money, they should feel free to do so. Upon entering the room, each subject was asked to sign a sheet acknowledging that he or she had received the money, and each was given approximately thirty seconds to sign and make whatever contribution he or she chose. Subjects then left the room and were asked to complete another short questionnaire. The goal of this design was to create a personal incentive (individual payout) that competed with the expected norm of group behavior—contributing to Obama.

Table 5.6 describes the experimental treatments tested in this study. For subjects in the control condition, the foregoing protocol describes their entire experience—they participated in the interview and entered

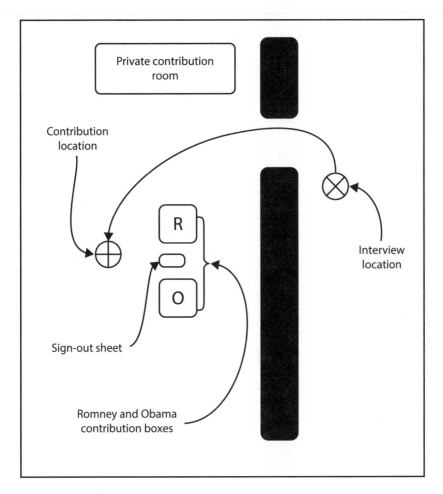

FIGURE 5.1. 2012 Obama/Romney experiment

the private contribution room alone. Subjects in the treatment conditions, however, were told that they would be interviewed at the same time as another student. In all cases, this other student was a confederate. The black confederate condition, designed to create racialized social pressure, paired the subject with a black student of the same sex. The white confederate condition paired the subject with a white student of the same sex. Pairing subjects and confederates of the same sex ensured that the social pressure was limited to race. We confirmed that the confederates were strangers to the subjects through after-reporting by the confederates.[3] Confederates and subjects were simultaneously given the protocol instructions and each

TABLE 5.6. Description of Experimental Treatments in Contribution Study

Condition 1: No confederate (control)	Contribution made in private
Condition 2: Black confederate	Contribution made in the presence of a black confederate who contributes all $10 to Obama
Condition 3: White confederate	Contribution made in the presence of a white confederate who contributes all $10 to Obama

given the ten dollars in one-dollar bills. The confederate and subject were then instructed that they were to enter the contribution room together. The social pressure treatment was implemented by the confederates' actions upon entering the room: they walked immediately to the Obama box; said, "I am giving all of my money to Obama"; inserted the entire ten dollars in the box; and then signed the sheet acknowledging that they had received the money. In all cases, the confederate completed the protocol before the subject made any contribution. To induce a sense of social monitoring, the confederate waited until the subject was done before leaving the room. When the subject was done, both exited the room and were asked to complete the final questionnaire.[4]

HYPOTHESES

Our expectations for this experiment are simple. In the control condition, which lacks any social pressure, we expect that most blacks will maximize their personal gain and will keep most or all of the money given to them. If our argument about the process of conformity to group-based norms is correct, however, we expect significantly more money to be given in the black confederate condition, but not in the white confederate condition. These expectations, again, rest on the argument that supporting Obama and the Democratic Party is defined by an in-group norm of political behavior, and the consequence of deviating from such a norm invites social sanctions within the black community. In other words, black subjects are expected to be concerned *uniquely* about having other blacks question their commitment to racial group goals and be constrained accordingly.[5] We also expect, as we did in the race-of-interviewer analysis presented in Chapter 4, that racialized social pressure will constrain ideological defection and also prevent defection regardless of the level of black linked fate.

RESULTS

We tested these expectations by comparing the mean Obama campaign contributions across each of the experimental conditions. The results are presented in Figure 5.2. Our expectation about the unique ability of racialized
social constraint to compel black political behavior away from self-interest
is supported by these results. When black subjects entered the contribution
room alone, they clearly acted on their self-interest; they kept most of the
money given to them. Subjects in the control group contributed an average of only $3.74 to the Obama campaign.[6] About 30 percent of subjects
in this condition kept *all* the money for themselves. Also, consistent with
our expectations, the presence of a white confederate who made his or her
intentions to support Obama very clear had no effect, relative to the control,
on the Obama contributions. Subjects in the white confederate condition
gave on average only $4.45 to the Obama campaign. The net increase in
contributions relative to the control was only $0.71, which is both substan-
tively small and statistically indistinguishable from the control ($p < .45$). In
the presence of the black confederates, however, contributions to Obama
were significantly higher, with an average contribution of $6.85.[7] This is an

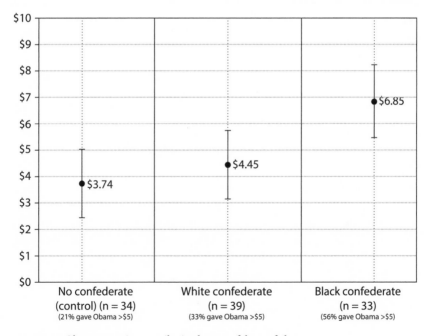

FIGURE 5.2. Obama campaign contribution by race of the confederate

increase of $3.11 contributed to the Obama campaign compared with the control. Just three subjects in this condition kept all of the money, while over half gave all the money to the Obama campaign. These results provide the first clear causal evidence that racialized social constraint is a powerful tool for imposing racial group norm compliance among African Americans. The presence of another black person clearly leads to compliance with racial group expectations of political behavior even in the face of monetary incentives to behave otherwise.

In the previous chapter, we saw that racialized social pressure effectively conditioned the effect of ideology on black political behavior. We now turn to examining whether ideology might also have played a role in how blacks evaluated whether to make contributions to the Obama campaign. Our expectations for the control and black confederate conditions are generally similar to those for the race-of-interviewer effects presented in Chapter 4. We expect to observe little or no relationship between ideology and Obama campaign contributions in the presence of a black confederate, and we would expect that in the control condition, conservatives would contribute less and liberals would contribute more to the Obama campaign. Our expectations with regard to how the white confederate condition might condition the effect of ideology on Obama campaign contributions are less clear. In the race-of-interviewer test presented in Chapter 4, we observed that white interviewers allow black conservatives to act on their conservative beliefs. We expected this outcome largely because of the ambiguity of partisan expectations in the presence of a white person. In other words, while ascriptive blackness carries with it signals of partisan preferences, no such expectations exist for white Americans, as they are fairly evenly distributed across the Democratic and Republican Parties. In this study, however, the partisan preferences of the white confederates are made clear by the design of the study. All confederates were instructed to make clear to the subjects that they were giving all of their money to the Obama campaign. We thus remain somewhat agnostic about our expectations for how black respondents of different ideological leanings will respond to this treatment.

The results of this analysis are presented in Figure 5.3. Before we begin our discussion, we should note that the results from tests of conditional effects using these data are largely suggestive given the relatively small sample size within each condition.[8] Although we cannot say whether any of the results presented in Figure 5.3 (and Figure 5.4) are statistically distinguishable, we note that the pattern of results presented is consistent with our general theoretical expectations. Beginning with the control condition,

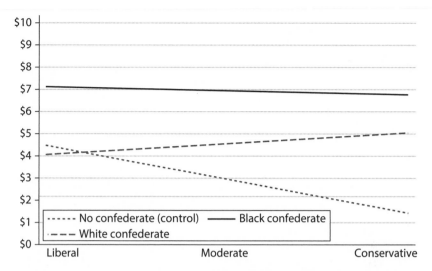

FIGURE 5.3. Effect of liberal or conservative ideology and race of confederate on Obama campaign contribution

we see that, as expected, the amount contributed to Obama appears to vary as a function of the individuals' ideological self-placement.[9] Self-identified liberal blacks appeared to contribute more (~$4.50) to the Obama campaign than self-identified conservative blacks (~$1.50) in this condition. Moving to the effect of ideology on Obama campaign contributions in the black confederate condition, we see essentially no change in Obama campaign contributions across the liberal-conservative ideological spectrum, as we expected. Obama contributions are generally much higher in this condition, with only a $0.33 decrease in Obama contributions as we move from liberals to conservatives.

The effect of the white confederate treatment on liberal or conservative ideology is interesting. It seems that while seeing a white person contribute to Obama does little to increase black liberals' willingness to contribute to Obama (relative to black liberals in the control condition), it does appear to inspire conservative blacks to contribute to Obama. While we are not sure why this is the case, given overall uncertainty about the results, it is nonetheless interesting. Might certain conservative blacks be swayed by whites who support Democratic or black candidates? This result points to an important area of future research.

Having seen that our experimental treatments are able to condition the effect of liberal or conservative ideology on blacks' willingness to contribute to the Obama campaign, we now turn to observing how they might also

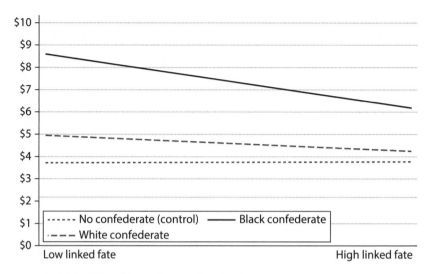

FIGURE 5.4. Effect of black linked fate and race of confederate on Obama campaign contribution

condition the effect of black linked fate on Obama campaign contributions. If black linked fate functions as Dawson (1994) and others (Tate 1993; I. K. White 2007) have argued—as a psychological constraint on black political behavior—then we should be able to observe, at the very least, Obama campaign contributions increasing as we move from low to high levels of black linked fate, particularly in the control condition. However, if our racialized social constraint argument is correct, we should not observe much of an effect of linked fate in the presence of black social monitoring. The results of this analysis are presented in Figure 5.4.

The results are somewhat inconsistent with any sort of predictions one might have about how linked fate might relate to willingness to contribute to the Obama campaign. In both the control and white confederate treatments, we see no relationship between black linked fate and blacks' Obama campaign contributions.[10] Although we should approach these results with some degree of skepticism given the small sample size, one likely reason for this particular pattern of results may be that the lure of monetary benefit and the lack of racial group accountability simply outweigh the psychological connection blacks have to the racial group. In the black confederate condition, the relationship between black linked fate and Obama campaign contributions is the opposite of what the linked fate research would predict. It appears that blacks with low levels of linked fate gave noticeably more to the Obama campaign in the presence of a black confederate than blacks with high levels of linked fate. While this particular pattern of results is somewhat unexpected, it is consistent with our racialized social constraint argument, which would suggest that even blacks with low levels of linked fate would be aware of the norms and expectations of the racial group and thus would conform to the group norm of political behavior.

These results highlight the work of racialized social constraint in preventing black defection from the norm of supporting Democratic candidates. Much like the results we saw from the survey data presented earlier in this chapter and in Chapter 4, the results of this experiment also support the idea that even social pressure from absolute strangers, as long as they are black, can influence black political behavior. The implications of these results are consistent not only with the argument that the racial in-group has a unique ability to constrain its members from maximizing self-interest at the expense of the group interest but also with the argument that such influence does not depend strictly on interpersonal connections between group members.[11] Consider, for example, how social pressure might influence how black Americans engage in public political discussions. Our results suggest that norms of political behavior within the black community ought to constrain black Americans who engage in political discussions in the presence of other black Americans, making them likely to censor norm-deviant opinions for fear of incurring sanctions. Unlike the survey results, however, this experiment's results offer us a glimpse of how blacks make political decisions in the face of real and identifiable incentives to their self-interest. What we learned is that some blacks are clearly susceptible to being "bought off," and neither ideological beliefs nor beliefs in black linked fate are able to constrain black partisan defection as effectively. It is clear, however, that racialized social constraint effectively deters defection from these group norms.

Experiment 2: The Limits of Racialized Social Pressure

The experimental results just discussed provide strong support for the idea that racialized social pressure from other black Americans can encourage compliance with racial group norms of political behavior. It is important to note, however, that there are limits to the ability of racialized social pressure to influence black political behavior. In the first few chapters of this book, we argued that racialized social pressure *must* work in conjunction with well-established group norms of political behavior. We argued in Chapter 1 that without a clear and common understanding of expected group behavior, social pressure from other racial in-group members can be easily dismissed as having little to do with the racial group. In this section, we put this idea to the test using another lab-in-the-field experiment, one in which we examine whether racialized social pressure can push blacks to work against group interest—in this case increasing support for the Romney campaign. Our analysis finds convincing evidence that social pressure from other blacks does not appreciably increase defection.

DESIGN

In this experiment we employ elements from the previous experiment to assess the effects of social pressure on *encouraging* defection from the group norm. The experiment was conducted from October 15 to October 20, 2012, on fifty-six self-identified African American subjects. All of the subjects in this study were recruited on or around the campus of a large, mostly white midwestern university. The black subjects in this experiment were told that they were going to participate in a short interview. As in the previous experiment, subjects participating in the interview were told that the researchers conducting the study were political scientists who had been awarded a grant from an organization called the Voter Turnout Project and that the funds from this grant were to be used to provide young people "like themselves" with an opportunity to contribute to presidential and congressional campaigns. Subjects were told by the interviewer that the Voter Turnout Project would like to provide them with one hundred dollars to donate to the presidential campaign of either Obama or Romney. Subjects were told that they could allocate the money any way they saw fit. They could donate it all to one candidate or split it across the candidates as long as their donations totaled one hundred dollars. Subjects were additionally instructed that the computer may provide them with an incentive to donate to one of the candidates. They were told that, in the interest of fairness, the computer would randomly determine for which candidate the incentive would be offered. In reality, the incentive was not randomly assigned—all subjects in the incentive conditions were provided an incentive to contribute to the Romney campaign. That is, we wanted to incentivize deviation from the (expected) black norm of behavior—contributing to Obama—with a personal monetary gain, but we did not want the subjects to suspect that the monetary incentive was driven by partisan motivations. Subjects in this experiment were told that for every ten dollars they donated to the Romney campaign, they would receive a one-dollar personal payout, implying a maximum payout of ten dollars if they allocated the entire one hundred dollars to the Romney campaign. These payouts, if chosen by the subjects, were actually paid in cash within the experiment. In this condition we expected to induce internal conflict among black subjects between their individual self-interest and their group interest, causing some to decide to stick with the Obama campaign and others to choose to take the payout and, as a consequence, provide financial support to the Romney campaign.

As in the previous experiment, the treatment was administered in the presence of a confederate. All subjects were told that they were to be interviewed along with another study participant. In each interview, however, the other subject was a black confederate, and the confederate was always asked by the interviewer to make his or her contribution decision first. What was manipulated here was whether the confederate openly forwent the incentive and gave all the money to the Obama campaign or openly took the incentive and gave all the money to the Romney campaign.

Our expectations for this simple experiment are a bit nuanced. We expect that another black student complying with the norm of supporting Obama and monitoring the subjects' contribution decisions should be an effective form of racialized social pressure. Thus, we expect that those in the Obama confederate condition will exhibit a high degree of compliance with the in-group norm to allocate all of the money to Obama despite the self-interest incentive to defect. Our theory implies, however, that the confederate's violation of the norm should not have the effect of racialized social pressure. Given the crystallized group norm of Obama support, we expect that the Romney confederate condition will only enable defection in favor of self-interest in the sense that it communicates that the other black person present is *not* performing the task of social monitoring. We expect that the Romney confederate condition will induce lower compliance than the Obama confederate condition but will not be effective at *pushing* acceptance of the self-interest payout for contributions to Romney to particularly high levels.

RESULTS

The results of this experiment are presented in Figure 5.5. What is shown is that subjects in the Obama confederate condition were nearly universal in allotting all of the possible campaign funds to Obama, despite the self-interest incentive to give to Romney. Subjects in this condition gave an average of $97.32 to the Obama campaign. Though subjects in the Romney confederate condition gave significantly less, their mean contribution to Obama was still over $70.00. These results suggest that the differences across these

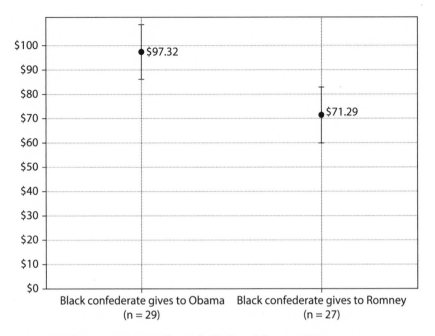

FIGURE 5.5. Obama campaign contribution by black confederate candidate support

two conditions are more consistent with an interpretation that holds that subjects in the Romney confederate condition perceived the confederate's actions as a cue that they were not being monitored for their adherence to the group norm, rather than as an effective act of racialized social pressure to violate the group norm. In the next chapter we will revisit elements of this design that will affirm our suspicion that the differences we see here are driven largely by the incentive and not by pressure to violate the norm.

Conclusion

In this chapter we offered our first bit of solid causal evidence in support of our racialized social constraint explanation. Here we were able to demonstrate the ability of racialized social constraint to inspire black Americans to engage in costly political activity to support the Democratic Party. We also explored the limits of racialized social pressure, demonstrating that although it can powerfully encourage compliance with well-established norms for black political behavior, it is less effective at encouraging defection from well-established group norms. The survey and experimental analysis presented here also offered evidence of how racialized social constraint can shape a broad range of black political behaviors, including black expression of an intention to vote, reported turnout levels, reported campaign activity, vote overreporting, and campaign giving.

In Chapter 6 we expand on our idea of how racialized social constraint can prevent black defection by showing how black institutions are enabled with the mechanisms to enforce compliance with black social norms and prevent self-interest defection. We posit that the ability of sanctions to be effective at constraining behavior requires the maintenance of said sanctions within racially homogeneous spaces. In fact, black institutions are vital for sanctioning because it is in these spaces that norms are reinforced and sanctions can be executed. Through another novel experimental design, we show how the social pressure created by black institutions is just as effective at constraining behavior as face-to-face encounters.

6

Institutional Constraints and the Enforcement of Racialized Social Pressure

To this point we have seen evidence that the social location of group members is essential to the effectiveness of social pressure to comply with norms. In this chapter, we will sharpen our focus on black social location by examining the role that black indigenous institutions play in enforcing norm compliance and overriding self-interest. Indigenous institutions have been vital to the black community and its survival. Born out of de jure and de facto efforts to segregate blacks from whites, black social and political institutions represent the cultural foundations of black communities. During periods of American history in which black access to spaces frequented by whites was restricted, black institutions were able to step in and provide the racial group with the material and cultural resources essential to civic progress. Spirituality, faith and hope have been centered in the black church. These places of worship have also served as the foci of organizing, politics, and social movements. Black educational institutions, created so that whites would not have to attend public schools with blacks, have provided group members with supportive environments in which they can pursue intellectual and academic endeavors along with technical training. Black broadcast and print news outlets have offered information and news about the black community that often go unacknowledged in the mainstream press.

Today, black institutions continue to exhibit high levels of racial homophily while also continuing to serve the communal needs of the group, informing, educating, and uplifting group members. Today's black institutions have also diversified using the internet and social media to reach broader black audiences. When it comes to politics, modern black institutions play an essential role in defining and enforcing racial group norms of political behavior, particularly around large-scale group mobilization efforts. As we discussed in earlier chapters of this book, social media and Black Twitter, in particular, were essential to the mobilization efforts of the Black Lives Matter Movement of 2014 and 2015. In this chapter we will explore the role that modern black institutions play in facilitating black political action. Specifically, we will discuss how individual self- and ideological interest can come into conflict with the broader group interest and how black institutions are designed to achieve group-based objectives effectively through the use of racialized social constraint.

In the first part of the chapter, we outline research on the political influence of black institutions. We discuss the presence of social pressure within black institutions and its role in constraining the behavior of group members. We then engage literature that discusses traditional black institutions and more casual manifestations such as what Melissa Harris-Lacewell (2004) calls "everyday talk" within black counterpublics and make the case for black institutions as venues for imposing racialized social constraint in large group settings. In the second half of this chapter, we empirically demonstrate the sustained relevance of black institutions in black social life through self-reported attendance in these institutions and establish the connection between institutional membership and adherence to norms of black political behavior.

We then move on to discussing the results of a behavioral experiment modeled after the experiments presented in Chapter 5. We leverage the structure of a black institution (a historically black college or university [HBCU]) to test our racialized social constraint argument. With this experiment, we are able to demonstrate the ability of black institutions to directly constrain black political behavior in the face of self-interest incentives. This design highlights the effectiveness of black institutions at executing social sanctions and preventing defection from racial group norms of political behavior. It also offers additional support for our argument that racialized social constraint is a powerful tool for ensuring group unity in the face of incentives to do otherwise.

Overview of Black Institutions in Politics

Black indigenous institutions have been an important resource for black political engagement (Francis 2014). Although blacks are frequently found to be lacking the economic and educational resources believed to facilitate greater political participation, they nonetheless continue to be heavily engaged in the political environment. As we have noted several times throughout this book, one of the more surprising findings of the research on American political behavior has been that black-white racial disparities in many low-cost forms of political participation tend to disappear when we account for the differences in socioeconomic status that exist across the racial groups (Verba and Nie 1972; Wolfinger and Rosenstone 1980). We have also noted that group consciousness is often cited as the primary means by which blacks have been able to overcome these barriers to political engagement. However, equally important in this research has been the connection between black institutional contact and increased political engagement among blacks. Researchers have found strong evidence to suggest that membership in black social and political organizations, membership in a black church, and the use of black media are all strongly associated with greater levels of black political engagement (Calhoun-Brown 1996; Cohen 1999; Dawson 1994, 2001; F. C. Harris 1994; McDaniel 2008; Tate 1993).

The black church, for example, has historically been one of the most important indigenous institutions for black political organizing and is formative in shaping black political culture (Higginbotham 1993; Lincoln and Mamiya 1990; McClerking and McDaniel 2005; Smith 1996; Wilcox and Gomez 1990). Katherine Tate (1993) argues in *From Protest to Politics: The New Black Voters in American Elections* that the black church has used its collective nature both to pool resources in a manner that can offset inequalities and disadvantages experienced by blacks and to provide members with information about political issues that can motivate blacks to become more politically engaged. Voting initiatives through black churches like Souls to the Polls and voter registration drives have been effective at encouraging and promoting black political participation.[1] Furthermore, Tate argues that the black political church and black political life are significantly intertwined. In her discussion of the 1984 presidential election, Tate (1993, p. 77) notes, "Contrary to their depiction as separate spheres, black religious life and political life have historically commingled. It is well known that the black church served as the 'institutional center' of the black civil rights movement. Most recently, black churches have been active in electoral politics. Jesse

Jackson's 1984 bid for the Democratic Party's presidential nomination was greatly aided by the black church. Jackson relied upon a network of black ministers and churches to raise campaign funds and to mobilize black voters." The 1984 presidential bid by Jackson clearly demonstrates that the black church does not do its political work without consideration of the racial group interests. Tate convincingly argues that black church leaders played a vital role in convincing blacks that it was possible for black interests to be incorporated politically into the executive branch and that the election of Jackson was the means by which that could happen. The information that black churchgoers received from the church told them of the group's interest in electing Jackson and mobilized them to participate in the campaign. The black church continues to play an important role in Democratic Party mobilization and played a vital role in black voter mobilization efforts around the 2008 election and 2012 reelection campaigns of Barack Obama (Saulny 2012), as well as the 2016 campaign of Hillary Clinton (E. Green 2016).

Building on Tate's observations about the importance of black institutions to black political engagement, Michael Dawson (2001) argues that black institutions are essential to black politics and the formation and maintenance of black racial ideologies. African Americans have frequently found themselves on the outside of what Dawson calls the "American bourgeois public sphere" (p. 24), or mainstream American political and social institutions. These efforts at racial exclusion, as well as blacks' embrace of their own autonomy, have, according to Dawson, facilitated the creation of a black counterpublic that engages politics in largely black-only spaces. In these counterpublics, blacks discuss issues concerning the black community and strategize to empower the black community and ensure civil rights protections. Dawson notes that historically, the black church has served as the primary location for this discourse. Specifically, Dawson (2001, p. 51) argues for the importance of the black church by also acknowledging the practices that contributed to its centrality in black politics: "The forcible separation of blacks from whites in the late 19th century led to the formation of a separate black counterpublic. The separate counterpublic had as its institutional foundation the set of autonomous organizations that the black community had built since the Civil War. The black church was particularly critical for providing an independent secular as well as sacred organizational basis for the black community." The segregation of blacks was integral to the creation of black institutions and the prominence of the black counterpublic. Dawson maintains that these black counterpublics are where various black racial ideologies have developed and where competing priorities for the improvement of the status of the group emerge. The ideologies that emerge from these institutions sharply diverge in their paths for the achievement of racial equality. For example, black conservatives might promote an agenda that encourages self-help, attack the state for slowing black progress, and lobby for antidiscriminatory markets. Black Marxists, according to Dawson, might emphasize issues with the capitalist system and argue that there should be a united front of progressive allies within and outside the black community.

Counterpublics also play a key role in Harris-Lacewell's (2004) account of how blacks learn about the diversity of black political beliefs. In her book *Barbershops, Bibles, and BET: Everyday Talk and Black Political Thought*, she expands on the notion of black counterpublics and asserts that these differing ideologies concerning race can even be found in "everyday" black spaces like barbershops, beauty salons, and just about any other place that black social interactions occur. According to Harris-Lacewell, "everyday talk" is how blacks become aware of the views of other group members, and although they may not be convinced by the arguments presented, what they gain through these conversations is a general perspective on the diversity of black political beliefs. Harris-Lacewell also asserts the importance of the black church as a central institution for political thought and discourse. She argues that it is where differing black ideologies intersect through everyday talk. Harris-Lacewell (2004, p. 39) contends that through the church, "African Americans use the cues and messages of their organizational life to inform their political worldviews."

Despite the array of perspectives that Dawson and Harris-Lacewell contend emerge from the black political discourse found in black social and political organizations, there is reason to believe that the political discussions occurring within these black spaces might not be quite as democratic as either Dawson or Harris-Lacewell seems to suggest. Cohen (1999), for example, argues that black America's response to the HIV/AIDS crisis was fraught with constraints created by black institutions that resulted in the black community's non-response to the crisis. Black elites have historically policed the behavior and actions of the community with concern for how the racial group will be perceived by the white gaze. Cohen (1999, p. 51) highlights the significance of black institutions for black life, noting, "Recognizing the inaccessibility of dominant systems, marginal groups often turn inward, redirecting their resources, trust and loyalty toward community-based institutions and relationships that more directly address their needs.

They rely upon indigenous organizations, leaders, networks, and norms to provide some version of the resources and information that are unavailable from dominant institutions and relationships." Cohen goes on to advance a framework she calls secondary marginalization, in which black elites will minimize the concerns of certain segments of the racial group because of the need to portray a unified group position. According to Cohen, black elites have an interest in portraying a unified image of black America and would not want the group to be generalized about based on the actions or behaviors of individuals who may be seen as engaging in a lifestyle that is contrary to mainstream values. This perspective centers on the need of black elites to define blackness in a way that is consistent with the objectives of the ruling elite within the black community. Cohen (1999, p. 71) states, "Leaders, organizations, and institutions in the black communities have consistently attempted to redefine and indigenously construct a new public image or understanding of what blackness would mean. This process of reconstructing or (im)-proving blackness involves not only a reliance on the self-regulation of individual black people, but also includes significant indigenous policing of black group members." We agree with Cohen's characterization that one of the chief roles of black indigenous institutions has been to "police" the behavior of group members and define acceptable forms of blackness. In fact, this is, in essence, what our racialized social constraint argument implies: that Democratic partisanship has been defined into black identity by black institutions and elites and has become an expectation of how one should behave politically as a black person. We also generally agree with Cohen's normative claim that this policing can have the effect of unjustly marginalizing certain group members. Clearly the interest of large segments of the black community in the 1980s, in the 1990s, in the first decade of the twenty-first century, and today have been defined outside the boundaries of blackness simply because their gender, class, or sexual identities are seen as threatening to dominant narratives of what it means to be black in America.

Where we disagree with Cohen, however, is in her implication that the policing or the enforcement of group boundaries is an intrinsically bad practice. In fact, we believe that a group's ability to define its boundaries is essential to its existence and its ability to mobilize. For groups to effectively make demands on government, they must have some means for defining where the group begins and ends, who is part of the group and who is not, and what constitutes the group's interest. Ideally this would involve some open democratic process in which all the voices of potential group members could be heard; however, even this requires a reliable definition of who is allowed to engage in such a debate. Black institutions have historically filled this role, functioning as venues for the definition of black interest and enforcement of group norms. Certainly these institutions are not attended by every black person, nor are they always particularly democratic, but given black Americans' fairly widespread contact with them, they likely represent the best hope of identifying anything approximating a democratic consensus within the black community, beyond perhaps elections.

We contend that black institutions continue to play a vital role in the enforcement of norms of black political behavior. While we have shown in previous chapters that interpersonal social contact can constrain black political behavior, black institutions expand the scope of racialized social constraint by offering a mechanism for large-scale group accountability. In his 1965 book *The Logic of Collective Action*, Mancur Olson points out the role that group size plays in influencing the ability of a group to organize. He persuasively demonstrates how as groups grow in size, so do the organizational costs associated with bringing about collective action. For small groups such as families or small friendship groups, social incentives for norm compliance are more obvious and easily implemented because sanctions (positive and negative) can be more directly administered. However, for larger groups, organization comes at a higher cost as social incentives for norm compliance become more difficult to administer. Individuals in large group settings can have greater anonymity, thus making them less accountable to group mobilization efforts and social sanctions. For black Americans, black institutions have historically helped to offset the organizational costs associated with large-scale collective organization by offering venues in which social sanctions can be more effectively administered. As we saw in Chapter 2, black organizations have a long history as venues for sanctioning defection and preventing free riding. This is made effective by the close-knit nature of membership in black institutions (Payne 2007). Black leaders and activists have frequently leveraged social investments and organizational positions within black institutions to pressure compliance with movement objectives, even in the face of incentives to do otherwise (Chong 1991). Recall the example in Chapter 2, where we described Charles Payne's (2007) detailed account of how civil rights activist Dick Gregory used a speech in a black church to publicly call out the principal of a local black school and local black preachers for their lack of support for the Freedom Rides. Gregory actually instructed parishioners to abandon black churches where the preachers were unsupportive and pray in the streets instead. Indeed, shortly after Gregory's speech, thirty-one local black ministers issued a joint statement expressing their unwavering support for the movement (Payne 2007, p. 198).

The organizational structure of the black church makes it particularly effective as a tool for countering incentives for free riding. Its strong leader structure, along with members' close social connections, makes it an almost ideal tool for implementing racialized social constraint. It was no accident that the first meeting of the Montgomery Improvement Association, the group that organized the Montgomery bus boycott, was held at one of the largest black churches in Montgomery. Martin Luther King Jr. and others used the structure of the black church to convince the black citizens of Montgomery to participate in the boycott. Black institutions continue to play a role in facilitating collective organization through the use of social pressure today. For example, in his 2012 reelection campaign, Barack Obama issued a campaign video in which he urged black Americans to work within black barbershops, HBCUs, and churches to encourage others to vote to support his reelection campaign so that we could "continue the progress we've made" (BarackObama.com 2012). Moreover, black social spaces online represent the new era of black institutions. As discussed in Chapters 1 and 2, Black Twitter has become an effective platform for black voices and the implementation of black social pressure.

In the pages that follow, we will demonstrate the ability of black institutions to use racialized social constraint to bring about conformity to norms of black political behavior. We will show first that most blacks still have significant contact with exclusively or largely black organizations and spaces. We will then show that this contact is related to greater norm compliance and reduced ideological defection, particularly contact with black churches. We will then show how black institutions can prevent self-interested defection from group norms of black political behavior. Here we will use an experimental design that leverages the structure of a black institution, in this case an HBCU, and its members to demonstrate how black institutions use racialized social pressure to constrain the behavior of their members.

Contact with Black Organizations

Although membership in black institutions has seen a decline over the last four decades, most black Americans still have some contact with at least one institution or organization that has a largely black membership.

Returning to data we discussed in Chapter 3 on black Detroit-area residents (the 1996 Detroit Area Study [DAS]), we find that 83 percent of all black Detroit residents and 93 percent of black Detroit churchgoers reported attending a church that is mostly or all black. Similarly, over 47 percent of the black Detroit residents sampled in these data described the most important organization with which they were affiliated as being mostly or all black.

To get a better sense of the scope of black organizational membership, we conducted our own survey of black Americans. Although our sample is not a probability sample, it does contain responses from 717 blacks in at least twelve different states and the District of Columbia. The data were collected in March 2012. In this survey, we probed deeper into black organizational membership, asking blacks about the racial makeup of their churches, high schools, colleges, and friendship networks. The results of this survey are striking. Looking at Table 6.1, we see that 81 percent of black respondents in this sample reported attending a church that is at least 50 percent black, while only 19 percent reported attending a church that is less than 50 percent black. We also find that the majority of the black respondents (61 percent) reported that they attended a high school that is at least 50 percent black. And similar to what we observed in previous chapters, over 80 percent of respondents reported that their friendship networks are at least 50 percent black.

We also asked respondents in this survey about the specific types of black indigenous institutions they had contact with. These results are presented in Table 6.2. We see that 16 percent of blacks with some college or junior college reported that they at some point attended an HBCU. Similarly, roughly 7 percent of blacks with at least some college or junior college reported that they are members of a historically black fraternity or sorority. Our survey respondents also reported varying amounts of exposure to black media: 28 percent read a black newspaper, 43 percent read a black news magazine, 73 percent watched a black television program, and 50 percent listened to a black news program on the radio. We also created a composite measure of media exposure, the Black Media Index, which shows that over 80 percent of the sample engages with at least one black media source.

These findings describe the scope of black Americans' day-to-day experiences and interactions with black institutions. As we have seen, black Americans' interactions with black institutions are both widespread and common. Given that these spaces are largely free of the influence of whites, we see the potential that black institutions have as tools for the political

TABLE 6.1. Black Homogeneity in Institutions and Social Networks

	<50% black (n)	>50% black (n)
Church[†]	18.93% (106)	81.07% (454)
High school	38.77% (278)	61.23% (439)
Friends	18.83% (135)	81.17% (582)

Note: Data from the 2012 African American Qualtrics Quota Survey.
† Percentage based only on respondents who indicated that they attend church.

mobilization of the black community. In the next sections of this chapter, we will evaluate the effects of black institutional contact on black political behavior, specifically the ability of black institutions to enable the use of racialized social constraint as a means of constraining black political behavior.

To pin down exactly how racialized social constraint might work within black institutions to influence black political behavior, we examine differences in conformity to the norms of identifying with the Democratic Party among blacks who are members of a black institution and those who are not. Despite their role as social and spiritual organizations legally bound to abstain from endorsing political candidates, black churches have historically been one of the more effective organizations at influencing black political engagement (Morris 1984). Thus, if our racialized social constraint argument is correct, we should observe more norm-consistent behavior exhibited by blacks who attend black churches than among blacks who are members of churches with mostly non-black congregations. To evaluate this expectation, we return to the data from the 1996 DAS and the 2003 and 2010 Kinder Houston Area Survey. Using these data, we examine how the likelihood of identifying as a Democrat changes as a function of whether the respondent attends a church with a largely black congregation or a church with a largely non-black congregation.

The results of this analysis are presented in Figures 6.1a–b. We can clearly see that attending a church with a black congregation is strongly related to greater Democratic Party identification among blacks. In the Houston-area

TABLE 6.2. Participation in Black Organizations, Institutions, and Media

	Yes (*n*)	No (*n*)
Attended an HBCU[†]	15.64% (86)	84.46% (464)
Member of historically black fraternity or sorority[†]	6.91% (38)	93.09% (512)
Read a black newspaper (online or print)	28.31% (203)	71.69% (514)
Read a black news magazine (*Ebony* or *Jet*)	43.10% (309)	56.90% (408)
Watched a black TV program	72.94% (523)	27.06% (194)
Listened to a black news program on the radio	50.21% (360)	49.79% (357)
Black Media Index (at least one black media source)[‡]	82.71% (593)	17.29% (12)

Note: Data from the 2012 African American Qualtrics Quota Survey.

† Percentage based on respondents who indicated that they have attended some college or higher on the education measure.

‡ The Black Media Index is an additive scale of all black media types in the survey, which are (1) reading a black newspaper, (2) reading a black news magazine, (3) watching a black TV program, and (4) listening to a black news program on the radio.

data, we observe a more than 20-percentage-point increase in the probability of identifying as a Democrat when the respondent attends a black church compared with those blacks who do not. In the Detroit-area data, we see that this gap in the probability of Democratic Party identification increases to over 30 percentage points.[2]

While attending a church with a mostly black congregation appears to be strongly related to adherence to the norm of black Democratic Party identification, we have also argued that racialized social constraint works by curtailing the defection of those individuals who have incentives to defect from the norm of black political behavior. Just as we did in the social networks analysis presented in Chapter 3 and the race-of-interviewer analysis presented in Chapter 4, the results presented in Figure 6.2 demonstrate the effectiveness of attending a black church at constraining the defection of black conservatives from the Democratic Party. The results from this analysis are again consistent with the expectations of our racialized social constraint argument. As we can see, among those blacks who attend churches with

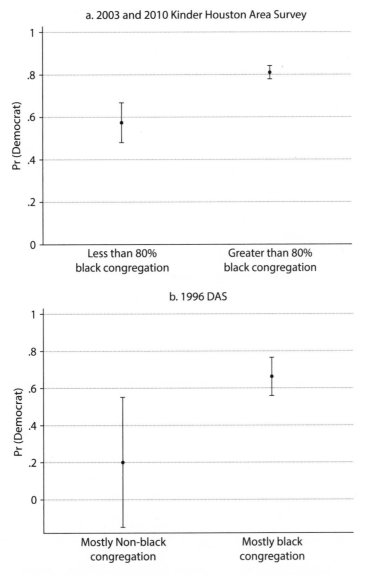

a. 2003 and 2010 Kinder Houston Area Survey

b. 1996 DAS

FIGURE 6.1. Black Democratic Party identification by attending a church with a largely black congregation. *Note:* The DAS does not distinguish party leaners.

largely non-black congregations, a moderate to strong relationship between liberal or conservative ideology and Democratic Party identification exists. In these data, we see a nearly 40-percentage-point decrease in the probability of Democratic Party identification among blacks who do not attend a black church as we move from strong liberals to strong conservatives.

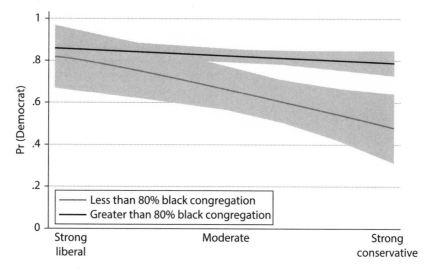

FIGURE 6.2. Black Democratic Party identification by percentage of black associates or friends and ideology, 2010 Kinder Houston Area Survey

Among blacks who do attend mostly black churches, however, we see no identifiable difference between black liberals and conservatives in the probability of Democratic Party identification.

While these results are strongly suggestive of the fact that racialized social constraint can effectively constrain ideological defection through black institutions, we still want to know more about the actual process by which racialized social constraint might interact with black institutional structure to constrain black political behavior. Also, while we are able to observe ideological constraint, we know little about the process by which black institutions might use racialized social constraint to prevent self-interested defection.

Black Institution Experiment

To test our argument about black institutions and racialized social constraint around group norms of black political behavior, we designed an experiment that enables us to observe the trade-offs blacks make between their racial group interest and simple self-interest under different social pressure constraints in the context of a black social institution. In this experiment, our aim was to attain as much clarity as possible about the causal effects of both self-interest and social pressure around norms of group interest, while also maintaining as much ecological validity as possible. Our design attempts to strike a balance between abstraction and reality as we once again leverage the real-world scenario of the 2012 presidential election and appear to provide subjects real opportunities to contribute financially to it. Here, self-interest and social pressure are independently manipulated, enabling unconfounded assessments of the causal connection between each and political behavior. We also observe and describe the traits of blacks willing to set aside their simple self-interest in favor of the group norm, do the same for those who defect, and test how and on whom racialized social pressure constrains this defection.

In this experiment, we leverage the role of a black institution in facilitating racialized social constraint within the black community. We conducted this study on students at a large HBCU located in the southern United States. We implemented the study at an HBCU because it provides an especially clean experimental test of how social pressure within the black community works. By using an HBCU, not only can we be confident of subjects' awareness of the group norms about politics and of likely social sanctions, but we can also leverage the institution's structure as a means of potentially implementing these sanctions. In this case, we take advantage of the school's student newspaper as a known mechanism for the dissemination of information through these black social networks to provide a cue to likely in-group social sanctions for deviation from a black political norm.

Like the experiments in Chapter 5, we use the candidacy of Barack Obama in the 2012 election and an opportunity to donate money to the Obama campaign as the basis for creating a black political norm-conforming action for our subjects. The experiment involved 148 self-identified African American subjects and was conducted approximately two months before the general election, from September 7 to September 20, 2012. Subjects were recruited to participate in the study through classes at the university and were rewarded with extra credit for their participation. Upon agreeing to participate in the study, subjects were asked to read and sign a written consent document. After providing their consent, subjects were then asked to fill out a short pretest questionnaire and were told that they were to participate in a five-minute one-on-one interview about the upcoming presidential election. Subjects were randomly assigned to receive one of three messages during the interview. As in the experiments presented in Chapter 5, all subjects were told that the researchers conducting the study were political scientists from a public university and had been awarded a grant from an organization called the Voter Turnout Project, and that the funds from this grant were to be used to provide young people with an opportunity to contribute to campaigns. Just like experiment 2 (on limits to racialized social pressure) in Chapter 5, subjects were told that the project would provide them with one hundred dollars to donate to the presidential campaigns of Barack Obama and Mitt Romney and that they could allocate the money any way they chose. They could donate it all to one candidate or split it across the candidates, as long as their donations totaled one hundred dollars. In the control condition, this was all subjects were told before the interviewer then directed their attention to a webpage on a nearby laptop where the donation amounts were entered. Once the subject determined how he or she wanted the money donated, the interviewer entered the amount into the website, asked the subject if he or she was sure about the donation, and then submitted the contribution. Again, no money was actually donated to the campaigns, and subjects were debriefed as to this fact upon completion of the study.

This experiment involved two treatment conditions. The second row of Table 6.3 highlights the manipulations of the first treatment condition, which we call the incentive condition. This condition is identical to the incentive condition in experiment 2, presented in Chapter 5. Subjects in this condition were given the same ability to allocate one hundred dollars in campaign contributions, but they were additionally informed that the computer might provide them with an incentive to donate to one of the candidates. Further, subjects were told that in the interest of fairness, the computer would randomly determine for which candidate the incentive would be offered. In reality, the incentive was not randomly assigned—all subjects in the incentive condition were provided an incentive to contribute to the Romney campaign. That is, we wanted to incentivize deviation from the black norm of behavior—contributing to Obama—with a personal monetary gain, but we did not want the subjects to suspect that the monetary incentive was driven by partisan incentives. Subjects in the incentive condition were told that for every ten dollars they donated to the Romney campaign, they would receive a one-dollar personal payout, implying a maximum payout of ten dollars if they allocated the entire one hundred dollars to the Romney campaign. These payouts, if chosen by the subjects, were actually paid in cash within the experiment. In this condition, we expect to induce conflict for black subjects between their individual self-interest in money in their own pockets and their awareness of the expected group behavior of supporting the Obama campaign over the Romney campaign.

In the second treatment condition, the incentive and newspaper condition, highlighted in the bottom row of Table 6.3, we add a manipulation for examining the effect of social pressure in restraining self-interest-incentivized

TABLE 6.3. Description of Experimental Conditions and Hypotheses

Control (n = 48)	• Asked to distribute $100 of project-provided funds
H1: Most subjects donate their funds to Obama	• Money can go to Obama or Romney campaign or split across campaigns

Incentive condition (n = 50)	• Asked to distribute $100 of project-provided funds
H2: Subjects donate significantly less to Obama	• Money can go to Obama or Romney campaign or split across campaigns • **$1 for every $10 donated to Romney**

Incentive and newspaper condition (n = 50)	• Asked to distribute $100 of project-provided funds
H3: Subjects donate significantly more to Obama than in the incentive (only) condition	• Money can go to Obama or Romney campaign or split across campaigns • ***Told contribution and name would appear in school newspaper*** • **$1 for every $10 donated to Romney**

defection from the group norm. This condition is identical to the incentive condition with the exception that we informed subjects—before they were asked to make their donation decisions—that all donations and donor names would be publicized in the university's newspaper. In the context of this HBCU, this manipulation represents quite well the threat of racialized social sanctions. This university has a newspaper (both paper and online) that is well read by the predominantly black student body, meaning that exposure of their choices to their black peers and social networks was likely to be anticipated by the subjects. Thus, the treatment should provide a sense of social pressure to conform to the black norm of expected behavior— contributing to Obama—and reduce defection, as subjects fear the social consequences of being seen as someone who deviates from that norm.

Our expectations for this experiment can also be found in Table 6.2. We will use the control condition, where the subjects were simply asked to allocate the money to the candidates of their choosing, as our baseline contribution condition. We assess the baseline "norm" of black political behavior in the form of campaign contributions. If supporting Obama is in fact a norm of black political behavior, then control subjects should choose to have the majority of the funds donated to support the Obama campaign (H1). In the second condition, we expect to observe the effect of self-interest. We expect that personal monetary incentives (self-interest) for defection from the norm of supporting Obama will decrease contributions to Obama (H2). We believe that in the face of the contribution being publicized in the university's newspaper, the effect of the incentive will be attenuated because social pressure enforces compliance with the group norm (H3).

As with the experiment in Chapter 5, we also examine the possible moderating effects of linked-fate attitudes and ideology, as these are the other predispositions that are often implicated in African Americans' political decision-making calculus. Once again, we do not expect these dispositions to moderate the effects of our treatments. We expect the social pressure from our racialized social constraint treatments to apply broadly, as both those low in black linked fate and black conservatives are aware of and concerned about how they are viewed in the eyes of other blacks.

RESULTS

Figure 6.3 presents the basic results of this experiment: the average amount of money allocated to the Obama campaign across each of the experimental conditions. We see that, consistent with the idea that support for Obama is a normalized form of black political behavior, subjects in the control condition demonstrated a clear preference for supporting the Obama campaign, with a mean donation of ninety dollars. Indeed, in the absence of any incentive to do otherwise, most of the subjects in this condition allocated all of the money provided to them to the Obama campaign. Similarly, only 2 percent of the control condition subjects gave the Obama campaign less than fifty dollars ($n = 1$), and about 75 percent of subjects gave the Obama campaign ninety dollars or more.

Having established a benchmark contribution amount, we now turn to examining the results of our other experimental conditions. In the incentive condition, where subjects were offered the self-interest payout of one dollar for every ten dollars they allocated to the Romney campaign, we expected to observe less adherence to the norm of supporting Obama. Indeed, in the face of an incentive to defect, allocation to the Obama campaign dropped off significantly compared with the control.[3] As displayed in the second column of Figure 6.3, the mean Obama contribution dropped by more than twenty dollars, to sixty-eight dollars. Twenty-two percent of subjects maximized their self-interest and donated the entire one hundred dollars to the Romney campaign. In the face of self-interest incentives to defect, individuals who

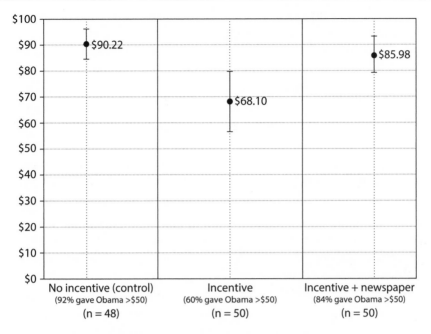

FIGURE 6.3. Obama contribution by experimental condition (95% CIs)

may have ordinarily behaved in a manner consistent with the expected group norm (supporting the Democratic candidate) defected and chose instead to support the Romney campaign.[4]

This result is also interesting considering the findings of experiment 2 presented in Chapter 5. That experiment sought to assess the ability of black social pressure to encourage defection from the group norm of supporting the Obama campaign. In that experiment, blacks were faced with an identical choice to the one presented in this condition—an incentive to contribute to Romney—however, in that experiment, subjects faced pressure from a black confederate to either contribute all the funds to Obama in one condition or, in another condition, contribute all the funds to Romney. In the treatment that sought to encourage defection to Romney, the average contribution amount was about seventy dollars, which is only two dollars more than we see here, suggesting that the degree of defection is no different from that in this incentive-only condition with no social pressure.[5] This further affirms our conclusion that the contribution difference in that experiment reflects a sense that racial monitoring was not occurring, and black social pressure cannot encourage norm-inconsistent behavior.

If social pressure can prevent this defection, we should observe an attenuated effect of the incentive in the form of a smaller difference from the
control condition in Obama contributions in the incentive and newspaper
condition than in the incentive-only condition. Indeed, this is exactly what
we observe. As shown in Figure 6.3, we see that when the incentive was
combined with information that the donations would be published in the
university's newspaper, defection from the group norm was reduced significantly. Mean contributions to the Obama campaign in the incentive and
newspaper condition were eighteen dollars higher than in the simple incentive condition. Contributions in the incentive and newspaper condition are
also statistically indistinguishable from the control ($p < .49$), suggesting that
this social pressure resulted in a return to normalized behavior.

These findings provide strong support for our racialized social constraint
argument and demonstrate how racialized social constraint might work
within black institutions to constrain black political behavior. Social location in these organizations makes those who might deviate from the group
norms easily subject to social sanctions that can be implemented through
structured communication channels within these institutions. What is clear
from these results is that black political solidarity is vulnerable to the influence of self-interest incentives, yet social pressure appears to be an effective
tool for keeping defection from the group norm in check.

BLACK LINKED FATE

We turn now to examining whether black linked fate might also be working
to constrain black Obama contributions. Again, we expect that racialized
social constraint and self-interest will have an independent effect on black
Obama contributions. In other words, we expect that black linked fate will
not condition the effect of our treatment conditions and will not moderate how black Americans make political decisions that involve known
trade-offs between self- and group interests. Figure 6.4 presents predicted
Obama campaign contributions by treatment condition and level of black
linked fate. We can see that while those high in linked fate appear to contribute, on average, a little more to the Obama campaign than those low
in linked fate, across each of the conditions the overall effect of linked
fate appears to be unrelated to the contribution decisions. The correlation
between black linked fate and Obama contributions is 0.15 ($p < .29$) in the
no incentive (control) condition, 0.13 ($p < .31$) in the incentive condition,
and 0.18 ($p < .21$) in the incentive and newspaper condition. Consistent

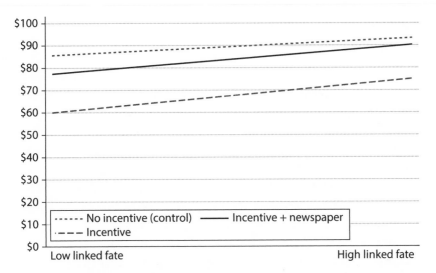

FIGURE 6.4. Obama contribution by condition and black linked fate disposition

with our expectation that linked fate is less effective at constraining black political behavior in the face of self-interest incentives than racialized social pressure, we continue to observe somewhat large, statistically significant decreases in contributions among both high- and low-linked-fate blacks from the control to the incentive condition. In a separate analysis, we found that among high-linked-fate blacks (those who scored above the mean on the black linked fate measure), those in the no incentive control contributed, on average, $92 (95% confidence interval [CI] = $86 to $97), while those in the incentive condition contributed, on average, $71 ($57 to $86). This is a statistically significant ($p < .05$) decrease of $21. Among low-linked-fate blacks (those who scored below the mean on the black linked fate measure), this difference is essentially the same. Those in the no incentive control contributed, on average, $87 ($71 to $100) to the Obama campaign, and those in the incentive condition contributed, on average, $61 ($38 to $83). This is a statistically significant ($p < .05$) decrease of $26. In sum, the psychological ties that bind many blacks to identify with the group are no match for the power of financial incentives. Regardless of one's level of black linked fate, racialized social constraint effectively constrains defection from the norm of black political behavior. This evidence also generally supports our argument that the linked fate paradigm is not especially effective at constraining black political decisions in which blacks must navigate between group and self.

IDEOLOGY

Next, we test the ability of our racialized social pressure treatment to constrain ideological defection from the norm of supporting the Obama campaign. Support for Obama is not just a racialized political choice but also an ideological one. We might thus expect a pattern of racialized social constraint similar to what we have seen throughout this book: that racialized social constraint will most effectively constrain the defection of black conservatives. Figure 6.5 presents the observed amount of Obama campaign contributions by experimental treatment and liberal or conservative ideology. While the results generally suggest that ideology plays very little role in shaping blacks' contribution decisions, it does appear that the incentive condition may encourage greater defection among black conservatives and that the racialized social pressure treatment has the ability to rein in that defection. We see in both the no incentive control and the incentive and newspaper condition that conservatives are no different from liberals in their Obama campaign contributions. While it may seem somewhat counterintuitive that the contributions of black conservatives are no different from those of black liberals in the control condition, it is important to remember that even in the control condition, respondents were interviewed by ascriptively black interviewers in a black institutional context. Thus, given that the interviewers were black and that in previous chapters we have seen that

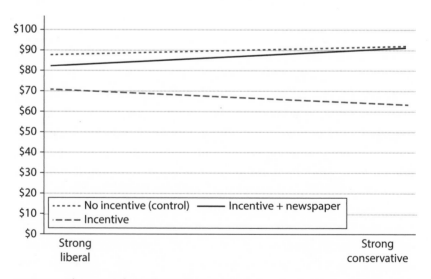

FIGURE 6.5. Obama contribution by condition and ideology

black interviewers are particularly effective at constraining norm defection among black conservatives, this pattern of results should come as no surprise.

The differences between the incentive condition and the incentive and newspaper condition are also consistent with the findings from previous chapters about the effect of racialized social constraint on the political behavior of black conservatives. Indeed, the biggest difference between the incentive condition and the incentive and newspaper condition appears to be among black conservatives. Among self-identified black conservatives, those in the incentive and newspaper condition contributed, on average, $92 (CI $78 to $105) to the Obama campaign and those in the incentive condition contributed, on average, $53 (CI $27 to $79). This is a statistically significant $39 difference in contributions. This result suggests a couple of things. First, in the face of incentives, black conservatives appear to defect from the norms of black political behavior—even in the presence of a black interviewer. Second, these results once again confirm our expectations that black conservatives are very much aware of the social cost of publicly defecting from the norm of black political behavior.

OTHER MODERATORS OF NORM COMPLIANCE

Having examined the principal factors that should moderate racialized social constraint, we now turn to examining other possible individual-level dispositions that might condition the processes of defection and constraint in the face of monetary incentives and racialized social pressure. Our pretest questionnaire included a number of measures that capture not only blacks' attitudes about race and the appropriateness of racialized social sanctioning but also respondents' beliefs about money and the value they place on it. We examine across each of the experimental conditions the relationships among blacks' willingness to contribute to the Obama campaign, their belief in the enforcement of group solidarity, and the value they place on money. We see each of these dispositions as a factor that should condition how blacks respond to our treatments; our expectations for how these dispositions might shape black contribution decisions in the face of monetary incentives and racialized social pressure are more instrumentally based than they are theoretically derived. We expect that blacks who value the idea of "policing" compliance with group norms of political behavior will be internally constrained by this belief and will likely not accept incentives for defection. On the other hand, we believe that individuals who place a high value on money will likely not be moved by racialized social pressure, as they are likely to place a higher premium on money than on social relationships.

ENFORCEMENT OF BLACK GROUP SOLIDARITY

Thus far in this book we have focused only on how contextualized social pressure from other African Americans can constrain black political behavior. We have shown how in a number of different social contexts, racialized social pressure and expectations of black political behavior can constrain a broad range of black partisan political behaviors and beliefs. What we have yet to discuss, however, is how this "belief" in the appropriateness of maintaining unified group behavior through social sanctions might be internalized and what that means for black political behavior. As we stated briefly in Chapter 1, we expect that long-term black political socialization around adherence to group norms of political behavior can result in internalized beliefs in black political solidarity. We thus expect that such beliefs might condition responses to the treatments in much the same way that social monitoring has done: by making subjects less likely to accept the self-interest incentive to deviate from the group norm. We operationalized these solidarity beliefs with a measure of subjects' level of agreement with the appropriateness of referring to blacks who support the causes of white Americans at the expense of causes supported by other blacks with the social sanction terms "sellout" and "Uncle Tom." We believe that this particular measure reflects blacks' acceptance of social pressure to enforce behavior in the group's interest, capturing the solidarity attitude's connection to the social process of norm enforcement. The distribution of responses to this measure in our sample is presented in Figure 6.6. Black subjects in our experiment are largely split in their belief about the appropriateness of such terms. A little over 50 percent believe that the use of such terms is never appropriate given the context, and a little less than 50 percent believe that the use of these terms is at least sometimes appropriate. Thus, about half of our sample has some measure of internalized support for the enforcement of norms of black political behavior. Keep in mind that this is not a belief that the norm exists, just a belief in appropriateness of this manner of enforcement in this particular situation.

Next we test how responses to this measure might condition the average contributions to the Obama campaign in our experimental treatments. The results of this analysis are presented in Figure 6.7, which shows the predicted Obama contribution amount by experimental condition and belief in

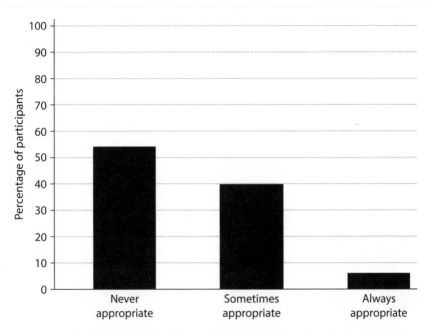

FIGURE 6.6. Distribution of measure of appropriateness of social sanction. *Note:* Participants responded to the following question: Black people have often used the terms "sellout" and/or "Uncle Tom" to refer to those Blacks who support the causes of White Americans at the expense of causes supported by other Black Americans. Do you think the use of these terms ("sellout" and/or "Uncle Tom") is ever appropriate?

the appropriateness of social sanctions. What we see here is that solidarity beliefs do appear to be important to constraining self-over-group behavior. Across the experimental conditions, we observe very little change in Obama contributions among those blacks who see social sanctioning for group defection as appropriate. Even in the face of monetary incentives to defect from the group norm of behavior, blacks who believe in the use of these sanctions continued to contribute to the Obama campaign. Thus, it seems that internalized beliefs in the use of social sanctions for preventing defection, much like social pressure, can be an effective tool for preventing black defection from group norms of political behavior.

Blacks who did not see the use of sanctioning terms as appropriate were less constrained in the face of incentives but, given their awareness of the possible sanctions, exhibited norm-consistent behavior in the social pressure condition. Among this set of black subjects, the predicted Obama contribution dropped from ninety-three dollars in the control condition to fifty-six dollars in the incentive condition. Yet when faced with a relevant

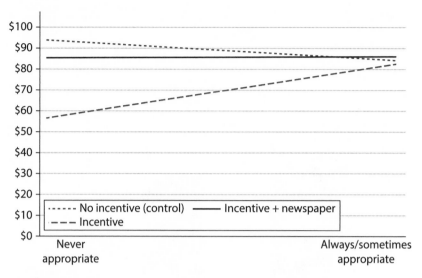

FIGURE 6.7. Obama contribution by condition and belief in the enforcement of "sellout" and "Uncle Tom" sanctions

mechanism for enabling social sanctioning, even those who rejected the use of sanctioning terms conformed. The predicted Obama contribution among individuals in the incentive and newspaper condition was eighty-five dollars, an amount much higher than what they gave when faced *only* with the self-interest incentive, and far closer to and statistically indistinguishable from the amount allocated by their counterparts in the control condition ($p < .35$). It seems that, regardless of what blacks normatively think about this method of enforcing group norms, awareness of the potential for social sanctions, combined with the presence of mechanisms for delivering them, is effective in preventing group defection.

THE IMPORTANCE OF MONEY

Because our individual incentives came in monetary form, we think it prudent to test the moderating effect of the personal value respondents place on money. We expect that more valued self-interests might be more difficult to overcome with social pressure. Because of the relative homogeneity of the economic standing of our college student sample, comparisons of the respondents' actual income are infeasible. We measure instead the extent to which the individual respondent values money with an attitudinal measure. We use a single question that contrasts the value the respondent places on money

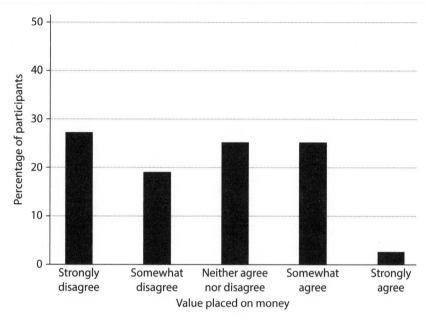

FIGURE 6.8. Distribution of value placed on money. *Note:* Participants responded to the question, Do you agree or disagree with the following statement: It is sometimes okay to abandon friends if they stand in the way of you making money.

with the value he or she places on personal friendships. The measure reads, "Do you agree or disagree with the following statement: It is sometimes okay to abandon friends if they stand in the way of you making money." As we have stated throughout this book, support for the Democratic Party is maintained in large part by blacks' concern for their valued social relationships with other blacks. If, however, an individual is willing to abandon friends if they stand in the way of some individual benefit, then we can likely assume that the individual will be less susceptible to social pressure efforts meant to override self-interest. We expect that respondents who answered this question in the affirmative would be more likely to accept incentives to defect from the group norm and would also be less likely to be affected by social pressure to conform to the group norm of supporting the Democratic Party. The distribution of this variable is presented in Figure 6.8. As we can see, while this variable is slightly skewed toward disagreement with this statement (47%), nearly 30 percent of the sample nonetheless agreed that it is sometimes OK to abandon one's friends if they get in the way of one making money.

Next, we analyze how this measure might condition the effect of the treatments on Obama campaign contributions. Again, we expect that

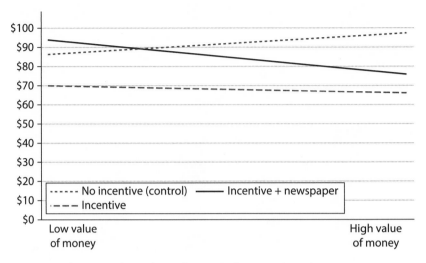

FIGURE 6.9. Obama contribution by condition and value respondents place on money

individuals who place greater value on money will be more likely to accept monetary incentives to defect from the group norm. The results for this analysis, presented in Figure 6.9, show that the only differential produced by an individual's valuation of money is his or her level of immunity from the threat of social sanctions. That is, while both low and high valuers of money defected in the incentive-only condition by giving significantly less than those in the control, only those who place a high value on money continued to defect in the face of the threat of social sanctions provided in the incentive and newspaper condition. In fact, the results are suggestive that individuals exposed to the social pressure treatment who placed a relatively low value on money were almost entirely constrained by the sanction threat; they gave just about the same as those in the control. Yet among those who value money over friends, the social pressure treatment is rendered ineffective, as these individuals appear to be overwhelmed by the draw of the monetary incentive. These results speak to the relative value of the self-interest gain in conditioning the trade-offs made between group and self. It mattered that though the individual incentives we offered were equal, not all subjects valued them equally. The important conclusion here is that groups may increase group-interest behavior in part by working to define possible self-interest incentives as less valuable, making group members more susceptible to the effects of social pressure to choose group interests over individual gains.

Conclusion

In this chapter, we looked at the role of black institutions in developing racial group norms and enforcing norm compliance. Black institutions have served as the backbone of black life and also as a resource for information and political organizing. The racial homophily present in black institutions has cultivated a system of accountability in which group members are often beholden to the expectations of the racial group. Although group members may have diverse opinions on a variety of issues, there is an unequivocal understanding that one must adhere to group norms or potentially risk one's social ties with in-group members. In the realm of politics, black institutions, and black churches in particular, have defined much of the political battleground and the strategy for achieving the group's goals of equal rights, access, and opportunity.

Black churches provide resources for achieving these goals, using their facilities as sites for organizing, platforms for the political leadership of institutional actors, and forums for informing blacks about political issues that are pertinent to the group. The campaigns of numerous Democratic candidates have been supported and strengthened by the black church. The Civil Rights Movement was fundamentally shaped by the efforts of the black church. From the Montgomery bus boycott to the March on Washington, the church has been a dominant force for black politics. The institution's regular contact with blacks often makes it the front line for political efforts on behalf of the group.

The emergence of the black counterpublic as a space for predominantly black political discourse is the direct consequence of racial isolation from the mainstream political domain. Blacks, wanting to discuss the issues of the day, had to convene in spaces that were all black, but in these "safe spaces" diverse opinions and ideologies were allowed to flourish (see Spence 2011). These spaces for political discourse have even expanded beyond formal institutions and can be found in more casual locations like the barbershop or beauty salon and online (e.g., Black Twitter). With the proliferation of diverging views (black Marxist, womanist, black nationalism, etc.), how do blacks maintain such strong political cohesion when it comes to Democratic partisan support?

Black institutions are ground zero for an accountability system for collective behavior. They are the information source for what is top priority for the black agenda, and they are able to hold individuals responsible for their actions as a result of the strong social ties that are also racially homogeneous.

Racialized social pressure is an effective mechanism for maintaining group cohesion. Group members with opinions that may differ from the norm understand that they must perform the expected behavior or risk social sanctions. Individuals that opt not to perform the expected behavior find themselves isolated or even marginalized within the group for their lack of compliance.

Key to the influence of indigenous institutions on black political behavior is the racial homogeneity within them. The results presented here demonstrate the prominence of indigenous institutions in black communities. These findings provide strong support for our racialized social constraint argument and demonstrate how that constraint might work within black institutions to constrain black political behavior. Social location in these organizations makes those who might deviate from the group norms easily subject to social sanctions that can be implemented through structured communication channels within these institutions. What is clear from these results is that black political solidarity is vulnerable to the influence of self-interest incentives, yet social pressure appears to be an effective tool for keeping defection from the group norm in check. Chapter 7 will sum our concluding thoughts about the contributions of this book and the implications for understanding black politics as we enter into a new period of American politics—the post-Obama era.

Conclusion

Across the previous chapters, we have offered an explanation for how it is that black Americans as a group have been able to maintain a unified voice in partisan electoral politics for over fifty years. We have shown that racialized social constraint, or the social process by which compliance with norms of black political behavior gets enforced within the black community, is indeed an effective means by which black Americans have been able to encourage prosocial political behavior among group members. Realizing that their ability to effectively make demands on government is conditional on their capacity to engage in unified political action, black Americans have actively sought ways of maintaining group unity in the face of individual incentives to betray group interest or free ride on the efforts of others. Our evidence supports the argument that racialized social constraint works to maintain black collective action in partisan politics through reputational rewards for compliance with expected group behavior and sanctions for defection from this behavior. More specifically, we demonstrated how this process undergirds contemporary black support for the Democratic Party, showing how it has become a normalized form of black political behavior and how an ongoing process of enforcement through black social relations maintains high levels of Democratic Party support within the black community even as that community increasingly diversifies.

In this chapter we explore the broad political implications of our racialized social constraint framework and consider what the future might hold for black unity in partisan politics. We begin by discussing what some may see as a normatively problematic feature of racialized social constraint: its seemingly coercive nature. While we take this concern seriously, we also take seriously counterweights against it, including the ways in which racialized social constraint may not be as repressive of individual freedom as some critics argue and how little progress toward racial equality we might expect without it. We then move on to the explanatory potential of our argument for the politics of other racial groupings in America. While there are certainly reasons to believe that racialized social constraint would be ideal for explaining the political behavior of similarly situated racial, ethnic, or gender minority groups in the United States, we examine how our social constraint explanation might best apply to the politics of Southern white Americans—wherein an ongoing effort to repress black Americans seems to have constructed a version of white identity politics that uses well-defined social expectations of "whiteness" to ensure partisan political solidarity. We discuss the potential scope of partisan consequences of "white" racialized social constraint, particularly as Southern political culture becomes more mainstream and spreads outside the South.

We close with a contemplation of the implications that our social constraint argument might have for the future of black politics. We pay particular attention to what the decline in brick-and-mortar black social and political institutions might mean for the maintenance of political unity as a tool for racial liberation and black political power. Does the decline of these institutions mean an end to black politics as we know it? We conclude by charting a course for future research to further assess the utility and the boundaries of our racialized social constraint framework.

Coracial Policing and Norm Compliance

Although we have demonstrated that racialized social constraint helps black Americans solve a collective action problem for the sake of gaining political power otherwise outside their reach, for some the ends of black political unity may not justify the means. As we noted briefly in the introductory chapter, critics of this model may see the kind of social constraint we outline in this book as coercive or illiberal. After all, we have demonstrated that group expectations of political behavior and threats of social sanctions can prevent black Americans from acting on what they would clearly see as either their ideological or economic self-interest. Moreover, the notion of a politics based on a group's best interest raises questions about the in-group dynamics that define the group norms, including the normatively concerning one of whether in-group power dynamics necessarily lead to strict priority of "group interests" only as defined by the most privileged members of the group. Both of these concerns merit nuanced consideration.

In a fundamental sense, our racialized social constraint framework broadens the notion of self-interest to include the social self. That is, we conceive of the in-group as providing social benefits that fulfill real human needs, *including* those of belonging, friendship, and a socially derived sense of self-concept. Individuals value the relationships they have that meet these needs. Within our framework, then, individuals are weighing the trade-offs between their own self-interests in meeting those needs and their other self-interests. The choice between paying the social cost of defecting from group norms of political behavior and maximizing self-interest on another dimension is in a real sense just that: a choice between one's own conflicting self-interests. In this way, the racialized social constraint framework is a truly "rational" explanation of black political decision making. For some black Americans, ideological or material self-interests are more highly valued than their racial in-group social connections. These individuals may choose to identify with and support Republican or independent candidates—and indeed we have documented that they do.

When contemplating the notion of the racialized social constraint model as coercive, it also seems important to be clear about the meaning of that term. Although our historical review of previous eras of black politics revealed that violence or threats thereof have in some moments been used to incentivize group-interest compliance—notably in eras in which violence marked many parts of the American political system—we have no evidence that such tactics are the foundation of modern black in-group sanctioning. Indeed, our evidence indicates that the social pressure mechanisms around group-interest norms in modern black politics are fairly mild ones: having one's willingness to support others questioned or simply knowing that in-group members approve of the choices one is making is quite far from physical violence. Again, the racialized social constraint model functions in connection with the value an individual assigns to social relations. That social needs can only be fulfilled in a relational way does mean that they come with relational obligations—having others help to fulfill one's needs does leave one open to claims for reciprocation. Certainly, it is important to question the boundaries of what we can and should expect from each other within human relationships. That there are any expectations at all, however, does not itself define a moral dilemma of "coercion."

Those concerned about the boundaries of social expectations ought to take seriously the potential for harm to marginalized subpopulations within the black community. We consider, for example, the argument made by Cathy Cohen (1999) that concern about the effect of the white gaze on black behavior has resulted in a *secondary marginalization* of segments of the black community that do not align with notions of respectability promoted by black elites. Black elites, Cohen argues, have both the incentive and the capacity to police the behavior of other blacks, demanding that they live lifestyles that are consistent with "mainstream" values and defining their specific concerns in light of the black political agenda. In some ways our racialized social constraint explanation is consistent with Cohen's secondary marginalization thesis. The use of threats of social sanctions to increase the likelihood of compliance with an expected group behavior can be seen as a form of coracial policing. But Cohen's concern is rightly not simply about the practice of coracial policing but fundamentally about policing to what and whose ends. We think this implies two fundamental considerations for normatively evaluating the practice of racialized social constraint: (1) what norms it centers and (2) who does and does not have influence over what those norms are.

What norms define the doing of black politics was a question we took up empirically in Chapter 2. Our lens of a broad historical overview was a good one for its purpose: identifying central, definitional norms of black political behavior that characterized eras of politics. Through that lens, the black group-interest norms looked normatively unproblematic. In each era, from that of slavery to the modern one, we identified norms that were in fundamental agreement with a black politics aimed toward the broad group interest in racial liberation—ones whose aim was to help the group toward freedom from enslavement, Jim Crow, and widespread racial segregation. Our theoretical framework helps explain why it is these sorts of broad group-interest goals that define central norms of expected political behavior: racialized social constraint is more effective when it rests on norms that are both broadly descriptive and injunctive—when the political behavior can be something most in the group can and should do. That a group interest is a broadly shared one across individuals within that group and that the norms most effectively "policed" via racialized social constraint are ones linked to those broad interests are implications that make the racialized social constraint model one productive for racial liberation and greater racial equality in the American system.

And yet Cohen is right to raise concern that this model of black politics is not ideally suited to serve all liberation-seeking interests within the black community. The concerns of intersectionality theorists generally loom large here. If black political power comes in unity, and unity is best achieved around broadly shared interests and through political behaviors that can be commonly expected across the group, where is the political hope for the specific needs of those members of the black community who are marginalized by systemic oppression beyond race? If black political tools are not built for their needs, can they still serve them?

These important questions, we think, imply a more general one about whether the interests of relatively disadvantaged black Americans are fundamentally closed off from the black agenda via this model of doing black politics or whether there are avenues to their inclusion. We do think there are ways that racialized social constraint can actually be a tool for the empowerment of marginalized subpopulations of black Americans. There are at least questions worth asking about ways for the relatively disadvantaged to exercise some constraint over the relatively privileged within the racial group.

Let us consider more concretely a specific group, that which is sometimes termed "the black underclass" (Drake and Cayton 1945; Wilson 1984)—the most economically disadvantaged. Intersectional race scholars including Cohen have argued that what motivates much of respectability politics among elite black Americans is a need to control the narrative of blackness in the minds of white Americans. Of central concern to black elites, these scholars argue, is the perception that white Americans see most black Americans as poor, as well as the consequences of that narrative for how they are seen. Indeed, as Robert Entman and Andrew Rojecki (2000, p. 8) find, "The average White mistakenly believes that Blacks constitute one-third of the American population, a majority of the poor, and the bulk of welfare rolls." In an effort to control this narrative, black elites seek to rein in the behavior of black Americans of the lower socioeconomic classes by imposing strict moral standards on their behavior. A good example of this would be the debate about young black men wearing sagging pants. In an interview with NPR's blogger Gene Denby (2014), Mary Sue Rich, a black city council member from Ocala, Florida, who proposed a ban on the fashion statement, lamented, "I'm just tired of looking at young men's underwear, it's just disrespectful. . . . I would wager nine out of ten of them don't have jobs." These respectability politics, then, center on policing in-group behaviors linked with "undesirable," "poor" representations of black Americans—and raise the flag of concern that the needs and interests specific to the least privileged, the black underclass, might get swept off the political agenda.

While we do not argue that the in-group policing of respectability politics is unproblematic, we do think it suggests a crosscutting implication: that the black underclass in America has some ownership over the definition of blackness, within the minds of both white Americans and the black elite, which may give it some agency when viewed through our racialized social constraint model. To the extent that black elites are invested in their identities as black Americans, the seeming unquestionable blackness of the black underclass might actually give the latter the capacity to use racialized social constraint to constrain the behavior of black elites. Black elites have their own interest in reshaping the definition of blackness to include behaviors that might reflect their lifestyles, personal tastes, or economic and ideological interests. These attempts to expand the range of acceptable black behaviors, importantly, might include attempts to justify behaviors that enable them, personally, to be more integrated into white society: living in neighborhoods with few or no other black residents, dating or marrying outside the race, having exclusively white associates—or supporting the Republican Party. The tools of social pressure, then, become important to reining in or at least defining as "not black" the behaviors of black elites understood as being at odds with black collective empowerment. From a position well insulated from accusations of "acting white," members of the black underclass may have unique leverage to define as "beyond blackness" at least some behaviors that would suit black elites or upper classes but be at odds with black collective empowerment. Thus, a form of racialized social constraint may be one of the ties that bind black elites to the black underclass in collective politics. It is worth investigating further, we think, whether such leverage exists—and if it does, whether and how it might be used to shape black politics in ways that better serve secondarily marginalized group members' interests.[1]

Racialized Social Constraint beyond Black Americans

While our racialized social constraint model was developed to explain the partisan political behavior of black Americans, there are reasons to ask whether and how this framework might apply to other social groupings. None of the basic social or psychological mechanisms underpinning the model are particularly unique to African Americans. At first glance, other racial minority groups, such as Latino and Asian Americans, might seem to have social group characteristics that could make racialized social constraint a useful model of their in-group politics, suggesting the potential for group interest to define their partisan political choices. Each group is marked by at least some spatial isolation, and within each group we find unique social institutions, some built around a shared cultural heritage.

One significant challenge to group-based politics through a racialized social constraint model among Asian or Latino Americans, however, might be their larger recent immigrant populations. Immigration patterns can add levels of socioeconomic and cultural diversity that could make the definition and maintenance of norms of political behavior within these groups difficult. Perhaps more important to consider, however, is the fact that Latino and Asian immigrants come from nations structured by different racial contexts, and it can take time for recent immigrants to fully appreciate where they fit in the American racial order. Indeed, political scientist Candis Watts Smith (2014) has shown that even for black immigrants, different understandings of race brought with them from their countries of origin can impede political and racial socialization. The timeline for such integration, Smith shows, may be as long as a generation or two. Without a clear appreciation of where they fit in the American racial order, immigrants may be less likely to see why they should be accountable to racial in-group members and their expectations of political behavior. When immigrants are faced with pressure to conform to racial in-group expectations of political behavior, crosscutting national or ethnic identities may be more salient, particularly if these identities more closely fit immigrants' ideological or self-interests. Localized subpopulations, however, may be marked by less heterogeneity and stronger—local—social ties. Application of our framework, then, may be more likely to be useful in explanations of ethno-racial group behavior in local politics.

Another potential application of the racialized social constraint framework may be to explain the political behavior of white ethno-political subgroups in America. White subpopulations such as Mormons, Jewish Americans, and Southern whites all have strong culturally defined social institutions and well-defined norms of partisan political behavior that could enable racialized social constraint. The largest of these groups, Southern whites, presents a particularly interesting case on which the racialized social constraint model could be tested. White Southerners have long had their own segregated institutions that imposed political loyalty—perhaps in the name of fending off Northern aggression but also, foundationally, to preserve a racial order of white supremacy (Acharya, Blackwell, and Sen 2018). It is in these social spaces—white social clubs, neighborhoods, and schools—that white Southerners ensured political and racial loyalty within the white community by defining norms of political behavior and sanctioning the defection of group members. Terms such as "scalawags" and "race traitors" describe those within the Southern white community who aligned themselves with the interest of African Americans. Sanctions for in-group defection included social shunning and isolation but also violence and even death (Walton 1975). The Southern Poverty Law Center, for example, documented at least eight cases in which white civil rights activists were murdered by white Southerners while campaigning for black rights in the 1950s and 1960s (Southern Poverty Law Center n.d.).

Like black Americans, Southern whites have use racialized social constraint to gain political power within partisan politics. The history of Southern whites is, for the most part, that of party loyalty, from the unflinching loyalty of "yellow dog Democrats" in the late 1800s, to the "Solid South" Democratic politics of the early to mid-twentieth century, to the Republican revolution of the 1990s and the apparent embrace of Trumpism today. Southern whites, like blacks, appear to have intertwined their culture and politics in a way that ensures group loyalty in partisan politics. As the Republican Party's most loyal supporters, Southern whites have so shaped the identity of the Republican Party that it has now become synonymous with a style of politics, as well as cultural appeals, that are foundational to the South (Maxwell and Shields 2019).

The Republican Party's Southern Strategy of appealing to white identity through the use of white cultural tropes and ethnocentrism is paying dividends today.[2] Not only has the "Solid South" reemerged as the base of Republican Party support—white Southerners vote for Republican presidential candidates at about the same rate that blacks vote for Democratic candidates—but this identity politics strategy is gaining traction outside the South. As Southern whites effectively laid claim to many of the last remaining vestiges of exclusively white rural culture, such as NASCAR, country music, and white evangelical Christian beliefs, the Republican Party's ability to associate itself with a politics of ethnocentrism has expanded the party's base particularly among rural white Americans in the Midwest and western states (Jardina 2019). The expansion of a Southern white identity politics outside the South presents a new challenge to the resolution of racial conflict in America, not because the Republicans have found new voters but because if whites' level of racialized social constraint both within and outside the South reaches anything approximating that of blacks, greater polarization and heightened racial conflict in America will take hold more broadly.

The Future of Racialized Social Constraint for Black Americans

As we have shown throughout this book, black Americans continue to reside in spaces, attend schools, and worship in churches that are predominantly black. Although the experiences of most black Americans today are defined by this segregation, that does not mean this will always be true. By many measures, the isolation of black Americans has, in fact, declined in the post–civil rights era, albeit very slowly. As black Americans break through glass ceilings and economic prosperity enables them to seek opportunities outside coracial enclaves, for some, racial integration has become a reality. For example, the rates of interracial marriage within the black community are the highest they have ever been (Davenport 2018). Access to predominantly white institutions at the collegiate level is increasing (M. Anderson 2017). Traditional black political organizations such as the NAACP (Dickerson 2007) and National Urban League (Fears 2008) have seen a steady decline over the last fifty years. What does all this mean for racialized social constraint and consequently black Americans' ability to politically mobilize as a unified bloc?

We believe that increased contact with non-blacks and a decline in attendance at black institutions, in favor of more integrated spaces, would threaten the stability of black Democratic partisan loyalty. The result, we believe, would be a slow but steady diversification of black partisanship because leveraging social sanctions for racial group norm compliance would become much more difficult in integrated spaces. Blacks would no longer have to rely on their coracial social ties for resources and opportunities. Non-black relationships could offer access and benefits that would make the social cost of norm defection a moot point. It would also become difficult to socialize blacks to the group norm and the consequences of defection without racial homophily in everyday life. Scholars have written on the declining influence of black institutions and organizations in politics (Dawson 2001, 2011), but another consideration should be what the loss of these indigenous institutions will do to the long-term maintenance of black Democratic Party loyalty.

There may, however, be some hope for the maintenance of a unified black politics. The creation of black social spaces online may offer an effective means by which black Americans can exercise racialized social constraint. We have discussed the emergence of digital social spaces such as Black Twitter and Facebook, as well as the possibility that these may replicate the sort of accountability mechanisms that exist within brick-and-mortar black institutions. We have seen how the sanctioning of black celebrities through Black Twitter can effectively constrain their partisan political behavior, and one can only imagine how the close familial ties of Facebook friends limit the expression of party politics among black Facebook users. While on one hand, we can certainly see how online social networks would be important, especially for norm definition and enforcement, on the other hand, online social communities can also open the door for party polarization within the black community. Online networks can offer black conservatives a means of expanding their social networks in ways that were significantly more difficult before. Digital social media greatly increases individuals' social connections, allowing them access to people of all different viewpoints. For black conservatives, this essentially allows them to sort themselves by political beliefs, giving them access to more racially and politically diverse individuals who would be more supportive of them identifying as something other than Democrats. Will these types of social connections be able to override familial and kinship ties? That remains to be seen; however, the role that social media plays in imposing black political accountability is certainly an important area of future study.

Racialized Social Constraint and Private Ballot Voting

An important question that we have yet to fully engage has been the role that racialized social constraint plays in the voting booth. Racialized social constraint is a social accountability process, which implies that in order to hold individuals accountable to group norms, their behavior must be observable by others. Indeed, although turnout can be observed, the actions of individuals within the voting booth cannot be. So how would racialized social constraint constrain black voting decisions?

Although vote choice is unobservable, this does not necessarily mean that racialized social constraint is not playing a role in constraining the vote decisions of black Americans. Network effects can take hold long before an individual reaches the voting booth. Many of the events that lead up to the act of voting are socially structured, such as norm definition and norm enforcement of public political expressions. The constant sanctioning of defection and rewarding of norm-consistent political behaviors can lead to the internalization of norm-consistent behavioral practices, which voters can bring with them to the voting booth.

Additionally, while voting-booth behavior may not be directly observable, the anticipation of rewards for compliance and the threat of sanctioning can still constrain vote choice. For example, if a black conservative with a largely black social network were to consider voting for Donald Trump or some other Republican candidate, he would be doing so knowing that his friends and family would not likely approve. While he may understand that they cannot possibly know how he voted, he may anticipate that they might ask. In which case, he is faced with the choice of (1) telling the truth, in which case he would almost certainly incur social sanctions, or (2) lying to his friends and family, a behavior that for many people creates its own psychological distress (Kenny 1992; Mutz 2006). Given this and the possible social rewards of conformity, supporting the Democratic candidate is almost certainly the least costly option.

NOTES

Introduction

1. No such trend exists for white Democrats. White Democrats were never particularly supportive of any of these initiatives; their support has remained flat over time.

Chapter 1

Portions of this chapter are reprinted from Ismail K. White, Chryl N. Laird, and Troy D. Allen. (2014). Selling Out? The Politics of Navigating Conflicts between Racial Group Interest and Self-Interest. *American Political Science Review*, *108*(4), 783–800.

1. According to the National Urban League's 2016 State of Black America report, the black/white gap in home ownership grew six percentage points from 1976 to 2016 (National Urban League 2016).

2. Gurin, Hatchett, and Jackson (1989) find that only 33 percent of blacks believe that some or a lot of what happens to blacks as a group has something to do with what happens in their own lives.

3. Certainly, blacks also faced social pressure to abstain from participation in movement activities. Given the dangerous nature of political action during the Civil Rights Movement, particularly among those in the Southern United States, family members and loved ones commonly discouraged participation (Payne 2007).

4. That is, at least at times, movement participants were well aware that their participation came with real risk of imprisonment, police or mob brutality, and even death.

5. Chong, however, never actually directly acknowledges the use of the phrases "Uncle Tom" and "sellout."

6. These phrases are also at times used to describe those blacks who might fail to support the causes of black Americans because they perceive some personal benefit from abstaining.

7. However, deviations to the right of the group norm are much more likely to incur criticism than deviations to the left (see Carter 1991).

8. These are Protestant churches of historically black denominations.

9. Much of this is probably due to the denominator—blacks who go to college—increasing rather than the numerator (HBCU attendance) decreasing.

10. This is also referred to as "identity theory" but should not be confused with "social identity theory."

11. This is also not to say that social pressure is the only thing that influences black political behavior. The point here is that social pressure and reputational cost are often overlooked as factors contributing to black political behavior.

12. Feeling thermometer measures in the ANES range from 0 to 97. For consistency within the time series, values from 98 to 100 were recoded to 97. We recoded scores of 0 to 2 to 3 to recode the scale from −47 to 47.

Chapter 2

1. Slave codes also sought to reduce the incentives for slave revolts by regulating the treatment of slaves. Despite giving great leeway to slave owners in how they treated their slaves, such codes also sought to regulate the harsh treatment of slaves in the United States. These restrictions were not necessarily meant to ensure the humane treatment of slaves as much as they were tools for discouraging insurrection, as it was thought that if slaves were treated too harshly they would see no other choice but to revolt. The "humane" treatment of slaves, along with the ever-present idea that their situation could be worse, also presented an obstacle to the collective organization of slaves since threats of death for revolting or escaping loomed larger than the status quo.

2. The black Democratic vote was believed to be decisive in both the 1882 and 1886 gubernatorial elections in Louisiana. Democrat Murphy J. Foster, who campaigned on a platform of "white supremacy," was believed to have received some of his strongest support from parishes with the largest percentage of black voters (see *United States v. State of Louisiana* 1963).

3. Differences are statistically significant ($p = .000$) for all years.

4. "Dragging" or "to be dragged" is a slang term used to describe a person being embarrassed by others in a digital forum. Urban Dictionary describes it as "being disrespected or humiliated on an internet forum" (format916 2011).

5. A trending topic is a topic that is listed among the most popular topics people are tweeting about on Twitter (K. Lee et al. 2011).

6. Retweets and likes are used by Twitter users to signal their endorsement of or support for a particular tweet. At times a retweet could be an attempt to draw attention to a tweet, but in most cases people retweet to show their approval unless otherwise noted.

7. Although some scholars have found that descriptive norms can constrain political behavior on their own (Nickerson and White 2010), we should point out that black partisan political behavior is characterized by overlapping descriptive and injunctive norms related to black Democratic Party support. In other words, not only do nearly all black Americans support the Democratic Party, but many black Americans see Democratic Party support as an expected group behavior.

8. Data are Gallup (2008–2010) opinion poll data.

9. Research examining the effects of descriptive norms of black political behavior has found only small or conditional effects (Nickerson and White 2010). However, this research has focused only on this condition of normative behavior. Our interest here lies specifically in the trade-offs blacks make between norm compliance and self- or ideological interest; thus, we think that normative expectations and social sanctions are both essential to the ability of norms to offset self-interest incentives.

10. Descriptive norms can legitimate normative expectations. If, for example, evidence existed that most black voters regularly *did not* support Democratic candidates, this would weaken any claims that Democratic Party support is a behavior specific to the group and would undermine group member expectations of Democratic support.

Chapter 3

1. According to the 2010 U.S. Census, Houston and Detroit have the fourth- and sixth-largest populations of African Americans, respectively, and Detroit has the nation's highest percentage of black residents (82%) among large major cities.

2. Note that these places, Detroit and Houston, have much larger proportions of blacks than the U.S. population, yet segregation persists.

3. Because of the categorical nature of the social networks measure (all, most, some, or none) in the 2015 Pew Research Center survey of multiracial Americans, we only examine the difference between the proportions of black and white friends.

4. Fourteen percent of blacks reported that less than 50 percent of their associates were black.

5. Neither the 2015 Pew multiracial survey nor the 2006 Social Capital Community Survey included a measure of candidate choice or support.

Chapter 4

1. We use only face-to-face interviews because they more accurately capture meaningful social interactions.

2. The ANES began recording the race of the interviewer in 1988. The analysis of the cumulative ANES includes all years that the ANES recorded interviewer race (black or white) for face-to-face interviews. These years are 1988, 1992, 1996, 2008, and 2012. For many of the midterm elections, the ANES conducted only telephone interviews, making them unsuitable for analysis for this purpose. The 2000 ANES was also conducted via telephone. We did not use the 2004 ANES since interviewer race was only recorded as white or non-white. To avoid contamination effects, all analysis relies only on preelection interviews.

3. Others have analyzed race-of-interviewer effects using earlier years of the ANES, but this information is not included in the current ANES cumulative data file.

4. Given that all of these studies are done by the same organization, there certainly could be something related to how all these studies are conducted that could confound our results. This is why we also employ multiple adjustment procedures.

5. The 2012 and 2016 ANES did not include a sufficient number of Asian Americans to replicate this analysis.

6. We limit our analysis to the 1988, 1992, 1996, 2008, and 2012 ANES. We are aware that race-of-interviewer information was collected for earlier years, but it is not included in the ANES cumulative file. See Anderson, Silver, and Abramson (1988) for information on other years.

7. ANES only.

8. As all questions are asked during the survey process, we do not adjust for any measures that would likely be influenced by the treatments. We adjust on age, sex, region, and year of survey because we see these as the variables least likely to be influenced by the treatment; any differences across black and non-black interviewers are likely the result of preexisting differences that could potentially contaminate our treatment effect.

9. The advantages of using Pew and Gallup data rather than pooling the few academic phone surveys of African Americans are (1) the Pew surveys give us relative consistency in sample design and data collection procedure, (2) both Pew and Gallup data are clustered around the same time period as our face-to-face surveys, while most of the well-known academic phone surveys of blacks were done in the 1980s and 1990s, (3) we can have much more statistical power using Pew and Gallup data.

10. The 2012 ANES has a more nuanced measure of race than that included in the cumulative file. Here we include all individuals who identify as black, while the ANES cumulative file only includes non-Hispanic blacks.

11. Because there is not a well-understood norm in the black community with regard to ideology, we do not expect it to vary as a function of the interviewer's race. In the 2012 ANES the correlation between race of interviewer and ideology is 0.02 ($p = .53$), in the GSS it is 0.00 ($p = .88$), and in the cumulative ANES it is 0.07 ($p = .00$).

12. The lack of a statistically significant interaction result in the Democratic Party identification models for the 2012 ANES may be the result of a lack of statistical power, particularly at the tails of conservative ideology. While we would ideally like a larger sample, our ability to find statistically significant interaction effects in the cumulative ANES and the GSS, as well as in all of the seven-point party identification scale models, makes us confident that black interviewers are in fact altering the effect of ideology on black party identification.

13. Here black linked fate may play a role in distinguishing black opinions. There does appear to be a slight conditional effect of race of interviewer (black interviewer vs. online) on how black linked fate relates to the candidate difference measure. We observe that while low-linked-fate blacks are somewhat similar in their evaluations of candidate difference in aid to blacks, there was significant divergence among high-linked-fate blacks.

14. The results included here are only for face-to-face interviews.

Chapter 5

1. Note that for this study we use the postelection waves rather the preelection waves we used in previous chapters.

2. The 1996 survey only had a small number of black interviewers.

3. The confederates self-identified as white or black, and their physical appearances (including skin tone) were such that they were unlikely to be misidentified by the subjects.

4. No money was actually donated to the campaigns, and subjects were debriefed accordingly following their participation.

5. We would have the same moderating expectations for the response to the black confederate treatment as for the two treatments from experiment 1, but our smaller case base does not enable us to test those here.

6. We focus on money kept versus money given to Obama because only two subjects in the experiment made any contribution to Romney.

7. Using analysis of variance, differences from the control and white confederate conditions are both significant ($p < .01$). Inferences from an independent sample Fisher-Pitman randomization test are indistinguishable.

8. We did not design this experiment with the intent of testing conditional effects.

9. Ideology is measured with the three-point scale of liberal, moderate, and conservative.

10. Black linked fate is measured with the traditional four-point scale of none, not very much at all, some, and a lot.

11. One might question whether the presence of a black confederate simply increases the salience of racial considerations (primes race) in the minds of black subjects, rather than working by a mechanism of racialized social pressure. A significant reason to doubt the racial priming explanation is the baseline salience of race with respect to Obama. Given that Obama was the first black president, it is unlikely that blacks would ever not think of him in racial terms. Indeed, recent research has shown that Obama's popularity among blacks appears directly related to their sense of racial group pride and solidarity (Abrajano and Burnett 2012). If blacks already have a racialized view of Obama, it is not likely that any treatment could further racialize their judgments. We also tested this question within these data and found no empirical evidence to support the priming explanation.

Chapter 6

1. Souls to the Polls is a movement in which churches, many of them African American, will transport congregants to the polling stations after Sunday church services in states with early voting (American Civil Liberties Union 2012).

2. There are only ninety-three black respondents in the 1996 DAS data. Also, the lower overall levels of Democratic Party identification in the DAS can be attributed to the fact that the DAS does not distinguish party leaners.

3. We also implemented nonparametric randomization inference tests (see Keele, McConnaughy, and White 2012). The inferences derived from those tests are indistinguishable from those produced using analysis of variance.

4. Despite the considerable defection in the presence of an incentive, 60 percent of respondents still gave more than fifty dollars to the Obama campaign in this condition. Although we would caution against making comparisons across experiments, this may reflect a race-of-interviewer effect similar to what we observed in the black confederate condition in experiment 1 presented in Chapter 5. The black interviewer is consistent across all conditions here, so its impact is controlled.

5. We acknowledge concerns about comparing results of two different experiments run on separate populations at different times. These comparisons are largely meant to put the results of experiment 2 in Chapter 5 in context and to illustrate that if we were in fact able to encourage defection from the norm of black behavior through the use of racialized social pressure, we would expect a much larger decrease in blacks' willingness to contribute to Obama.

Conclusion

1. Even the accumulation of individual wealth can be seen as outside the bounds of acceptable black behavior, given that it places one closer to white Americans than to the black urban underclass.

2. In a telling anecdote of the Southern Strategy, Ronald Reagan launched his 1980 campaign with a states' rights speech at the Neshoba County Fair in Mississippi, just seven miles from the location of the 1964 Freedom Summer murders of three civil rights activists. One Republican official said of the choice of location, "It was not a mistake that Reagan went to the Neshoba County Fair. . . . We were just obsessed with how you turn around these rural counties and get them started voting with us" (Nash and Taggert 2009, p. 119). For more on the Southern Strategy, see Lassiter (2006) and Maxwell and Shields (2019).

REFERENCES

Abrajano, M., & Burnett, C. M. (2012). Polls and Elections: Do Blacks and Whites See Obama through Race-Tinted Glasses? A Comparison of Obama's and Clinton's Approval Ratings. *Presidential Studies Quarterly, 42*(2), 363–375. https://doi.org/10.1111/j.1741-5705.2012 .03970.x

Abramowitz, A. I., & Webster, S. W. (2016). The rise of negative partisanship and the nationalization of U.S. elections in the 21st century. *Electoral Studies, 41*, 12–22.

Acharya, A., Blackwell, M., & Sen, M. (2018). *Deep Roots: How Slavery Still Shapes Southern Politics*. Princeton, NJ: Princeton University Press.

American Civil Liberties Union. (2012, March 6). Take Your Souls to the Polls: Voting Early in Ohio [Podcast]. Retrieved from https://www.aclu.org/podcast/take-your-souls-polls-voting -early-ohio

Allport, G. W. (1954). *The Nature of Prejudice*. Oxford: Addison-Wesley.

Amir, Y. (1976). The Role of Intergroup Contact in Change of Prejudice and Ethnic Relations. In P. A. Katz (Ed.), *Towards the Elimination of Racism* (pp. 245–308). New York: Pergamon.

Amir, Y. (1998). Contact Hypothesis in Ethnic Relations. In E. Weiner (Ed.), *The Handbook of Interethnic Coexistence* (pp. 162–181). New York: Continuum.

Anderson, B. A., Silver, B. D., & Abramson, P. R. (1988). The Effects of Race of the Interviewer on Measures of Electoral Participation by Blacks in SRC National Election Studies. *Public Opinion Quarterly, 52*(1), 53–83.

Anderson, M. (2017, February 28). A Look at Historically Black Colleges and Universities as Howard Turns 150. *Pew Research Center*. Retrieved from https://www.pewresearch.org/fact-tank /2017/02/28/a-look-at-historically-black-colleges-and-universities-as-howard-turns-150/

Andriot, A., & Owens, T. (2014). Identity. In *Sociology: Oxford Bibliographies*. Retrieved from http://dx.doi.org/10.1093/obo/9780199756384-0025

Aptheker, H. (1937). American Negro Slave Revolts. *Science and Society, 1*(4), 512–538.

Aptheker, H. (1943). *American Negro Slave Revolts*. New York: Columbia University Press.

Arceneaux, M. (2017, January 27). Chrisette Michele's Decision to Perform for Trump Wasn't for the People . . . It Was for Her. *Essence*. Retrieved from https://www.essence.com/celebrity /chrisette-michele-trump-inauguration-opportunistic

Banks, A. (2018). With Voting Rights Act Weakened, Black Church Networks Seek More Voters. *National Catholic Reporter: The Independent News Source*. Retrieved from https://www.ncronline .org/news/politics/voting-rights-act-weakened-black-church-networks-seek-more-voters

Banks, A. J., White, I. K., & McKenzie, B. D. (2018). Black Politics: How Anger Influences the Political Actions Blacks Pursue to Reduce Racial Inequality. *Political Behavior*, 1–27. https:// doi.org/10.1007/s11109-018-9477-1

BarackObama.com. (2012). *President Obama Announces the 2012 Launch of African Americans for Obama* [Video file]. Retrieved from https://www.youtube.com/watch?v=BdjoHA5ocwU

Behrend, J. (2015). *Reconstructing Democracy: Grassroots Black Politics in the Deep South after the Civil War*. Athens: University of Georgia Press.

Bicchieri, C. (2006). *The Grammar of Society: The Nature and Dynamics of Social Norms*. Cambridge: Cambridge University Press.

Bicchieri, C., & Xiao, E. (2008). Do the Right Thing: But Only If Others Do So. *Journal of Behavioral Decision Making, 22*(2), 191–208. https://doi.org/10.1002/bdm.621

Blalock, H. M. (1967). *Toward a Theory of Minority-Group Relations*. New York: Wiley.

Bledsoe, T., Welch, S., Sigelman, L., & Combs, M. (1995). Residential Context and Racial Solidarity among African Americans. *American Journal of Political Science, 39*(2), 434–458. https://doi.org/10.2307/2111620

Bobo, L., & Gilliam, F. D. (1990). Race, Sociopolitical Participation, and Black Empowerment. *American Political Science Review, 84*(2), 377–393. https://doi.org/10.2307/1963525

Brewer, M. B. (2001). The Many Faces of Social Identity: Implications for Political Psychology. *Political Psychology, 22*(1), 115–125. https://doi.org/10.1111/0162-895X.00229

Brown, R. K., & Brown, R. E. (2003). Faith and Works: Church-Based Social Capital Resources and African American Political Activism. *Social Forces, 82*(2), 617–641. https://doi.org/10.1353/sof.2004.0005

Brown-Dean, K., Hajnal, Z., Rivers, C., & White, I. (2015). *50 Years of the Voting Rights Act: The State of Race in Politics*. Washington, DC: Joint Center for Political and Economic Studies. Retrieved from http://jointcenter.org/sites/default/files/VRA%20report%2C%208.5.15%20%28540%20pm%29%28updated%29.pdf

Browning, R. P., Marshall, D. R., & Tabb, D. H. (1984). *Protest Is Not Enough: The Struggle of Blacks and Hispanics for Equality in Urban Politics*. Berkeley: University of California Press.

Calhoun-Brown, A. (1996). African American Churches and Political Mobilization: The Psychological Impact of Organizational Resources. *Journal of Politics, 58*(4), 935–953. https://doi.org/10.2307/2960144

Campbell, A., Converse, P. E., Miller, W. E., & Stokes, D. E. (1960). *The American Voter*. Chicago: University of Chicago Press.

Carter, R. T. (1991). Racial Identity Attitudes and Psychological Functioning. *Journal of Multicultural Counseling and Development, 19*(3), 105–114. https://doi.org/10.1002/j.2161-1912.1991.tb00547.x

CensusScope. (n.d.). CensusScope: Your Portal to Census Data. Retrieved from http://www.censusscope.org

Charles, C. Z. (2000). Neighborhood Racial-Composition Preferences: Evidence from a Multiethnic Metropolis. *Social Problems, 47*(3), 379–407. https://doi.org/10.2307/3097236

Charles, C. Z. (2003). The Dynamics of Racial Residential Segregation. *Annual Review of Sociology, 29*, 167–207. https://doi.org/10.1146/annurev.soc.29.010202.100002

Chong, D. (1991). *Collective Action and the Civil Rights Movement*. Chicago: University of Chicago Press.

Chong, D., & Rogers, R. (2005). Racial Solidarity and Political Participation. *Political Behavior, 27*(4), 347–374. https://doi.org/10.1007/s11109-005-5880-5

Cialdini, R. B., Reno, R. R., & Kallgren, C. A. (1990). A Focus Theory of Normative Conduct: Recycling the Concept of Norms to Reduce Littering in Public Places. *Journal of Personality and Social Psychology, 58*(6), 1015–1026. https://doi.org/10.1037/0022-3514.58.6.1015

Clark, P. B., & Wilson, J. Q. (1961). Incentive Systems: A Theory of Organizations. *Administrative Science Quarterly, 6*(2), 129–166. https://doi.org/10.2307/2390752

Cohen, C. J. (1999). *The Boundaries of Blackness: AIDS and the Breakdown of Black Politics*. Chicago: University of Chicago Press.

Cohen, C. J., & Dawson, M. C. (1993). Neighborhood Poverty and African American Politics. *American Political Science Review, 87*(2), 286–302. https://doi.org/10.2307/2939041

Cook, S. W. (1984). The 1954 Social Science Statement and School Desegregation: A Reply to Gerard. *American Psychologist, 39*(8), 819–832. https://doi.org/10.1037/0003-066X.39.8.819

Cowen, T. W. (2017, January 13). Steve Harvey Absolutely Destroyed on Social Media after Meeting with Trump. *Complex*. Retrieved from http://www.complex.com/pop-culture/2017/01/steve-harvey-trump-meeting

Dash, S. (2012, November 7). Stacey Dash: Epic 1,344 Word Rant about Election Depression. *TMZ*. Retrieved from https://www.tmz.com/2012/11/07/stacey-dash-epic-1-344-word-dissertation-about-election-disappointment/

Davenport, L. D. 2018. *Politics beyond Black and White: Biracial Identity and Attitudes in America.* New York: Cambridge University Press.

Davis, D. W. (1997a). The Direction of Race of Interviewer Effects among African-Americans: Donning the Black Mask. *American Journal of Political Science, 41*(1), 309–322. https://doi.org/10.2307/2111718

Davis, D. W. (1997b). Nonrandom Measurement Error and Race of Interviewer Effects among African Americans. *The Public Opinion Quarterly, 61*(1), 183–207. https://doi.org/10.1086/297792

Davis, D. W., & Silver, B. D. (2003). Stereotype Threat and Race of Interviewer Effects in a Survey on Political Knowledge. *American Journal of Political Science, 47*(1), 33–45. https://doi.org/10.2307/3186091

Dawson, M. C. (1994). *Behind the Mule: Race and Class in African-American Politics.* Princeton, NJ: Princeton University Press.

Dawson, M. C. (2001). *Black Visions: The Roots of Contemporary African-American Political Ideologies.* Chicago: University of Chicago Press.

Dawson, M. C. (2011). *Not in Our Lifetimes: The Future of Black Politics.* Chicago: University of Chicago Press.

Dawson, M. C., & Popoff, R. (2004). Reparations: Justice and Greed in Black and White. *Du Bois Review: Social Science Research on Race, 1*(1), 47–91. https://doi.org/10.1017/S1742058X04040056

Denby, G. (2014, September 11). Sagging Pants and the Long History of "Dangerous" Street Fashion. *National Public Radio*. Retrieved from https://www.npr.org/sections/codeswitch/2014/09/11/347143588/sagging-pants-and-the-long-history-of-dangerous-street-fashion

Dennis, A. (2013). A Snitch in Time: An Historical Sketch of Black Informing during Slavery. *Marquette Law Review, 97*(2), 279–334. https://scholarship.law.marquette.edu/mulr/vol97/iss2/4

Dickerson, D. (2007, June 19). The NAACP's Sad Decline. *Salon*. Retrieved from https://www.salon.com/2007/06/19/naacp_9/

Dinan, S. (2015, September 29). Ben Carson Uses Empowerment Message in Bid to Sway Black Voters. *Washington Times*. Retrieved from //www.washingtontimes.com/news/2015/sep/29/ben-carson-uses-empowerment-message-in-bid-to-sway/

DKT [darleneturner53]. (2017, January 18). Chrisette Michele, Jim Brown, Steve Harvey, Kanye West—Added to the cancelled list [Tweet]. Retrieved from https://twitter.com/darleneturner53/status/821767156610306048

Downs, A. (1957). An Economic Theory of Political Action in a Democracy. *Journal of Political Economy, 65*(2), 135–150. https://doi.org/10.1086/257897

Drago, E. L. (1999). *Hurrah for Hampton! Black Red Shirts in South Carolina during Reconstruction.* Fayetteville: University of Arkansas Press.

Drake, S. C., & Cayton, H. R. (1945). *Black Metropolis: A Study of Negro Life in a Northern City.* New York: Harcourt, Brace, and Company.

Duggan, M., Ellison, N. B., Lampe, C., Lenhart, A., & Madden, M. (2015, January 9). Social Media Update 2014. *Pew Research Center: Internet & Technology*. Retrieved from http://www.pewinternet.org/2015/01/09/social-media-update-2014/

Engel, C. (2011). Dictator Games: A Meta Study. *Experimental Economics, 14*(4), 583–610. https://doi.org/10.1007/s10683-011-9283-7

Entman, R. M., & Rojecki, A. (2000). *The Black Image in the White Mind: Media and Race in America*. Chicago: University of Chicago Press.

Faussett, R., & Robertson, C. (2017, December 13). Black Voters in Alabama Pushed Back against the Past. *New York Times*. Retrieved from https://www.nytimes.com/2017/12/13/us/doug-jones-alabama-black-voters.html

Fears, D. (2008, April 5). Civil Rights Groups Seeing Gradual End to Their Era. *Washington Post*. Retrieved from http://www.washingtonpost.com/wp-dyn/content/article/2008/04/04/AR2008040403589.html?noredirect=on

Fields, C. (2016). *Black Elephants in the Room: The Unexpected Politics of African American Republicans*. Oakland: University of California Press.

Foner, E. (1988). *Reconstruction: America's Unfinished Revolution, 1863–1877* (H. S. Commager & R. B. Morris, Eds.). New York: HarperCollins.

Foner, E. (1993). *Freedom's Lawmakers: A Directory of Black Officeholders during Reconstruction*. New York: Oxford University Press.

Fong, C. M., & Luttmer, E. F. P. (2009). What Determines Giving to Hurricane Katrina Victims? Experimental Evidence on Racial Group Loyalty. *American Economic Journal: Applied Economics, 1*(2), 64–87. https://doi.org/10.1257/app.1.2.64

format916. (2011, February 20). Dragged. In *Urban Dictionary*. Retrieved from https://www.urbandictionary.com/define.php?term=dragged

Francis, M. M. (2014). *Civil Rights and the Making of the Modern American State*. Cambridge: Cambridge University Press.

Franklin, J. H., & Moss, A. (1994). *From Slavery to Freedom: A History of African-Americans* (7th ed.). New York: Knopf.

Frymer, P. (1999). *Uneasy Alliances: Race and Party Competition in America*. Princeton, NJ: Princeton University Press.

Gallup. (2017, January 23). Obama Weekly Job Approval [Excel file]. Retrieved from https://news.gallup.com/poll/122465/obama-weekly-job-approval.aspx?g_source=link_newsv9&g_campaign=item_121199&g_medium=copy

Gallup News Service Polls. (2011–2015). Data collection, Roper Center for Public Opinion Research. Retrieved from https://ropercenter.cornell.edu/featured-collections/gallup-data-collection

Gates, H. L. (2019). *Stony the Road: Reconstruction, White Supremacy, and the Rise of Jim Crow*. New York: Penguin Press.

Gay, C. (2004). Putting Race in Context: Identifying the Environmental Determinants of Black Racial Attitudes. *American Political Science Review, 98*(4), 547–562. https://doi.org/10.1017/S0003055404041346

Gay, C., Hochschild, J., & White, A. (2016). Americans' Belief in Linked Fate: Does the Measure Capture the Concept? *Journal of Race, Ethnicity, and Politics, 1*(1), 117–144. https://doi.org/10.1017/rep.2015.3

Gerber, A. S., Green, D. P., & Larimer, C. W. (2008). Social Pressure and Voter Turnout: Evidence from a Large-Scale Field Experiment. *American Political Science Review, 102*(1), 33–48. https://doi.org/10.1017/S000305540808009X

Gerber, A. S., Green, D. P., & Larimer, C. W. (2010). An Experiment Testing the Relative Effectiveness of Encouraging Voter Participation by Inducing Feelings of Pride or Shame. *Political Behavior, 32*(3), 409–422. https://doi.org/10.1007/s11109-010-9110-4

Gillion, D. Q. (2013). *The Political Power of Protest: Minority Activism and Shifts in Public Policy*. Cambridge: Cambridge University Press.

Gloster, N. (2017, January 24). Chrisette Michele on "No Political Genius" & Performing at Trump's Inaugural Ball: "It Was My Responsibility to Say Yes with Purpose." *Billboard*. Retrieved from http://www.billboard.com/articles/columns/hip-hop/7668871/chrisette-michele-no-political-genius-donald-trump-inaugural-ball-performance-interview

Golding, S. (2017, January 16). Steve Harvey Won't Be at Anybody's Inauguration Because His Wife Said No. *Vibe*. Retrieved from http://www.vibe.com/2017/01/steve-harvey-marjorie-harvey-inaguration/

Green, D. P., & Cowden, J. A. (1992). Who Protests: Self-Interest and White Opposition to Busing. *Journal of Politics*, *54*(2), 471–496. https://doi.org/10.2307/2132035

Green, E. (2016, August 8). Black Pastors Are Breaking the Law to Get Hillary Clinton Elected. *The Atlantic*. Retrieved from https://www.theatlantic.com/politics/archive/2016/08/black-pastors-pulpit-hillary-clinton/494876/

Griffin, J., Nickerson, D., & Wozniak, A. (2012). Racial Differences in Inequality Aversion: Evidence from Real World Respondents in the Ultimatum Game. *Journal of Economic Behavior & Organization*, *84*(2), 600–617. https://doi.org/10.1016/j.jebo.2012.09.010

Gurin, P., Hatchett, S., & Jackson, J. S. (1989). *Hope and Independence: Blacks' Response to Electoral and Party Politics*. New York: Russell Sage Foundation.

Hajnal, Z. L., & Lee, T. (2011). *Why Americans Don't Join the Party: Race, Immigration, and the Failure (of Political Parties) to Engage the Electorate*. Princeton, NJ: Princeton University Press.

Harrington, H. J., & Miller, N. (1992). Social Categorization and Intergroup Acceptance: Principles for the Design and Development of Cooperative Learning Teams. In R. Hertz-Lazarowitz & N. Miller (Eds.), *Interaction in Cooperative Groups: The Theoretical Anatomy of Group Learning* (pp. 203–227). New York: Cambridge University Press.

Harris, D. R. (1999). "Property Values Drop When Blacks Move in, Because . . .": Racial and Socioeconomic Determinants of Neighborhood Desirability. *American Sociological Review*, *64*(3), 461–479. https://doi.org/10.2307/2657496

Harris, F. C. (1994). Something Within: Religion as a Mobilizer of African-American Political Activism. *Journal of Politics*, *56*(1), 42–68. https://doi.org/10.2307/2132345

Harris-Lacewell, M. V. (2004). *Barbershops, Bibles, and BET: Everyday Talk and Black Political Thought*. Princeton, NJ: Princeton University Press.

Harvey, Steve. (2017, January 16). Interview: Steve in His Own Words. On His Meeting with Trump. *The Steve Harvey Morning Show*. Premier Radio Networks. https://www.iheart.com/podcast/51-the-steve-harvey-morning-27928551/episode/interview-steve-in-his-own-words-47504732/

Higginbotham, E. B. (1993). *Righteous Discontent: The Women's Movement in the Black Baptist Church, 1880–1920*. Harvard University Press.

Hogg, M. A., Terry, D. J., & White, K. M. (1995). A Tale of Two Theories: A Critical Comparison of Identity Theory with Social Identity Theory. *Social Psychology Quarterly*, *58*(4), 255–269. https://doi.org/10.2307/2787127

Howard, V. B. (1982). The Civil War in Kentucky: The Slave Claims His Freedom. *Journal of Negro History*, *67*(3), 245–256. https://doi.org/10.2307/2717389

Huckfeldt, R., Johnson, P. E., & Sprague, J. (2002). Political Environments, Political Dynamics, and the Survival of Disagreement. *Journal of Politics*, *64*(1), 1–21. https://doi.org/10.1111/1468-2508.00115

Huckfeldt, R., Johnson, P. E., & Sprague, J. (2004). *Political Disagreement: The Survival of Diverse Opinions within Communication Networks*. Cambridge: Cambridge University Press.

Huckfeldt, R., Plutzer, E., & Sprague, J. (1993). Alternative Contexts of Political Behavior: Churches, Neighborhoods, and Individuals. *Journal of Politics*, 55(2), 365–381. https://doi.org/10.2307/2132270

Huckfeldt, R., & Sprague, J. (1995). *Citizens, Politics and Social Communication: Information and Influence in an Election Campaign*. Cambridge: Cambridge University Press.

Hutchings, V. L., & Jefferson, H. (2014). *Out of Options? Blacks and Support for the Democratic Party*. Presented at the 2014 World Congress of the International Political Science Association, Montreal, Canada.

Hutchings, V. L., Valentino, N. A., Philpot, T. S., & White, I. K. (2006). Racial Cues in Campaign News: The Effects of Candidate Strategies on Group Activation and Political Attentiveness among African Americans. In D. P. Redlawsk (Ed.), *Feeling Politics: Emotion in Political Information Processing* (pp. 165–186). New York: Palgrave Macmillan. https://doi.org/10.1057/9781403983114_9

Hyman, H. H. (with Cobb, W. J., Feldman, J. J., Hart, C. W., & Stember, C. H.). (1954). *Interviewing in Social Research*. Chicago: University of Chicago Press.

Inside Edition. (2017, January 17). Steve Harvey Breaks Silence after Trump Meeting: "I Didn't Expect the Backlash to Be So Fierce." Retrieved from https://www.insideedition.com/headlines/21066-steve-harvey-breaks-silence-after-trump-meeting-i-didnt-expect-the-backlash-to-be-so

Jackson, J. (1965). Social Stratification, Social Norms, and Roles. In I. Steiner & M. Fishben (Eds.), *Current Studies in Social Psychology* (pp. 301–308). New York: Holt, Rinehart and Winston.

Jackson, J. W. (1993). Contact Theory of Intergroup Hostility: A Review and Evaluation of the Theoretical and Empirical Literature. *International Journal of Group Tensions*, 23, 43–65.

Jardina, A. (2019). *White Identity Politics*. New York: Cambridge University Press.

Johnson, T. (2015, September 7). Can the Democratic Party Retain Its Hold on Black Voters? *The Atlantic*. Retrieved from https://www.theatlantic.com/politics/archive/2015/09/the-changing-outlook-for-black-voters/403975/

Jones, N. T. (1990). *Born a Child of Freedom, Yet a Slave*. Hanover, NH: Wesleyan University Press.

Jones, R. P. (2014, August 24). Self-Segregation: Why It's So Hard for Whites to Understand Ferguson. *The Atlantic*. Retrieved from https://www.theatlantic.com/national/archive/2014/08/self-segregation-why-its-hard-for-whites-to-understand-ferguson/378928/

Keele, L., McConnaughy, C. M., & White, I. K. (2012). Strengthening the Experimenter's Toolbox: Statistical Estimation of Internal Validity. *American Journal of Political Science*, 56(2), 484–499.

Keith, B. E., Magleby, D. B., Nelson, C. J., Orr, E. A., & Westlye, M. C. (1992). *The Myth of the Independent Voter*. Berkeley: University of California Press.

Keith, B. E., Magleby, D. B., Nelson, C. J., Orr, E., Westlye, M. C., & Wolfinger, R. E. (1986). The Partisan Affinities of Independent "Leaners." *British Journal of Political Science*, 16(2), 155–185. https://doi.org/10.1017/S0007123400003872

Kennedy, R. (2008). *Sellout: The Politics of Racial Betrayal* (Repr. ed.). New York: Vintage.

Kenny, C. B. (1992). Political Participation and Effects from the Social Environment. *American Journal of Political Science*, 36(1), 259–267. https://doi.org/10.2307/2111432

Key, V. O. (1949). *Southern Politics: In State and Nation*. New York: Vintage Books.

Klar, S. (2014). Partisanship in a Social Setting. *American Journal of Political Science*, 58(3), 687–704. https://doi.org/10.1111/ajps.12087

Koger, L. (1985). *Black Slaveowners: Free Black Slave Masters in South Carolina, 1790–1860*. Jefferson, NC: McFarland.

Krysan, M., & Farley, R. (2002). The Residential Preferences of Blacks: Do They Explain Persistent Segregation? *Social Forces, 80*(3), 937–980. https://doi.org/10.1353/sof.2002.0011

Laird, C. (2019). Black like Me: How Political Communication Changes Racial Group Identification and Its Implications. *Politics, Groups, and Identities, 7(2)*, 324–346. https://doi.org/10.1080/21565503.2017.1358187

Lassiter, M. D. (2006). *The Silent Majority: Suburban Politics in the Sunbelt South*. Princeton, NJ: Princeton University Press.

Laumann, E. O. (1973). *Bonds of Pluralism: The Form and Substance of Urban Social Networks*. New York: J. Wiley.

Lee, K., Palsetia, D., Narayanan, R., Patwary, M.M.A., Agrawal, A., & Choudhary, A. (2011). Twitter Trending Topic Classification. In M. Spiliopoulou, H. Wang, D. Cook, J. Pei, W. Wang, O. Zaïane, & X. Wu (Eds.), *Proceedings: 11th IEEE International Conference on Data Mining Workshops, Vancouver, Canada, 11 December 2011* (pp. 251–258). Los Alamitos, CA: IEEE Computer Society.

Lee, T. (2000). Racial Attitudes and the Color Line(s) at the Close of the Twentieth Century. In P. Ong (Ed.), *The State of Asian Pacific America: Transforming Race Relations* (pp. 103–158). Los Angeles: LEAP Asian Pacific American Policy Institute and UCLA Asian American Studies Center.

Leighley, J. E., & Vedlitz, A. (1999). Race, Ethnicity, and Political Participation: Competing Models and Contrasting Explanations. *Journal of Politics, 61*(4), 1092–1114. https://doi.org/10.2307/2647555

Levitan, L. C., & Visser, P. S. (2009). Social Network Composition and Attitude Strength: Exploring the Dynamics within Newly Formed Social Networks. *Journal of Experimental Social Psychology, 45*(5), 1057–1067. https://doi.org/10.1016/j.jesp.2009.06.001

Lilly, C., & Barris, K. (2015). Elephant in the Room. In Anthony Anderson, *Black-ish*. Burbank, CA: American Broadcasting Company.

Lincoln, C. E., & Mamiya, L. H. (1990). *The Black Church in the African American Experience*. Durham, NC: Duke University Press.

Massey, D. S., & Denton, N. A. (1993). *American Apartheid: Segregation and the Making of the Underclass* (Repr. ed.). Cambridge, MA: Harvard University Press.

Maxwell, A., & Shields, T. G. (2019). *The Long Southern Strategy: How Chasing White Voters in the South Changed American Politics*. New York: Oxford University Press.

McAdam, D. (1982). *Political Process and the Development of Black Insurgency, 1930–1970*. Chicago: University of Chicago Press.

McClerking, H. K., & McDaniel, E. I. (2005). Belonging and Doing: Membership in Black Political Churches and Political Participation. *Political Psychology, 26*, 721–733.

McConnaughy, C. M. (2013). *The Woman Suffrage Movement in America: A Reassessment*. New York: Cambridge University Press.

McCrummen, S., Reinhard, B., & Crites, A. (2017). Woman Says Roy Moore Initiated Sexual Encounter When She Was 14, He Was 32. *Washington Post*. Retrieved from https://www.washingtonpost.com/investigations/woman-says-roy-moore-initiated-sexual-encounter-when-she-was-14-he-was-32/2017/11/09/1f495878-c293-11e7-afe9-4f60b5a6c4a0_story.html?utm_term=.6235f823c405

McDaniel, E. (2008). *Politics in the Pews: The Political Mobilization of Black Churches*. Ann Arbor: University of Michigan Press.

Mckenzie, B. D. (2004). Religious Social Networks, Indirect Mobilization, and African-American Political Participation. *Political Research Quarterly, 57*(4), 621–632. https://doi.org/10.1177/106591290405700402004

Mead, G. H. (1934). *Mind, Self, and Society*. Chicago: University of Chicago Press.

Morris, A. D. (1984). *The Origins of the Civil Rights Movement: Black Communities Organizing for Change.* New York: The Free Press.

Mutz, D. C. (2006). *Hearing the Other Side: Deliberative versus Participatory Democracy.* Cambridge: Cambridge University Press.

Myrdal, G. (1944). *An American Dilemma: The Negro Problem and Modern Democracy.* New York: Harper and Bros.

Nash, J., & Taggert, A. (2009). *Mississippi Politics: The Struggle for Power, 1976–2008* (2nd ed.). Jackson: University of Mississippi Press.

National Advisory Commission on Civil Disorders. (1968). *Report of the National Advisory Commission on Civil Disorders.* Washington, DC: Government Printing Office.

National Urban League. (2016). Locked Out: Education, Jobs, and Justice. *2016 State of Black America: Executive Summary and Key Findings.* http://soba.iamempowered.com/sites/soba.iamempowered.com/themes/soba/flexpaper/SOBA2016-ExecutiveSummary/docs/SOBA2016-ExecSumm-5.25.16_FINAL_forweb.pdf

Naylor, B. (2017, December 13). "Black Votes Matter": African Americans Propel Jones to Alabama Win. *National Public Radio.* Retrieved from https://www.npr.org/2017/12/13/570531505/black-votes-matter-african-americans-propel-jones-to-alabama-win

New York Times. (2017, August 1). Alabama Results. Retrieved from https://www.nytimes.com/elections/2016/results/alabama

Nickerson, D., & White, I. (2010). *The Effect of Priming Racial In-Group Norms of Participation and Racial Group Conflict on Black Voter Turnout: A Field Experiment.* Retrieved from https://polisci.osu.edu/sites/polisci.osu.edu/files/PrimingGroupConflict.3.15.13.pdf

Obama, B. (2014, July 21). *Remarks by the President at My Brother's Keeper Town Hall.* Speech, Washington, DC. Retrieved from https://obamawhitehouse.archives.gov/the-press-office/2014/07/21/remarks-president-my-brothers-keeper-town-hall

Oliver, J. E., & Mendelberg, T. (2000). Reconsidering the Environmental Determinants of White Racial Attitudes. *American Journal of Political Science, 44*(3), 574–589. https://doi.org/10.2307/2669265

Olson, M. (1965). *The Logic of Collective Action: Public Good and the Theory of Groups.* Cambridge, MA: Harvard University Press.

Omi, M., & Winant, H. (1996). Contesting the Meaning of Race in the Post–Civil Rights Movement Era. In S. Pedraza & R. G. Rumbaut (Eds.), *Origins and Destinies: Immigration, Race, and Ethnicity in America* (pp. 470–479). Belmont, CA: Wadsworth.

Payne, C. M. (2007). *I've Got the Light of Freedom: The Organizing Tradition and the Mississippi Freedom Struggle* (2nd ed.). Berkeley: University of California Press.

Perez, T. (2017, December 13). Let me be clear: We won in Alabama and Virginia because #BlackWomen led us to victory. Black women are the backbone of the Democratic Party, and we can't take that for granted. Period [Twitter post]. Retrieved from https://twitter.com/tomperez/status/940968519088386049?lang=en

Pettigrew, T. F. (1998). Intergroup Contact Theory. *Annual Review of Psychology, 49*(1), 65–85. https://doi.org/10.1146/annurev.psych.49.1.65

Pew Research Center. (2008–2010). Datasets. Retrieved from http://www.people-press.org/category/datasets/

Pew Research Center. (2009, January 30). A Religious Portrait of African-Americans. *Pew Research Center: Religion & Public Life.* Retrieved from https://www.pewforum.org/2009/01/30/a-religious-portrait-of-african-americans/

Philpot, T. S. (2007). *Race, Republicans, and the Return of the Party of Lincoln.* Ann Arbor: University of Michigan Press.

Philpot, T. S. (2017). *Conservative but Not Republican: The Paradox of Party Identification and Ideology among African Americans.* New York: Cambridge University Press.

Philpot, T. S., & White, I. (Eds.). (2010). *African-American Political Psychology: Identity, Opinion, and Action in the Post-Civil Rights Era*. New York: Palgrave Macmillan.

Provasnik, S., Shafer, L., & Snyder, T. (2004). *Historical Black Colleges and Universities, 1976 to 2001* (NCES 2004-062). Washington, DC: National Center for Education Statistics, Department of Education. Retrieved from https://nces.ed.gov/pubsearch/pubsinfo.asp?pubid =2004062

Rhodes, P. J. (1994). Race-of-Interviewer Effects: A Brief Comment. *Sociology, 28*(2), 547–558. https://doi.org/10.1177/0038038594028002011

Rice, F. (2015, May 15). Black Republican Frequently Asked Questions. *Black Republican Blog*. Retrieved from http://blackrepublican.blogspot.com/2015/05/black-republican-frequently -asked.html

Rigueur, L. W. (2015). *The Loneliness of the Black Republican: Pragmatic Politics and the Pursuit of Power* (Repr. ed.). Princeton, NJ: Princeton University Press.

Saulny, S. (2012, October 28). With Less Time for Voting, Black Churches Redouble Their Efforts. *New York Times*. Retrieved from https://www.nytimes.com/2012/10/29/us/politics/black -churches-in-florida-urge-congregations-to-vote.html

Schickler, E. (2016). *Racial Realignment: The Transformation of American Liberalism, 1932–1965*. Princeton, NJ: Princeton University Press.

Schuman, H., & Converse, J. M. (1971). The Effects of Black and White Interviewers on Black Responses in 1968. *Public Opinion Quarterly, 35*(1), 44–68. https://doi.org/10.1086/267866

Scott, S. (2017, January 19). Chrisette Michele Responds to Trump Inauguration Performance Criticism: "I Don't Mind These Stones." *Essence*. Retrieved from https://www.essence.com /celebrity/chrisette-michele-trump-inauguration-performance-response/

Sigelman, L., & Welch, S. (1991). *Black Americans' Views of Racial Inequality: The Dream Deferred*. Cambridge: Cambridge University Press.

Sellers, B. [Bakari_Sellers]. (2017, January 13). On one side you have @repjohnlewis on the other you have @IAmSteveHarvey and @kanyewest. I'm rocking with the civil rights hero! [Tweet]. Retrieved from https://twitter.com/bakari_sellers/status/819999149223329793

Sharma, S. (2013). Black Twitter? Racial Hashtags, Networks and Contagion. *New Formations: A Journal of Culture/Theory/Politics, 78*(1), 46–64. https://doi.org/10.3898/NewF.78.02.2013

Shelby, T. (2005). *We Who Are Dark*. Cambridge, MA: Harvard University Press.

Shingles, R. D. (1981). Black Consciousness and Political Participation: The Missing Link. *American Political Science Review, 75*(1), 76–91. https://doi.org/10.2307/1962160

Sidanius, J., Laar, C. V., Levin, S., & Sinclair, S. (2004). Ethnic Enclaves and the Dynamics of Social Identity on the College Campus: The Good, the Bad, and the Ugly. *Journal of Personality and Social Psychology, 87*(1), 96–110. https://doi.org/10.1037/0022-3514.87.1.96

Sinclair, B. (2012). *The Social Citizen: Peer Networks and Political Behavior* (Chicago Studies in American Politics ed.). Chicago: University of Chicago Press.

Sitkoff, H., & Foner, E. (1993). *The Struggle for Black Equality*. New York: Hill and Wang.

Smith, A. (2014). *African Americans and Technology Use: A Demographic Portrait. Pew Research Center*. Retrieved from http://pewinternet.org/Reports/2014/African-American-Tech-Use .aspx

Smith, C. W. (2014). *Black Mosaic: The Politics of Black Pan-Ethnic Diversity*. New York: New York University Press.

Smith, R. C. (1996). *We Have No Leaders: African Americans in the Post-Civil Rights Era*. Albany: State University of New York Press.

Southern Poverty Law Center. (n.d.). Civil Rights Martyrs. Retrieved from https://www.splcenter .org/what-we-do/civil-rights-memorial/civil-rights-martyrs

Spence, L. K. (2011). *Stare in the Darkness: The Limits of Hip-Hop and Black Politics*. Minneapolis: University of Minnesota Press.

Spingarn, A. (2010, May 7). When "Uncle Tom" Became an Insult. *The Root*. Retrieved from https://www.theroot.com/when-uncle-tom-became-an-insult-1790879561

Spingarn, A. (2012). When Uncle Tom Didn't Die: The Antislavery Politics of H. J. Conway's *Uncle Tom's Cabin*. *Theatre Survey, 53*(2), 203–218. https://doi.org/10.1017/S0040557412000051

Starkey, B. S. (2012). Uncle Tom and Justice Clarence Thomas: Is the Abuse Defensible? *Georgetown Journal of Law & Modern Critical Race Perspectives, 4*, 101–148. https://heinonline.org/HOL/P?h=hein.journals/gjmodco4&i=117

Stewart, Nikita. (2018, April 2). "I've Been to the Mountaintop": Dr. King's Last Sermon Annotated. *New York Times*. Retrieved from https://www.nytimes.com/interactive/2018/04/02/us/king-mlk-last-sermon-annotated.html

Stryker, S. (1980). *Symbolic Interactionism: A Social Structural Version*. Menlo Park, CA: Benjamin/Cummings.

Tajfel, H., & Turner, J. (1979). An Integrative Theory of Intergroup Conflict. In W. G. Austin & S. W. Worchel (Eds.), *The Social Psychology of Intergroup Relations* (pp. 33–37). Monterey, CA: Brooks Cole.

Tate, K. (1991). Black Political Participation in the 1984 and 1988 Presidential Elections. *American Political Science Review, 85*(4), 1159–1176. https://doi.org/10.2307/1963940

Tate, K. (1993). *From Protest to Politics: The New Black Voters in American Elections*. Cambridge, MA: Harvard University Press.

Tate, K. (2010). *What's Going On? Political Incorporation and the Transformation of Black Public Opinion*. Washington, DC: Georgetown University Press.

Taylor, P. (2012, December 26). The Growing Electoral Clout of Blacks Is Driven by Turnout, Not Demographics. *Pew Research Center*. Retrieved from https://www.pewsocialtrends.org/2012/12/26/the-growing-electoral-clout-of-blacks-is-driven-by-turnout-not-demographics/

TheGrio. (2016, January 22). Damon Dash Calls Out Cousin Stacey Dash for "Cooning." Retrieved from http://thegrio.com/2016/01/22/dame-dash-stacey-dash-cooning/

Turner, R. H. (1978). The Role and the Person. *American Journal of Sociology, 84*(1), 1–23. https://doi.org/10.1086/226738

United States v. State of Louisiana, 225 F. Supp. 353 (E.D. La. 1963).

U.S. Census Bureau. (2011, February 8). Census Bureau Reports the Number of Black-Owned Businesses Increased at Triple the National Rate. Retrieved from https://www.census.gov/newsroom/releases/archives/business_ownership/cb11-24.html

U.S. Census Bureau. (2018, August 28). Historical Income Tables: Households. Retrieved from https://www.census.gov/data/tables/time-series/demo/income-poverty/historical-income-households.html

Uzee, P. (1961). The Republican Party in the Louisiana Election of 1896. *Louisiana History: The Journal of the Louisiana Historical Association, 2*(3), 332–344. https://www.jstor.org/stable/4230624

Verba, S., & Nie, N. (1972). *Participation in America: Political Democracy and Social Equality*. New York: Harper and Row.

Verba, S., Schlozman, K. L., & Brady, H. E. (1995). *Voice and Equality: Civic Voluntarism in American Politics*. Cambridge, MA: Harvard University Press.

Verba, S., Schlozman, K. L., Brady, H., & Nie, N. H. (1993). Race, Ethnicity and Political Resources: Participation in the United States. *British Journal of Political Science, 23*(4), 453–497. https://doi.org/10.1017/S0007123400006694

Walsh, E. (1986, November 7). Four New Southern Senators Owe Victories to Black Vote; Allegiance to Democrats as High as 90%. *Washington Post*.

Walton, H. (1975). *Black Republicans: The Politics of the Black and Tans*. Metuchen, NJ: Scarecrow Press.

Walton, H. (1985). *Invisible Politics: Black Political Behavior*. Albany: State University of New York Press.

Warren, L. [iamlaurenp]. (2017, January 13). "Name someone who just sold their soul." "OOOH! Steve Harvey!" "Survey says—" [Tweet]. Retrieved from https://twitter.com/iamlaurenp /status/820003887172161537?lang=en

Wattenberg, M. P. (2009). *The Decline of American Political Parties, 1952–1996*. Cambridge, MA: Harvard University Press.

Wax, D. D. (1982). "The Great Risque We Run": The Aftermath of Slave Rebellion at Stono, South Carolina, 1739–1745. *Journal of Negro History, 67*(2), 136–147.

White, I. K. (2007). When Race Matters and When It Doesn't: Racial Group Differences in Response to Racial Cues. *American Political Science Review, 101*(2), 339–354. https://doi .org/10.1017/S0003055407070177

White, I. K., Laird, C. N., & Allen, T. D. (2014). Selling Out? The Politics of Navigating Conflicts between Racial Group Interest and Self-interest. *American Political Science Review, 108*(4), 783–800. https://doi.org/10.1017/S000305541400046X

Wilcox, C., & Gomez, L. (1990). Religion, Group Identification, and Politics among American Blacks. *Sociology of Religion, 51*(3), 271–285. https://doi.org/10.2307/3711178

Willie, S. S. (2003). *Acting Black: College, Identity and the Performance of Race*. New York: Routledge.

Wilson, W. (1984). The Black Underclass. *Wilson Quarterly (1976–), 8*(2), 88–99.

Wimmer, A., & Lewis, K. (2010). Beyond and below Racial Homophily: ERG Models of a Friendship Network Documented on Facebook. *American Journal of Sociology, 116*(2), 583–642. https://doi.org/10.1086/653658

Wolfinger, R. E., & Rosenstone, S. J. (1980). *Who Votes?* New Haven, CT: Yale University Press.

Wong, W., Wang, L., & Kangasharju, J. (2012). Neighborhood Search and Admission Control in Cooperative Caching Networks. In *2012 IEEE Global Communications Conference (GLOBECOM)* (pp. 2852–2858). Piscataway, NJ: IEEE. https://doi.org/10.1109/GLOCOM.2012 .6503549

INDEX

Note: Figures and tables are indicated by page numbers in *italics*.